IN DEFENSE OF SEX

In Defense of Sex

NONBINARY EMBODIMENT AND DESIRE

Christopher Breu

FORDHAM UNIVERSITY PRESS   NEW YORK 2025

Library of Congress Cataloging-in-Publication Data available online at https://catalog.loc.gov.

Printed In the United States of America

27 26 25   5 4 3 2 1

First edition

For Gina, who brought me back from the land of the dead.

Contents

IN DEFENSE OF SEX

Preface: "This ain't by design, girl"

The needle drops on the opening cut of nonbinary artist Yves Tumor's brilliant 2020 album *Heaven to a Tortured Mind*.[1] "Gospel for a New Century" begins with a slinky rhythmic loop that finishes with a horn flourish sampled from a marching band. Absolute silence appears out of nowhere for a beat. The silence here is not the typical absence of sound that you encounter in a recording, where you may still hear certain sounds such as the whisper of guitar strings or the breathing of various band members (and while I prefer my music on vinyl, like any typical twenty-first-century hipster, the best way to really appreciate this silence is streaming or via CD and on headphones). This silence is absolute. Paradoxically, it takes on a forceful presence in the absolute absence it conveys. Like the silence in Prince's "Kiss," the silence in "Gospel for a New Century" becomes an active structuring element in the song. The allusion to "Kiss" here is not arbitrary. The Purple One is an artist to whom Yves Tumor is clearly indebted, from the tensions between rock and soul, the sacred and profane, and the carnal and the spiritual in their music to the complex, joyful, but also obsessive gender and sexual play that organizes both music and words. Both artists, despite Prince's later homophobic renouncement of his earlier, sexually explicit music, produce music that is queer in the most forceful sense of the word. Gender, sex, sexuality, and embodiment (including the signifiers of race) are remixed and radically restructured in sound. This restructuration is deeply sexy. This is not queerness as monstrous threat, but as joyfully freakish embodiment and desire.

In what follows in this book, I hope this vision of joyful freakishness persists as an erotic beacon, indexing what is possible to build and sustain where a collective sense of queerness as solidarity, desire, and embodiment is produced,

even as we also recognize that our "minds" have been "tortured" by class inequality, transphobia, homophobia, racism, misogyny, and ableism. The song
is freakish in the best sense of the word. It upholds freakishness as an embodied
ideal. It also freaks you. It invites you to freak your desire, your embodiment,
and the larger society in which you live. If Funkadelic invited you to "free your
mind and your ass will follow," Yves Tumor presents the opposite yet comple-
mentary injunction.[2] Their music feels like it is about freeing your ass so that
your mind can follow. Through material instantiations of queer embodiment,
our minds can become free of binary genders, sexes, and conceptions of desire
and begin to imagine anticapitalist, antiracist, and queer forms of solidarity.
Of course, the mind/ass dialectic works both ways. This book will attempt to
free our minds so our asses will follow, but it is important to realize that both
are necessary. Freak your mind! Freak your ass! You have nothing to lose but
capitalism, normativity, and your tightly scripted, egoic identity.

Let us return to the silence, which recurs throughout the song. It functions
as an active negativity, existing in tension with the looped rhythm and brass.
This forceful negativity, the active presence elsewhere of something that is
neither visible nor present for immediate apprehension, is central to the logic
of sex articulated, indeed defended, in this book. Sex, as a dimension of both
embodiment and desire, is in a negative relationship to the ways in which
gender and our ego identifications structure our active relationship to and
appearance as a gendered and sexual beings. It is a structuring absence. While
absence often implies a presence on another scene, the presence of sex elsewhere is both elusive and plural. Moreover, while it has material instantiations,
sex is anything but the rigidly binary site of material truth that normative and
transphobic discourses make of it in opposing it to gender. As Paisley Currah
and Dean Spade have differently documented, such discourses and their in-
stantiation in law have often formed the leading edges of transphobic and
reactionary movements and practices around sex and gender.[3] Sex, in its various
invocations, is hardly innocent as a category, and one can understand why
progressive, transpositive work may choose to focus on gender rather than sex.
Yet, this book argues that sex can be conceptualized otherwise. Indeed, if we
want to theorize intersex and trans together, we need a different conception of
sex. If we want to theorize how social and erotic desire functions within social
spaces, we need a different conception of sex.

In Defense of Sex argues for an understanding of sex as nonbinary, material
(thus having a positive dimension), and yet as also structured by a fundamental
negativity, resistant to any attempt at positivization. It is, as I argue in chapter
2, "extimate."[4] Lacan's neologism designates what is both an intimate exteriority
and an exteriorized intimacy. Sex is precisely such a thing. It is elsewhere, in

negative tension with the visible, yet experienced as an intimate alienness (the otherness within and the dimensions of ourselves that we experience as intersecting with the external world) that works to structure our relationship to both embodiment and desire.

Drawing on work in feminist new materialism, I theorize sex as material and "trans-corporeal," in Stacy Alaimo's sense.[5] Yet this understanding should be put into productive tension with the Lacanian account I have also just articulated, such that there is a not-all to sex. It cannot be fully positivized. This understanding of sex in the pages that follow is also articulated in relationship to recent work in theories of race and racialization that takes the flesh as a crucial category, one distinct from both gender and sex, in which forms of racialized and economic meaning, violence, and connection are inscribed and lived in the flesh. Finally, the understanding of sex articulated in this book is historicized within a larger Marxist framework. Desire and embodiment are historically shaped and transformed. They may become second nature at times (and psychoanalysis is one of the technologies we use to plumb this second nature), but they are still finally shaped and reshaped by historical and political-economic dynamics, however long and however seemingly fixed. In a more political dimension, I also draw on Marxism to theorize forms of solidarity and collective struggle that transcend the increasingly individualized and atomized structures of identity formation in recent accounts of gender and sexuality and in relationship to liberal to leftist political discourse in the United States more generally.

To return to "Gospel for a New Century," the song's racial resonances accrue around the reworking of the sample of the marching band. The sample does not merely repeat, even as the rhythm track recurs. Instead, after repeating three times, the repetition becomes difference. The horns amass, becoming discordant and strident. As they mix with cross-rhythms, they move from an invocation of the sweet horns associated with seventies soul to the warring brass in Duke Ellington's 1940 recording "Harlem Air-Shaft" all the way back to the beautiful cacophony of a New Orleans second-line performance or the collective music and dance of the "Buzzard Lope," analyzed brilliantly by R. A. Judy.[6] A whole history of racialized expression and its relationship to the physical embodiment of musical performance and the brutal physicality of forced labor is encoded in this track. Indeed, the acoustics become flesh, recording different forms of embodiment in relationship to the long history of Black musical forms. Music is rendered flesh here and a richly sentient and articulate flesh, as Judy posits it. The sexiness of the song and its enactment of gender is structured, in part, in relationship to this conception of flesh. Flesh here becomes a mediation between sex, as a structured silence, and gender, which is central to the performative dimensions of the song.

As a nonbinary artist invested in debinarizing and rerouting gender, many of Tumor's songs enact a powerful gender queerness. "Gospel for a New Century" is no exception. The song is addressed to a "girl," yet the more you listen to the song it is increasingly unclear whether the girl in question is referring to the diminutivized addressee of your conventional pop song or Yves themselves. This ambiguity richly persists throughout the song, situating its desires in an indeterminate relationship between self and other, reflexiveness and a reaching out toward otherness. This oscillation between self and other, in which neither yields a stable position, will be central to the account of desire in this book.

This reflexiveness is also apparent in the repeated phrase "this ain't by design girl," suggesting we are not fully in control of our subjectivities and our romantic entanglements. While we need designs for both individual and collective living—the socialist vision that this book articulates finally depends on the importance of design—we also need to recognize that design is always complicated by contingency and that which eludes or complicates its rational workings, including drives, the unconscious, chance events, new social, economic, and ecological developments, new social actors, and that which remains excluded (also called "the real" in Lacanian terms) from the symbolic our designs have produced. As I argue later in the book, we need a socialism and a conception of public sex that is both by design and that recognizes that designs always are incomplete. Design needs to be balanced with the workings of contingency, improvisation, split subjectivity, power from below, and the unpredictable. I call this socialism without mastery (grounded in a Marxism without mastery). It is a version of what Lauren Berlant calls the "inconvenience of other people," but I want to call it also the pleasure of other people.[7] It is the serendipitous encounter with otherness that startles, transforms, and pleases. We need a socialism that can account for this. While I advocate a socialism without mastery, our relationship to desire may, of course, be about fantasies of mastery. Any conception of public sex worthy of the name certainly would make room for fantasies of mastery (along with many other consensual fantasies and activities), but we should not confuse the fantasy of mastery as it plays out in kink with the drive toward mastery itself.

Samuel R. Delany's *Times Square Red, Times Square Blue* is a touchstone for any work that attempts to theorize public sex and what I describe in chapter 4 as the sexual commons.[8] Delany draws upon Jane Jacobs's critique of modernist planning to challenge the newly Disneyfied and neoliberal Times Square created around the turn of the twenty-first century and to defend the public sex cultures and cultures of interclass contact that occurred in the space before.[9] While Jacobs's critique makes sense in this context and in a moment when the

arrogance of capitalist top-down planning destroyed functioning neighbor-
hoods, our own moment is defined by uncontrolled capitalist speculation the
wholesale destruction of urban space in its name (take contemporary San
Francisco for one of its most dystopian instantiations), and the creation of
what Mike Davis terms a planet of slums.[10] From the contemporary vantage,
social planning looks like a lost art, one we need to renew. We need planning.
We also need play and improvisation. The best social visions (and the best
art—take jazz and other improvised music, for example) combine these two
approaches.

  In what follows, the world we need is both by design and finally "ain't by
design," girl. There is always the disruption via otherness including the otherness within. Otherness makes things complicated, but also sexy. Despite how
Yves Tumor begins the song ("I think I can solve it/I can be your all") we can
never be anybody's all (either to ourselves or others). Instead, we need to strive
toward solutions while recognizing the not all of anything we assay. It is to such
a joyful, yet responsible and just future that this book is written. Sex, to my
mind, needs to be a part of such a just future. I once had a friend tell me that
the problem with "Californians like me" (and I note that I lived there for only
eight years during graduate school) is that we confuse sex with revolution. I
invite that confusion. This book is my attempt to stay true to it.

Now that I have laid out the argumentative dimensions of this preface, a few
asides are in order. First, I have intentionally not written this book as a work
of autotheory. While I have written in an autotheoretical mode about intersex
before (see the preface to *Insistence of the Material* and my article "Middlesex
Meditations: Understanding and Teaching Intersex"), we are living in a time
when the theoretical imagination, like our relationship to otherness, is shrink-
ing.[11] As I will argue, the neoliberal atomization of society has not only affected
our visions of what is possible in social, economic, and ecological terms, but
it has also shaped, and attenuated, our very understanding of desire. Often the
drive to only write about oneself is cloaked in liberal or progressive injunctions:
"Don't appropriate the experience of others," "You can only write about what
you know," etc. Yet, there is nothing progressive, let alone radical, about the
proposition that we are sealed, hermetically, into our subjectivities and scripted
into our identities without any contradiction or relationship to the outside.
Indeed, this is a neoliberal dream state organized around what Anna Kornbluh
calls immediacy—where the private, individual, or the small group substitutes
entirely for the collective and the work of mediation is replaced by the immediate intensity of affects.[12] As much strong work as there is in autotheory and
autofiction in the present, I intentionally write this book to imagine collective

forms of solidarity around sexual, social, ecological, and economic struggles. Accordingly, I write using the pronoun "we" quite a bit. While there have been many critiques of the use of the third-person plural pronoun as imperializing, I use it as an invitation and an invocation, one that invites alliance and works to help bring collectivities into being. When I use "I" in what follows, I usually am emphasizing the particularity (but not exclusivity) of one of my positions, whereas "we" is used to intentionally invoke collectivity, one that I hope will be taken up.

Having said this, I should probably define my own subjective position, even as I want to resist the reduction of my argument to the same. Still, it can be important to know from what vantage an argument is being made.[13] I write from a relatively privileged position in terms of economics, race, nationality, and employment. I am a tenured professor at an embattled yet still functioning public (in name at least) university in the United States. In terms of race and class, I grew up privileged. I am white (in any meaningful sense of the word), and while my parents struggled and sacrificed to make it possible, I went to private school from kindergarten through college. In terms of my sexuality, I am straightish (whatever that means in terms of my embodiment and gender identity) but kinky and pleasurably contradictory (like many of us). In terms of my gender identity, I am a complicated mix of masculine and feminine (like many of us) but pass as masculine and have been inculcated with masculine values (some of which I have actively resisted and some of which I unconsciously reproduce) in my upbringing. In terms of my sexual embodiment, I am intersex (at least by most definitions of the word—I was born with a severe version of hypospadias) and have undergone at least sixteen surgeries (the medical records get murky the farther back you go) from the ages of two to fifty, the need for which were produced by complications from the unnecessary first surgery. These surgeries produced a rich yet often violent fantasy life and one that was split between masculine and feminine identifications. It also produced a strong sense of sexual guilt that I rebel against regularly.

I continue to use the word "intersex" rather than "disorders of sexual development" (DSDs) because I think "intersex" captures the nonbinary conception of sex that I articulate in the pages that follow. The DSD nomenclature also continues to pathologize something that should not be pathologized.[14] In terms of pronouns, I use either he/him/his (which I grew up with and that still feels, um, "natural") aor they/them/their (basically as a form of allegiance to other intersex folk as well as trans and nonbinary folk). It finally does not matter to me, though, how folks refer to me in terms of pronouns (she works, too!). While I respect that such terms are very important for others, I also think we need to

focus on larger material inequalities as much if not more than the specificities
of individual linguistic definition.

I always write into contradictions and ambivalences. In my first monograph,
Hard-Boiled Masculinities, I wrote into the contradictions that shape hegemonic masculinity.[15] In *Insistence of the Material*, I wrote into the contradictions of embodiment. This time I write into the contradictions of sex. Sex has
been perhaps the locus of my most intense and haunting contradictions.
Writing this book will leave me, hopefully, in a different place than where I
started. Yet the work that this book undertakes is only therapeutic accidentally
or in excess of its conscious aims. Instead, the work of this book is to imagine
sex and sociality in a different modality, one that challenges the privatized
and particularized microdefinitions of the present. Thus, when I use terms
like "intersex" or "nonbinary" or "trans," I do not use them as identity markers
but rather as adjectives.[16] I see our subjectivities as contradictory and complex,
opening both outward and inward in ways we are delightfully, and sometimes
hauntingly, not in control of. The insistence on reducing everything to a name,
which then can be invested with human and sometimes actual capital, is a
neoliberal fantasy *par excellence*. We are not our brand. Let us be anything
but "on brand" in the present. Instead, let us be collective, contradictory, and
desirous.

Introduction:
Sex for the Twenty-First Century

In other words—for the moment, I am not fucking, I am talking to you. Well! I can have exactly the same satisfaction as if I were fucking. That's what it means. Indeed, it raises the question of whether in fact I am not fucking at this moment.

JACQUES LACAN

Why would sex need defending in the present?[1] At first glance it is everywhere, from sexed-up advertising and the ubiquity of porn to the availability of various kinds of hookups and arrangements made even more frictionless via various dating apps. We also have a proliferation of different sexualities, orientations, and desires, from pansexuality and various kinds of kinks and fetishes to identities built on different relationships to desire, including asexuality, demisexuality, and aromanticism, to name only a few. Rather than a culture built around sexual repression, control, and exclusion, which was the basic thesis of most liberatory struggles around sex, gender, and sexuality in the twentieth century, from sex-positive feminism to queer theory and activism, we now seem to live in a culture in which one cannot escape sex.

Yet cultural attitudes toward sex have changed in the present. What Gila Ashtor terms "erotophobia" informs both theory and popular discourses.[2] Although her findings have been contested, Kate Julian claims that sex among young adults is on the decline.[3] David M. Halperin, pointing to the growth of legal and institutional regulations around even consensual sexual behavior, argues that there is a "war on sex" happening in the present.[4] Similarly, Oliver Davis and Tim Dean argue that present day Western society is organized around a hatred of sex.[5] In discussing sexual issues in the classroom or with friends, both younger and older, I often hear the word "sexualized" invoked as a negative term. Certainly, our relationship to sexuality does come from locations outside or in tension with the conscious subject, whether it be from cultural coding, drives that exist in what Lacan terms an "extimate" relationship with the subject (i.e., an intimate exteriority), or the workings of fantasy as it shapes these other materials.[6] So the idea of sexualization is not wrong. The culture sexualizes you. You are inserted, often against your conscious will or choice, into various sexualizing discourses, practices, and representations. What is missing from this account, however, is any recognition that one's relationship to sexuality is subjectified by people (initially retroactively), and with this subjectification comes an active and responsible, although not fully agential, relationship to it. As someone whose own relationship to sexuality was shaped by repeated forms of nonconsensual medical violence, designed to "fix" my intersex body, I think it is crucial to recognize that we have a subjective relationship to the forms of sexuality, desire, and embodiment that may start out as nonconsensual or thoroughly traumatic, but that becomes something we have an active, social, and hopefully pleasurable relationship to.

Defending Sex as Desire

Part of producing a better, more consensual, and pleasurable relationship to sex involves our ability to find ways of subjectively incorporating the forms of desire, enjoyment, and ambivalence that may have been generated outside of our conscious choosing. Given that many people's relationship to sex is shaped in part by trauma and violence and that these are unevenly distributed around race, gender, class, and sexuality, it seems critical to find a way of subjectifying this relationship. Otherwise it is only those who are untraumatized who are granted a relationship to sex. Similarly, one's active relationship to sex may not involve being physically sexual. In articulating an active relationship to sex I am arguing for the importance and possibility of a whole panoply of relationships to it, including many of the identifications covered under the concept of asexuality (which finally need to be understood, I want to suggest, as still involving a relationship to sex), various forms of eroticism and kink, forms of sexual and social fantasy, to physical relationships to sex within monogamy, polygamy (or "poly"), anonymity, ethical sluthood, and more. As the Lacan quote with which we began indicates, sex can be as much about talking as fucking, indeed it is often about taking as fucking and vice versa.

Yet too much contemporary discourse sees sex as something outside of us, unwanted, and always already traumatizing. In the paranoid structure of contemporary right-wing thought, sex is everywhere a threat, from the pedo-phile rings in pizza joints and the trans person in the bathroom to the instructor teaching queer theory or even sex education. Strikingly, while liberal and left-wing discourses around sex have been more truthful—there really was a pe-dophile ring being led by Jeffrey Epstein, and many of the people called out by #MeToo were indeed rapists and sex abusers—the logic of sex as threat is not dissimilar from that of the right wing. On the left there has been a flatten-ing of discourse around sexual violence, in which violent rapes were rendered interchangeable with nonconsensual, closed-mouth kissing (which turned out to be on the cheek, in one famous case).[7] Please don't get me wrong. #MeToo was absolutely necessary and long overdue. What I am calling attention to is the way in which discourses on sex have been rendered ubiquitous, amorphous, and threatening by a logic that seems to reproduce itself despite the differing political positions attaching to it. Part of this logic comes from the algorithmic workings of social media, which render all different kinds of discourse (true, false, localizable, generalizable) into the same viral and miasmatic structure. It is crucial for the left to remember that while it is imperative to combat sexual violence, we also want to produce a culture that affirms sex and sexual multi-plicity. These two should go hand in hand. The degree that they do not coincide suggests something about the negative status of sex in the present. Indeed, Halperin argues as much: "But preventing sexual abuse should not furnish a pretext for an all-out war on sex that permanently identifies sex itself with danger and with potential or actual harm. Nor should it provide a justification for dispensing with all measure and proportion in deterrence and punishment" (4). Moreover, as with any moral campaign and as has been typical of various wars on sex historically, it is those who are most marginalized and exploited who are disproportionately impacted. Queer folk, trans folk, intersex folk, sex workers, the poor, the racialized, are all the first people to experience the neg-ative effects of such a war.

Nudity itself has now become potentially traumatizing. I am not talking about the obviously aggressive and intentionally traumatizing actions that fall under the category of indecent exposure. We live in a culture where sexual violence and the straight, cis, male control of public space, through acts of symbolic and physical violence, are still much too prevalent. However, I am talking about the way in which even animal nudity is regularly blurred out in Facebook posts or moments in which the panoply of meanings attaching to the artistic display of nudity or scanty dress gets read as de facto traumatizing, like with the debate over the display of Tony Matelli's "Sleepwalker" sculpture at Wellesley (figure 1). The sculpture depicts a vulnerable, older man in

Figure 1. Tony Matelli's *Sleepwalker* on the High Line.

underwear. Some students who had experienced sexual assault found the statue triggering and went out of their way to not view it. I, of course, want to support students who are dealing with trauma produced by the prevalence of sexual assault in the United States. I also agree with Cynthia Barounis that the choice of a woman's college is perhaps less than ideal for the sculpture.[8] Its recent appearance on New York's High Line makes more sense and appears remarkably anodyne compared to the forms of explicit, public sex and sexual representation that have been part of Manhattan's history—from the abandoned warehouses where David Wojnarowicz documented his sexual encounters to Samuel R. Delany's blue Times Square to the leather clubs that intersex writer Thea Hillman chronicles.[9] Strikingly, all three of these public sexual spaces occupied the same space (or were only a short walk away) as the now posh area that the High Line traverses, suggesting a different allegory about gentrification and the fate of public sex in the present. Reading Matelli's figure as primarily traumatizing rather than as a figuration of a different kind of vulnerability suggests the way in which trauma has become the master signifier for interpreting representations of sexuality and nudity in the present.

In *Vulnerable Constitutions*, Barounis critiques what she theorizes as the implicitly macho stances that can inform otherwise progressive pro-sex queer positions like those of Samuel Delany, Paul B. Preciado, and Ann Pellegrini (205–8). While I admire her willingness to theorize the persistence of gender ideologies beyond gender identification and sexed embodiment, something that is necessary and risky in the present, she extends this to make a critique of "queer resilience" in general from a disabilities studies and asexual theory perspective. Yet, for me, resilience is a crucial category, particularly for leftist thought. Certainly we should not negate (and indeed affirm on a materialist level) various material, physical, and psychological limitations, forms of disability (or crip embodiment), and posttraumatic subjectivities. As I will argue, the negation of material limits in the name of resilience and self-branding are discourses that are profoundly tied up with neoliberalism and ever-growing global inequality. This is not the kind of resilience I mean when I argue that it is a key category of leftist thought. Instead, I am talking about hard-won material, psychological, and collective resilience that comes from the work of material, conceptual, and social activism, transformation, and resistance. It is a refusal to give in to the forces arrayed against us or that have scarred us while still recognizing the violence done by them. Pro-sex queer and feminist positions at their best were precisely such forms of resilience: an affirmation of sexual rights, provocations, pleasure, and responsibilities over against the necropolitical violence of the dominant response to AIDS in the 1980s through the 2000s.

While we need to attend to changing social contexts in which scholarly debates take place, we forget the lessons of the pro-sex moment at our peril. As Jordy Rosenberg persuasively argues, a revolutionary approach to trans political struggles around gender, sex, and sexuality is about transforming "vulnerabilities into pressure points to build power through the articulation of a demand."[10] This demand is one articulated in relationship to "our own pleasure" (267). We seem to have forgotten that pleasure itself can be a revolutionary demand, one of the fundamental ones.

Pro-sex relationships to embodiment, sexual activity, and representation can teach us to read in diverse ways, particularly in relationship to stuff that may initially challenge, disturb, or even trigger us (and part of the complication in all of these debates is the ways in which both "trauma" and "trigger" have evolved beyond their clinical definitions to become generalized buzz words in the present). It is important to remember that many of us have different (and changing) relationships between trauma and representation, ones that may not be well served by an increased curtailment of what can and should be part of representation and public sexual culture. As someone whose genitals were always already on display, being born with an intersex embodiment and having sixteen (initially unnecessary, if they had left me alone) surgeries, I find representations of nudity and consensual expressions of public sex and sexuality profoundly affirming. Moreover, even stuff I experience as too close to the source of embodied violence, such as films that involve medical horror, I often find later to be transformative on a psychological level. My argument here is not that we should ignore that representation holds the possibility to retraumatize folks. Indeed, good pedagogy should involve careful attention to when different students are able to productively engage with different texts and employ strategies for making these encounters as productive and supportive as possible. Moreover, I am not arguing that my own experience should trump that of others (although I think I am hardly alone in my different relationship to the intertwining of embodied trauma and representation). Our public sphere in the United States is already overrun with competing claims of the incommensurability of individual experience. I am not even arguing that the sculpture should have stayed where it was placed at Wellesley. Rather, I am arguing that we impoverish our understanding of representation and sexuality when we short-circuit the work it can do by assimilating it too quickly to the production of trauma. Reading the display of (almost) naked bodies primarily in terms of trauma puts us closer to Mussolini's insistence that nude Roman and Roman-styled statues be covered with fig leaves than with the serendipitous encounter with nudity I used to have when I was a graduate student at UC Santa Cruz, with its clothes-optional policies. I remember a wonderful conversation with the late (and much missed) Lauren Berlant that was gloriously interrupted by naked rollerbladers. It was a beautiful nude, queer moment, and it enriched the conversation with its pleasurable intrusion. I want to argue for a conception of sexuality, nudity, and sex as still potentially serendipitous and transformative rather than merely something that is threatening and thoroughly external to the subject.

The contemporary concept of sexualization as thoroughly external has a grounding in Foucault's critique of the repressive hypothesis.[11] If central to twentieth-century struggles around sex, particularly as articulated in relationship to accounts of sex framed within Marxism, psychoanalysis, and the complex group of struggles that went under the reductive banner of "sexual liberation," was the notion of sex as shaped by cultural repression, Foucault's argument against the notion of repression and for positive power as central to the production of sex and sexual subjectivities represented a major turning-point and break.[12] The discourse of sexualization represents one development of this framework—sex is a productive discourse that generates selves, bodies, and pleasures. In this sense it is literally sexualizing. However, even as the productive hypothesis came to replace the repressive hypothesis in a lot of queer and feminist work of the 1990s, it was still linked often to a sex-positive position. Queer theory typically posited sex as productive of bodies, pleasures, and perversities, and it celebrated them, while also attending to their ideological dimensions. Sex was productive here, but it was still seen as an affirmative dimension of subjectivity and culture in progressive circles. This is a very different usage of the productive hypothesis than is often invoked in the idea of sexualization in the present. The current version of sexualization does the work of earlier feminist discourses of objectification, criticizing the way consumer culture presents women and, to some degree and unevenly, other subjective positions as objects, but those earlier discourses also held out the concept of a more positive conception of sex. (I leave to the side, for the moment, whether a certain amount of objectification is necessary for desire to function.) Current uses of sexualization seem to want to be free of sex altogether.

The current account has brought to the fore the negativity lurking in Foucault's account of positive power. Of course, the positivity of Foucault's account was never about its results (which could indeed be constraining and negative), but it is striking that sexualization here seems to be about producing a negative state that is predicated on an earlier moment of nonsexualization or desexualization, if not innocence. The sex positivity of the 1990s has shifted to what can only be described as the strange sex negativity of the present moment in which sex is both ubiquitous and everywhere a threat. Given this emphasis in the present, it is perhaps not surprising that one of the most dynamic bodies of theory to have emerged in the past ten years or so is that around asexuality, which importantly attends to the conscriptive and violently compulsory dimensions of sexuality while also affirming a positive notion of asexuality as a lived subjectivity and relationality. Accounts of asexuality do not have to be erotophobic, indeed they can be central to producing a more affirmatively elective relationship to sex and sexuality, as Ela Przybylo has cogently argued, but a decent number of asexuality's more popular invocations seem to want to be rid of sex altogether.[13] Take, for example, the "Sex Is Obsolete" and "Sex Is Yucky" T-shirts seen in the storefront of a queer-positive shop in the Chicago neighborhood of Andersonville.

This attitude toward sex in the present has rendered it not only ubiquitous but also a ubiquitous problem. Sex, at least in terms of how we talk about it (and as Foucault and Lacan argue, in a rare moment of convergence, sex is as much about discourse as it is about acts), has stopped being primarily about pleasure, sensuality, desire, relationality, and the ecstatic ambivalence of jouissance.[14] It is not something we do, but something that is done to us. The way in which it complicates or negates our egoic conceptions of self increasingly presents itself as a problem. If it represents a breach of our egoic self, a complex and risky grappling with the otherness of both oneself and one's lovers, this breach itself is presented as traumatic. And trauma, itself an important if overused concept in contemporary theory and activist discourse, is a term, like sexualization, that has become ubiquitous, such that social struggles around, say, race and class that are political and macrological in their focus become imagined in relationship to trauma as an increasingly micrological category or as a medicalized reframing (as in inherited trauma) of macrological categories of struggle. I am not arguing that these understandings of trauma are wrong. What I am arguing is that trauma may not be the best way to frame fundamentally political, social, and economic struggles.

Powerful and necessary work on the pervasiveness of sexual violence in contemporary cultures articulated by the #MeToo movement in the United States and many other national contexts demonstrates that sex is too often bound up with trauma. It is too often used as a tool of domination, exploitation, and nonconsensual violence. Yet, in recognizing this reality and working to transform it, it is crucial that our theories of sex do not capitulate, by making it the dominant or even sole way in which we conceptualize sex, to the very ideology that we are trying to undo. The critique of the anti-sex understanding of sex as everywhere reinforcing unequal and nonconsensual forms of power was central to the queer, sex-positive positions of late twentieth-century thinkers like Gayle Rubin, Susie Bright, and Amber Hollibaugh, to name just three.[15] They, in turn, were responding to the foundational accounts of the centrality of rape and sexual violence to the maintenance of patriarchy by Catherine A. MacKinnon and Andrea Dworkin.[16] In order to produce a pro-sex position that does not just become sexual libertarianism or the justification of patriarchal business as usual (which is arguably, as Lorna Bracewell demonstrates, the fate of certain aspects of the pro-sex moment of the 1990s and early 2000s), we need to maintain both sets of insights at once.[17]

More than the unintentional effects of necessary struggles around sexual violence, however, I think the roots of the reconceptualization of sex as a problem, one that traumatically sexualizes one, is more directly related to transformations in subjectivity produced by neoliberalism and the uneven mediation of much of our sense of self through the ever-changing lens of social media and online culture more generally. Central to neoliberalism, as thinkers as diverse as Foucault, Wendy Brown, and David Harvey have argued, is the notion of human capital.[18] In place of collective notions of shared subjectivity, produced by shared yet unequal access to public sphere as a locus of collective rights and responsibilities, all of which are part of the long legacy of Fordism (for all of its contradictions) and the powerful forms of feminist, gay, and antiracist struggles of the 1960s and 1970s, we have instead a thoroughly individualized notion of one's relationship to the social, one that depends on how much human capital one has amassed. Human capital assumes that all aspects of human existence can be regulated and sorted by the market. In place of the society (so hated by neoliberal warriors like Margaret Thatcher and Ronald Reagan) as a locus of collective responsibility, positive liberty, and the possibility of collective flourishing, we instead have a collection of competing individuals whose right to social and economic goods depends on their individual performance of wealth, ability, health, morality, and visibility. In place of a social contract, however inadequate and bisected by the contradictions of capitalism, we instead have the imperative toward self-branding (you need to be "on brand," as the ironic internet lingo has it), self-promotion, and an individualist understanding of identity as personal property.

While the dynamics of human capital production characterize both phases of neoliberalism, I do think it is important to distinguish between early and late version of the phenomenon (which is simultaneously a set of policy prescriptions, a managerial strategy, a mode of class warfare, and a political-economic dynamic that unevenly characterizes the capitalist world system).

What I want to describe as the first phase of neoliberalism intersected with the dynamics of postmodernism and globalization such that subjectivity was imagined as reflexive, self-fashioned, and syncretic, and the political economy was imagined as thoroughly transnational. Our own moment of late neoliberalism (which can be dated since the economic collapse of 2008 but has taken on a new visage as it intersects with what Alberto Toscano has described as late fascisms of various sorts) is defined by walled conceptions of the nation state, walled identities, obsessions with racial and sexual purity, an economy that relies ever more on what Harvey theorizes accumulation by dispossession (the direct accumulation of capital via financialization, debt, and the privatization of public and common goods), and the ever growing warehousing of various populations (178–79).[19]

Wendy Brown provides an account of late neoliberalism as an unexpected antidemocratic growth out of its first phase:

> In short, while the book will argue that the constellation of principles, policies, practices, and forms of governing reason that may be gathered under the sign of neoliberalism has importantly constituted the catastrophic present, this was not neoliberalism's intended spawn, but its Frankensteinian creation. Fathoming how that creation came to be requires examining the imminent failures and occlusions of neoliberal principles and policy, as well as their admixture with other powers and energies, including those of racism, nihilism, fatalism, and ressentiment.[20]

Brown nicely historicizes the way in which neoliberalism has morphed into a version congruent with late fascism. She also indicates the way in which it has functioned as a social and political-economic pedagogy whose logic has profoundly reshaped our understanding of life and identity, both of which have been thoroughly privatized and shaped by the dynamics of human capital. So even if late neoliberalism is beginning to morph into something else (and it does feel like we are in a period of transition) such as new articulations of fascism, what Jodi Dean has theorized as a new form of feudalism (what I would call it, at the most, capitalism with feudal characteristics), what McKenzie Wark describes as a new political-economy dominated by information, or, more hopefully, a renewed socialism or communism, the logic of neoliberalism, particularly on the level of the individual subject is still very much with us.[21] Nowhere is this more evident than in how identity has been transformed within late neoliberalism. Moreover, capitalism may have changed visages, but it is still very much with us.

Identity, once a category of collective organizing and identification, has become primarily personal. Online it often also becomes a source of social capital, in which legitimate arguments around exploitation, oppression, and exclusion regularly morph into competing claims of greater marginality and authority (or marginality as authority) and lead to the proliferation of competing identity claims (including by members of groups that are already thoroughly privileged). I am not arguing that the subject positions and experience do not matter. I am arguing that we need to be able to create forms of solidarity and relationality that transcend increasingly micrological and local understandings of identity in addressing macrological inequalities. Given how intensively mediated our sense of identity (our brand) is, increasingly we experience any representation that does not affirm this identity as an affront or an attack, particularly since our subjectivity is conflated with its public status as an avatar and avatars become our primary form of property in the immiserated present.

Within this context, it is not surprising that one's relationship to sex itself has been fundamentally transformed for many people. As I argued, sex is increasingly seen as something both ubiquitous and alien. It impinges on one's identity and threatens to negate it. And while most psychoanalytic and constructivist accounts may locate the initial locus of sex outside the subject and, in Jean Laplanche's argument, the enigmatic signifier of sexuality is indeed experienced as potentially traumatizing, crucial to these earlier accounts is the way in which we subjectify sex in all its ambiguity.[22] Sex as a necessarily relationship to the self and the other has been lost in the present. Our understanding of sex constructs the other and the social as a threat to the ascendancy of one's identity and the careful cultivation of one's human capital. Sex has the uncomfortable taint of otherness, of other people, of the ghost of the social. It is also disruptive, disorienting and undoing of all the careful work one puts into presenting one's best self. It is much easier to just turn on porn. And while porn itself is as ambiguous as it is ubiquitous in the present, particularly as a locus of capitalist production/exploitation and as an alternately fascinating, disturbing, and boring mediation of our sexual fantasies, some of the phobic relationship to sex in the United States is shaped by the way in which graphic images online substitute for sex education, with its destruction by right-wing forces, and the ability to have mature discussions about sex, the body, and health. We have a proliferation of sexual images and a paucity of critical discourse and knowledge about sex and sexual representation. We also experience our embodiment increasingly as avatar-like.

In *Insistence of the Material: Literature in the Age of Biopolitics*, I argued that this becoming avatar-like is tied to a new form of commodity fetishism, which structures subjectification in the present. I call this new species of commodity fetishism avatar fetishism. Marx's account of commodity fetishism is about a dynamic of materialization, with the labor between people becoming perceived as a relationship between objects. In avatar fetishism commodities themselves have become thoroughly secondary (merely a means to an end) to the fetishized and thoroughly dematerialized self-image, the virtual self or avatar. This conception of self is tied not only to the domains of image, affect, information, and symbolic labor but even more to forms of social media and other forms of algorithmically driven and intensely mediated consumption. This fetish of the immaterial and customizable self forms as a fundamental class divide in contrast to those who are still consigned to physical labor, whether in industrial production, agricultural production, or sex work. These latter workers are often racialized or sexualized within both the dominant ideology and by the real segmentation of labor. They are abjected within the logic of avatar fetishism, but they also take on a kind of sexualized materiality, and thus become defined by what I term embodiment envy, in which those who have the privilege of conceptualizing themselves as immaterial become envious of those who they have reduced to an embodiment that can only appear excessive and hypersexualized. Sex (as both desire and embodiment) is shaped by these twin dynamics of avatar fetishism and embodiment envy. The strange sex negativity of the present is informed by these twin dynamics of wanting to transcend the physical while also imagining it as excessively embodied by the threatening yet erotic other.

Sex and sexual desire need to be discussed in pedagogical spaces as well as in the broader culture. Without discourse around sex and its contradictions, pleasures, and, yes, dangers, we are likely to produce a culture in which it is ever less consensual and ever more traumatizing. What is disavowed on the level of the subject returns on the level of action in particularly nonreflexive ways. Yet sex can be a powerful building block of the social. It insists that we have a relationship to otherness, even as that otherness necessarily remains opaque. It is a fundamental site of the ethical, precisely because we both must open up to otherness in acknowledging it and we must recognize the opacity of the other's desire. As Lacan famously argued, "there is no such thing as a sexual relation."[23] While this claim might seem to deny the sociality of sex and thus fundamentally run counter to the argument *In Defense of Sex* is advancing, Lacan's statement needs to be read in a dialectical relationship to his other argument that desire is always the desire of the other. Desire comes from the social, but our relationship to sex always remains opaque, precisely because of its otherness. Thus, sex in this understanding is fundamentally asymmetrical. We are in bed, or in a public park, or a kink club with our fantasies, and our sexual partner or partners are there with their fantasies, and while our bodies may join in all kinds of physical ways this joining is always mediated by the workings of fantasy and desire. The ethics of sex, including public sex, is about negotiating the opacity of this relationship. As with the social more generally, we both have a responsibility to the other and cannot fully know what motivates them. Consent is necessary but not sufficient in negotiating this opacity. To begin to build forms of collectivity that can sustain a common relationship to sexuality, we need to recognize both of these injunctions, that we have a responsibility to otherness and yet we need to recognize its opacity. Such becomes the necessarily democratic and collectivist negotiation that structures a radical politics, including a politics of sexuality.

Defending Sex as Embodiment

My defense of sex in this book is not only about defending sex as desire or act but also as a form of embodiment. Indeed, the roots of the book are here. I first began thinking about this question in relationship to the need to rethink embodied sex as a category, given the way in which, as Paisley Currah has cogently demonstrated, it is used in transphobic legislation and discourses to negate transgender rights and reproduce transphobia, while at the same time, abandoning it (or conflating it with gender) negates the crucial category by which intersex is understood.[24] Here too it may seem strange, at first glance, that sex needs defending. The sexed body, while maybe less of a focus in the present, is rendered evermore immanent to culture and evermore malleable, transformable, and biotechnical. If in the early twentieth century the body could be primarily grounded in nature, with gender designating its cultural superstructure, by the twenty-first century, with the growth of various biotechnologies, prostheses, and biopolitical interventions, both sex and gender have been folded into what Paul B. Preciado defines as the "pharmacopornographic regime," in which the body is not part of nature but is rather an artifact produced by "biomolecular" and "semiotic-technical" processes.[25] I finally prefer Rebekah Sheldon's term "somatic capitalism" to describe the way in which biology itself has become capitalized and biopolitically shaped. Preciado is a little too sanguine about the pharmacopornographic regime, and he overstates the medical capacity to unproblematically manipulate and reshape the body, yet he and Sheldon are both surely right that there is no simple nature/culture opposition at work in relationship to our current understanding of sex and gender. Sheldon's term remains more properly dialectical about what this process entails. I will thus use it with more regularity in what follows.[26]

The breaking of gender binaries is necessary and important, as is the vision of a world, as Susan Stryker and Aren Z. Aizura argue, that can "encompass new potentials for unexpected becomings and . . . accommodate the manifestation of unforeseen, emergent potentials of bodily being."[27] This work of generating multiple possibilities for gendered being is indeed crucial. Yet it is striking that gendered multiplicity is often narrated in terms of proliferating and individualized micro-identities, or what Kadji Amin describes as a return of sexology.[28] As trans activist Jennifer Finney Boylan quips, it is "not about who you want to go to bed *with*, it's who you want to go to bed *as*."[29] And certainly, who you go to bed as is important (all power to different versions of identification and sexual role playing in bed!), but certainly who you go to bed with matters too. In this context, is it any wonder that gender has everywhere replaced sex as the designation for subjective, identificatory, and embodied difference? Why would we need a concept of sex as an account of embodied morphology when gender seems to do the work that sex used to do and with much less potential for producing binaries or excluding specific forms of identification? Given the persuasive ways in which transgender and nonbinary theory and activism have challenged ideas of biomorphic sex as determining and foundational, sex as embodiment may seem not worth defending in the present. To defend it runs the danger of being reactionary. Perhaps it is best consigned to the dustbin of history.

In Defense of Sex argues otherwise. We lose something crucial when we stop talking about sex both in terms of embodiment and desire. Yet the different critiques of sex advanced by transgender theory, constructivist feminist theory, and asexual theory are crucial to engage. If we are going to defend sex, we are going to have to do so in a very different way from what has been done in the past. We are going to have to articulate a concept of sex for the twenty-first century, one that takes into account work in not only trans and queer theory but also in relationship to intersex theory and activism. The conception of sex I argue for is fundamentally nonbinary.

Much recent discourse in popular culture and in some trans and feminist theory have argued that the way forward for a nontransphobic conception of gender and embodiment is to eschew ideas of biological sex altogether. Of course, this position needs to be understood as being in dialectical tension with accounts of transgender subjectivity that emphasized the transformations of the sexed body, such as those of Preciado and Jay Prosser. Still, the argument that any reference to sex is potentially transphobic recurs regularly in the larger culture.[30] It is perhaps best captured in an antitransphobic meme that was circulated in response to some of the author J. K. Rowling's transphobic pronouncements:

Besides, you're saying it wrong.

@SH24_NHS

It's TRANSPHOBIA, not 'defending biological sex'

Figure 2. Anti-transphobic *Harry Potter* meme.

Certainly, the rhetoric of this meme is correct in naming the privileging of a binary understanding of biological sex as central to much transphobic discourse. Much transphobia, both online and in everyday life, is cast in the defense of an essentialist claim to the overarching truth of a binary conception of biological sex. Such claims are regularly used to trump the lived reality of gender. The position criticized by the meme negates the lived experience of gender and gendered identification as a central feature of subjectivity. It also is used to police the borders of the categories of man and woman, marking trans folk as somehow not true women and men. I affirm the work done by the meme for all these reasons. Yet the idea that any argument for biological sex is inherently transphobic shuts down what needs to be opened up: sex needs to be understood as nonbinary or can be visualized, in Amanda Montañez's terms, as a spectrum.[31]

Sara Ahmed, whose work on materiality and emotions I deeply admire, has made a similar if more nuanced argument as the meme in a blog post: "*Sex is real* is an assertion within a horizon of assertions. *Sex is real. Sex is material. Sex is immutable. Sex is biology. Sex is objective. Sex is science.* With these as- sertation about what sex is, come counter-implications about what gender is not. *Gender is not real. Gender is immaterial. Gender is subjective. Gender is stereotypes. Gender is ideology.*"[32] Again, Ahmed is certainly right about the way in which this discourse is being employed in transphobic contexts and anti-trans positions arising within essentialist feminism. Ahmed, Judith Butler, and other feminist scholars represent crucial voices in aligning progressive, anti-essentialist feminism with transgender theory and activism.[33] For this reason, again, their work here is necessary.

Yet the meme and Ahmed's argument also have the unintended effect of marking all discussions and defenses (to invoke the title of this book) of sex necessarily transphobic. To theorize in a way that can be aligned with intersex embodiments and identifications, we need not only a complex, multiple, and nonbinary conception of gender but one of sex as well. If we erase the materi- ality of the sexed body, we also erase the materiality of the intersex experience. Yet, as recent activism has maintained, intersex and trans struggles should be allied. Moreover, we need more solidarity and less factionalism around leftist struggles in general. To produce such a nonbinary conception of sex, one that can theoretically compliment a trans-affirmative conception of gender as mul- tiple, we need to decouple sex and gender further than Ahmed does in her argument. She assumes that a specific set of claims about sex (that it is material and biological) implies the nonreality of gender and gendered embodiment. Yet, this is only the case if we see sex as itself not multiply produced, complex, and historically and biomedically shaped as well as material. An assertion of the material and biological dimensions of sex does not necessarily imply that gender is secondary or immaterial and thus less true and real. Ahmed's argu- ment about the necessity of divorcing sex and gender here sees any account of sex as necessarily implying a concomitant conception of gender. Such a position still sees sex as necessarily tethered to and determining of gender. It is crucial that we think of sex and gender as radically distinct in terms of causality and identification, even as they are complexly braided on the level of embodiment. In arguing for a much more capacious and trans-affirmative conception of gender we should not unintentionally reify a traditional and binaristic (indeed transphobic) understanding of sex. Quite the opposite. This book proposes an alternate, multiple conception of embodied sex.

On the level of embodiment, I am arguing for a nonbinary yet materialist account of the category of sex. In doing so, my argument complicates much recent work in queer theory, trans theory, and gender theory, which has tended to privilege the category of gender and efface the category of sex as hopelessly retrograde, essentialist, and binary. Gender is a crucial category. In the largely psychoanalytic framework I am employing to define both gender and sex, gender is an identification that becomes an egoic mapping of the body. It is a version of what Freud describes as a body ego, Lacan calls the ideal ego as it functions in the imaginary, and what Didier Anzieu defines as a "skin ego."[34] The body or skin ego is a conceptual and affective mapping of the body and a sense of self that often intersects with the material body but is not reducible to it. The gendered body ego is not fully reducible to the surface of the body, but Anzieu is right to emphasize how much our imaginary constructions of our ego (and of gender, I would add) function as a skin, or what he defines as a "bridge and screen mediating between the psyche and the body" (4). Suggesting that gender is imaginary and structured around egoic identification is not to minimize it. On the contrary, it is central to the way in which we experience ourselves as a unified being, moving through the world and interacting with others, erotically or otherwise. It also can be understood as what Ben Spatz has discussed as a mode of technique—a way of inhabiting the physical and erotic body.[35]

If this is the account of gender I am operating with, my nonbinary account of sex sees it primarily as a material substrate, as Spatz also describes it, aspects of the material body that are related to desire, sexuality, and reproduction (180). A nonbinary understanding of sex is crucial to a materialist politics around embodiment, one that can help to envision better and more just embodied futures. Drawing on recent intersex scholarship, trans theory, critical race theory, psychoanalysis, queer theory, new materialist theory, and Marxist theory, *In Defense of Sex* argues for a nonbinary conception of the sexed body that intertwines with yet also importantly differs from nonbinary and transgendered understandings of gender. Sex and gender in this model are interwoven, yet they are not reducible to each other. Reducing sex to gender, as has been done in much recent theory and even more in popular discourse, renders intersex illegible.

It also erases specific histories of racial violence inscribed on what Hortense Spillers, C. Riley Snorton, R. A. Judy, Alexander G. Weheliye, and Marquis Bey theorize as the flesh, or the dimensions of the body that were radically degendered, commodified, and violently inscribed during slavery and its apartheid aftermath in Jim Crow.[36] As Spillers argues, we can only fully understand the violence of slavery as a process of degendering, which renders the enslaved person flesh. It also becomes the site in which enslaved people are produced as so-called thinking commodities or "sentient flesh," in Judy's terms (2). Flesh,

as Snorton argues, becomes the site of the racial body's "fungibility," its transformation into a serialized commodity (6). As he further demonstrates, the
fleshed body also became the locus of violent biomedical extraction and accumulation, with the emergence of modern gynecology produced out of the
experimentation on enslaved bodies and presaging the later production of
contemporary urology on intersex bodies (although it is, of course, crucial acknowledge the difference in terms of citizenship, racial privilege and often
economic privilege between medicalized intersex subjects and enslaved and/
or racialized ones). For Judy and Marquis Bey flesh is not just a negatively imposed category but also a locus of collective poesis, a mode of embodiment that
opens out to larger ecosystems. As I theorize more fully in the chapters that
follow, this version of flesh, one that parallels Marx's discussion of species being
and its destruction by dynamics of reification, also points toward collective and
trans-corporeal forms of embodiment that can be the basis for a genuinely materialist politics of embodiment would theorize both sex and flesh as sites of
both historical violence and potential liberation. We need struggles for liberation
in terms of not only gender but also sex, sexuality, race, class, and flesh. Such a
struggle would ally antiracist, intersex, feminist, Marxist, and trans struggles.

   In Defense of Sex draws upon materialist work by intersex scholars such as
Hil Malatino and David A. Rubin, as well recent gender, queer, psychoanalytic,
critical race, and new materialist theory to theorize anew the category of sex.[37]
Sex in this context refuses binaries. It is instead a nonbinary yet material dimension of the body, one that can intersect in complex was with flesh in Spillers's, Bey's, Snorton's, and Judy's different formulations. While the specific
racialized history of violence under and after slavery (including medical violence, which points to later—less thoroughly violent—experimentation on
intersex subjects, as I discuss in chapters 1 and 3) needs to be maintained,
Snorton also argues for "flesh as a capacitating structure for alternative modes
of being" (53). The concept of embodied sex I am proposing works as a similar
capacitating structure (as well as a potential site of both violence and sustenance), although one not necessarily experienced in the same way as the more
collectivized category that is flesh. Sex in this framework refers to the morphology of the biological body as it relates to issues of sexual desire, reproduction, and what has been called (rather reductively) primary (the formation and
development of the genitals) and secondary sex characteristics (for example,
the postpubescent development of breasts and facial hair).

   While we tend to think about this morphology in binary terms, feminist
biologist and critical theorist, Anne Fausto-Sterling, makes an argument for a
much more complex and capacious conception of sex as a category, in which
in which different aspects of the sexed body (including genetics, hormones,

gonads, organs, and genitals) can, and regularly do, produce or materialize a range of different sexed embodiments: "A newborn is a multilayered creature, the result of having a chromosomal sex, a fetal gonadal sex, fetal hormonal sex, a fetal internal reproductive sex . . . [and] an external genital sex."[38] We tend to frame the work of all of these bodily agents in relationship to the binary opposition male/female; yet the reality produced is multiple, generating different gradations of sexed embodiment. As recent work in epigenetics has demonstrated, even something as seemingly binary as genetic expression is shaped by environmental factors and the complexity produced by the interaction of different genes. So, even if we want to grant a basic binary logic to genetics, what this code produces is a composite of many different binary logics interacting and mixing with the nonbinary logic of environmental factors. Moreover, causality in the development of sex characteristics often works in relationship to feedback loops and chiastic exchanges between cause and effect. The development of a given morphology may be in part shaped by hormones, but this very morphology starts to inform the production of hormones. What emerges is material bodies that have certain tendencies, possibilities, and limits, but ones that only from a certain distance (and only if one is looking through ideological blinkers) look binary in their formation. This, then, is the nonbinary concept of sex that informs the book's larger arguments around the intersection of sex, class, gender, race, and sexuality in the present.

Rethinking the relationship between sex and gender, trans and intersex, embodiment and identification, reification and flesh, *In Defense of Sex* pushes contemporary queer discourse around gender beyond neoliberal notions of flexibility, micro-identity, self-fashioning, and personal choice. It instead articulates a materialist framework where the specificity of intersex, trans, queer, antiracist, and feminist struggles can be understood without giving in to the internecine and unproductive battles that sometimes play out between these different perspectives.

Theorizing Desire and Embodiment

In terms of thinking about sex in relationship to desire, *In Defense of Sex* argues for an understanding of desire that is materialist in the sense that it is a structuring element that exists in tension with our consciousness and symbolic forms of representation (while shaping both). While desire can be discursively shaped, it is not a passive element that is thoroughly flexible. As much as it is shaped by and intersects with representation and discourse, it exists in tension with both. It also forms in complex tension with our consciousness and moral dictates. If this account of desire seems familiar that is because it is.

My account of desire is fundamentally psychoanalytic. The version of psychoanalysis I employ, however, is broad and as informed by Marxist theory and its investment in desiring and building a collective and just world as it is informed by any specific tradition or school of psychoanalysis. [39] I primarily draw upon Jacques Lacan's understanding of subjectivity as oriented around a real to which it forms in contradiction. I also draw on Jean Laplanche's and Lacan's different account of the drive and sexuality as structured by an encounter with otherness. My understanding also works to be attentive to more recent developments in asexual theory, with its critique of compulsory sexuality, while articulating a fundamentally psychoanalytic framework. Thus, the version of psychoanalysis I am using here is invested in Freudian and post-Freudian accounts of the role of the drive(s). Sex, as drive, informs our speech and our desire to renounce it as much as it informs our embrace of it or our more embodied pursuits of it. It is important to theorize sexual desire in its broadest register as a desire for a relationship to the other, whether this other is manifested in the unconscious sexual messages of other people, in the language and practices of the culture, or in the forms of otherness that exist in our psyches and our relationship to our bodies.

In this way, the account of desire in the book emphasizes Lacan's understanding of desire as "desire of the other." [40] Lacan figures as central to my account of sex as both embodiment and desire. As Alenka Zupančič argues, "in psychoanalysis sex above all is a concept that formulates a persisting contradiction of reality." [41] In this specific sense, then, sex functions partially in the dimension of the real in Lacanian psychoanalysis. It exists in fundamental tension with symbolic and imaginary as they produce a shared sense of reality. Yet, my account of sex, both as embodiment and as desire, is less formalist than that proposed by strict Lacanianism. On the level of embodiment, as I detail more fully in chapter 2, I see the body as not constituted only in relationship to the imaginary body (where gender is central) but also by a real body (which is the domain, in part, of sex).

This real body is different from the reality of the body (although it can overlap with aspects of the latter) rather it represents both the uncoded and disavowed dimensions of embodiment (what is in tension with the mapping of the body ego). At the same time, as I will explore more fully in chapters 1 and 2, I am also interested in thinking about the material body in terms of a positive account of it as well as in relationship the persistent negativity of the real. For me, the body is extimate (and external intimacy, or intimate externality), to use another Lacanian concept. [42] Our maps of it always contain a not-all that haunts and exists in negative relationship to their topologies. Yet it is also important to provide a working account of sex as a dimension of the material body, and I will draw on recent work in feminist new materialism by Stacy Alaimo, Karen Barad, Mel Y. Chen, and Samantha Frost in order to situate a nonreductive and relational account of embodiment as it interacts with other bodies and the larger ecosystems in which it operates.[43] We need to understand our bodies and our conceptions of gender and sex as not privatized, but opening out, partially, to the larger ecological, economic, and social domains of the world in which we live.

Sex as desire can also be thought of as real in the Lacanian sense. As Zupančič argues, it forms a fundamental "contradiction" or "stumbling block" in reality (3). The real exists in fundamental tension with our symbolic accounts of reality. In positing sex as ontological in this manner, I do not think we need to dismiss the insights of asexual theory. Quite the opposite. This version of sex suggests why we often have a complicated, ambivalent, obsessive, or distant relationship to sex. Moreover, it also suggests the ways in which sex is often about our conversations, collective projects, and modes of producing in the world as much or more than it is about bodies fucking (as fun as that can be!). Sex in this expanded sense, also informs what Ela Przybylo, drawing on the foundational work of Audre Lorde, describes as a conception of erotics that is not attached to sex and the compulsory performance of sexuality (20–28). She may disagree that this should be described as sexual, but I think there is a space of productive overlap and alliance here. Finally, since I am proposing a non-binary model of sex and gender, the relationship of desire to embodiment is also not binary. As Tim Dean has argued, the model of partial objects (reworked as Lacan's *objet petit a*) and perversions (understood in the etymological sense of curving or turning away) provides a much more powerful, nonheteronor-mative understanding of desire.[44] If sex and gender are no longer necessarily binary, then our understanding of desire is even more polymorphous than initially proposed by Freud in *Three Essays on the Theory of Sexuality*.[45] There is no synthesizing genital stage (except as an ideology). Instead, we are in a world of perverse subjects and their relationship to other subjects, part objects, bodies, desires, acts, and fantasies.

There is a utopian dimension to what Przybylo describes as asexual erotics and my other borrowings from psychoanalysis also share this utopianism (even if they are more, focused on desire as central to their utopian vision) (23–24). To realize this utopianism, my argument combines its psychoanalytic focus with a Marxist emphasis on the production of desire as fundamentally social. In doing so, I am following in the long tradition, from the Frankfurt school to the recent work of Samo Tomšič, of thinkers who combine Marxism and psychoanalysis.[46] This tradition thinks of desire, subjectivity, and em-bodiment as thoroughly social. If many of us have learned to privatize each of these, this is an effect of specific forms of political-economic and social organization.

Contemporary capitalism, in its late neoliberal guise, has worked to privatize many domains that were once considered part of the social, and while access to this social was always uneven and structured by class, race, gender, and sexuality, these inequalities persist beyond formal rights and recognitions that may have been won in the meantime. As the public and commons have been transformed by new enclosures into forms of private property for the purposes of what David Harvey describes as accumulation by dispossession, contemporary capitalism continues to find new areas to privatize, commodify, and monetize all aspects of the lifeworld, most recently focusing on the body and subjectivity itself as prime sources of accumulation, from the appropriation of data on social media sites to the generation of human capital, the selling of organs and other body parts, and the growth of surrogacy, as Sophie Lewis has theorized, in all sorts of contexts (Harvey, 178–79).[47] Within such a context, it is not surprising that notions of identity have started to bleed into concepts of intellectual property, symbolic capital, and ideas of self-branding. The possibility of a collective and radically egalitarian and equal culture around embodiment, class, gender, race, and sexuality, which I explore more fully in chapter 4 on the bodily and sexual commons, becomes ever more necessary and yet ever more difficult to effect. The vision that this book hopes to articulate is one in which ideas of gender, sexuality, and sex can function as part of a larger socialist, queer, feminist, and antiracist transformation of culture and society, in which a new public culture can emerge that enables all to have a sustaining, consensual, and pleasurable relationship to embodiment, sex, and sexuality. To achieve this end, though, we need to rethink the way in which the concept of identity has functioned in increasingly micrological and exclusionary ways in our algorithm-driven and late neoliberal present.

Liberation or Reification?

Two edited collections of Marxist theory, *Totality Inside Out: Rethinking Crisis and Conflict under Capital* and *After Marx: Literature, Theory, and Value in the Twenty-First Century*, demonstrate the productive ways in which Marxist theory has transformed since 2000.[48] Central to this transformation is the growth of Marxist work in social reproduction theory, Black Marxism, Indigenous Marxism, queer Marxism, and eco-Marxism to theorize of not just class and economics but also race, gender, sexuality, and ecology as fundamentally shaped and unevenly structured by the logic of global capitalism. These works argue that waged work is structured around and enabled by the appropriation of various forms of nonwage value and labor including gendered forms of housework, caregiving, and other forms of social reproduction, various forms of forced, nonwage labor (from slavery to other coercive labor regimes), which are typically racialized, and the extraction of value from Indigenous lands and knowledge as well as the world ecology itself. It also argues, as Petrus Liu, Christopher Chitty, and Kevin Floyd have differently demonstrated, that sexuality emerges in a complex formation with the population displacements produced by emerging labor regimes and the uneven reification of the body under capitalism.[49] Thus, rather than a tradition that can speak only to class formation and the sphere of official economics, this new approach works to map capitalist totality and value on an expanded scale. The primary forms of social antagonism structuring our world are understood as central to an expanded conception of accumulation.

In Defense of Sex situates itself within these new developments in Marxist theory. As will be most evident in chapters 3 and 4, my own approach to sexuality, sex, and gender is fundamentally Marxist and relies on the expanded understanding of Marxism and the global dynamics of capitalism developed by this new work. Within such a framework, it is crucial that, even as I focus primarily on a few categories (sex, gender, and sexuality), these need to be understood as intersecting, in ways both uneven and structural, with other axes of difference and exploitation as well as with an expanded conception of sites of production, accumulation, appropriation, and value.

Yet, while I embrace this new approach to Marxist theory, there is one aspect of it about which I am skeptical. In their introduction to *After Marx*, Colleen Lye and Christopher Nealon map alternate trajectories for the development of Marxist theory since the mid-twentieth century.[50] In contrast to what they term the "Adornian" tradition that emphasizes the "commodification," and which finds its leading contemporary exponent in Fredric Jameson, they emphasize the Althusserian tradition, with its focus on multiple axes of overdetermination (7–8). They argue that this latter tradition has morphed into the version of Marxism they are advocating, with its emphasis on an expanded understanding of value production, the long-decline of capitalist profits since the beginning of the 1970s, and the "incorporation of ever more people into the ranks of what Marx called 'surplus populations'—those who are not worth incorporating into waged work on a regular basis" (8). While I absolutely agree that we need to think in terms of unwaged work as well as waged work and the crisis of profitability that has shaped capitalism in the last fifty years, it seems overly hasty to diminish the emphasis on commodification and ideology that were central to the Adornian tradition. In their argument, Lye and Nealon suggest that the Adornian tradition and its critique of ideology in relation to commodification is applicable only to the more privileged sectors of capitalism and effaces other axes of difference and value extraction outside of wage labor. While I too will theorize different positionalities within the world systems as enabling different worldviews and forms of embodiment (the concept of flesh being a privileged example in what follows), we let go of concepts of ideology and the transformation of the lifeworld (of which commodification is one key part) only at our peril. The notion that ideology stops at the edges of the official economy, and that people subject to more violent forms of accumulation are somehow positioned fully outside of it (they may be partially so), involves a fantasy of transparency, in which the subjective positions of the global precariat function much like the working class once did in Lukács as the subject-object of history.[51]

Obviously we need to theorize what insights and forms of collectivity as well as obfuscations are enabled by different positionalities within the world system and world ecology, but this does not mean that such positions are not themselves mediated by representation and shaped by historical contradictions and developments. For example, my discussion of flesh as a historically produced dynamic indicates the ways in which populations who are differently positioned in relationship to work and citizenship are shaped by their relationship to capitalist production in different ways, on the levels of both ideology and embodiment. The continuous growth that capitalism is organized around (even as it shuffles between exploitation and appropriation) should suggest that capitalist ideology, as well as ideological resistances to it, have also grown proportionately. Privatization and accumulation, not just commodification, produce capitalist ideology. Even if commodification is a partial dynamic, its logic still shapes nonwage labor relations and the logic of appropriation (the production of value itself is central to all of these dynamics). Similarly, while still quite uneven, the radical and commercial transformation of human communication systems via the cellphone, the internet, social media, and so on not just in the Global North but much of the Global South suggests that capitalist ideology and the commodification of the lifeworld has in fact grown exponentially in the last twenty years. We thus need to maintain an engagement with dynamics of commodification, reification, and ideology, even as we rethink them within an expanded Marxist frame.

These categories are also crucial to theorizing historical and contemporary conceptions of sex, gender, sexuality, and desire. There has been a sea change recently in how we think about these categories. Particularly in progressive circles, both within the academy and outside of it, the basic framework for how we understand sex, gender, and desire has undergone a mutation. As I argued earlier, gender, once seen as tied to and reflective of (although also able to differ from) a binary understanding of sex, has emerged as self-fashioned and multiple. Whereas our old understanding of gender and sex grounded the former on the latter and presented the latter as manifesting a binary form of embodiment (one was either male or female, and these were seen in opposition), the new conception importantly understands gender as both largely autonomous and definitional. Gender becomes the measure by which progressive folks apprehend the lived experience of themselves and others around sex, sexuality, and public life more generally. This transformation has been salutary. Much of this work to rethink gender has been produced by trans theory and activism in the last thirty years or so. It challenges the ways in which a still too binary and naturalized conception of gender contributed to an account of sexed and gendered embodiment that was structurally transphobic. In this context, trans theory dovetailed with and radicalized work that was also being done by gender theory (particularly in the wake of Judith Butler's crucial antifoundationalist reworking of gender), queer theory, and intersex theory to debinarize and denaturalize our understandings of both sex and gender.

This transformation has not merely taken place in the theoretical circles of the academy but has also found a strong grounding within progressive manifestations of popular culture. Of course, it is important to recognize the way in which this narrative is situated within a U.S.-centric understanding of these spaces. It is crucial to recognize the unevenness of the transformations I am talking about both globally and within U.S. culture. It is also just as important to recognize that along with this emergence there is a reactionary counterdiscourse that is challenging these developments, from the movements to deny gender-based social access to everything from bathrooms, shelters, and prisons to the ongoing presence of trans-exclusionary discourses about binary sex as the fundamental truth of being. These discourses are often tied to global rise of neofascism, with its atavistic conception of gender roles and biological understandings of both sex and race. So, in providing an account of the sea change around concepts in sex and gender, I want neither to overstate its reach nor to imagine that is not embattled. Yet, I also do not want to limit this transformation entirely to the United States or to academic or largely bourgeois culture. It has its roots in the activist redefinitions of gender and sexuality in various, globally situated queer communities, including queer working-class communities and queer communities of color.

While recognizing the unevenness of this discourse, it is striking how much of a change has taken place in the last ten years or so within progressive culture. The idea of gender as multiple has emerged as definitional. Similarly, understandings of one's relationship to sex and sexuality have multiplied and what were often more countercultural practices have become closer to the mainstream. If before we had the basic categories of gay/lesbian, straight, bi, trans, and people into BDSM, now we have a proliferation of categories around sex and desire. One can be gay, straight, bisexual, asexual, pansexual, demisexual, or sapiosexual, to just name some of the more popular categories. You also can mark the kinds of kink you are into in increasingly specific ways. What is more, you can find others in your community online or through various apps and hook up with the person who reflects or participates in your interests or fetishes. So not only is there a growing mainstreaming of these concepts, but they also seem to offer a level of precision that was not present before (even as, as Manuel Reza has noted, they become more privatized, moving from the club or bathhouse to the dating app).[52]

We are thus witnessing and participating in a cultural transformation in how we think about sex, gender, and desire. On one level, sex and gender have seemed never more liberated. And there is some truth to this narrative. The undoing of binary understandings of gender has been a crucial, if still too uneven, advance. On another level, though, our various relationships to sex, gender, and sexuality are more individualized and atomized in the present. The majoritarian or universal conception of queerness so powerfully articulated by Eve Kosofsky Sedgwick in the early 1990s has been replaced by an increasingly micrological account of ever more precise and often agonistic conceptions of identity.[53] Our discourses around sex and sexuality are less about desire and the relationship to otherness (including the intimate otherness of one's own body) than they are about enacting and affirming a specific conception of self. At least in terms of cultural representation (what people do in practice is always in a complex and contradictory relationship to cultural discourse), sex seem less interactive or other-directed. It is instead about affirming one's increasingly atomized and algorithmically shaped identity. Yet, as Ann Pellegrini and Avgi Saketopoulou argue, gender in its multiplicity may be better conceived outside of the framework of identity.[54] Moreover, at its best, queer universalism, as Madhavi Menon articulates it, "gathers together particularities across so-called identities and refuses to identify queerness in any particularity."[55] Menon provides a powerful rearticulation of queerness, one organized around "the impossibility of self-identity" and a conception of desire that "cannot suture bodies onto identities" (19, 16). Menon's version of queerness, like Sedgwick's before it, is central to the conception of queerness that animates In Defense of Sex.

If from one vantage the proliferation of different and ever more micrological identities looks like a conceptual revolution or, at the very least, a progressive social transformation, from another, it is an index of gender sex's increasing reification in the present, a specifically algorithmic reification. The reification of sex is not new to the present. Nor is it an unequivocally negative development. Combining the insights of Marxist and queer theory, Kevin Floyd has theorized the concept of reification to provide a historicist account of the emergence of (primarily male) homosexuality as a named identity, erotic embodiment, and a form of desire at the beginning of the twentieth century (39–78). Noting the historical overlap between Georg Lukács's account of the reification of labor and knowledge under Taylorism and Michel Foucault's articulation of the emergence of the figure of the homosexual as a minoritized (and stigmatized) identity within sexology and the human sciences more generally, Floyd argues that we can understand the (long and uneven) shift that Foucault charts from an earlier understanding of homoeroticism as primarily about acts, that is, the discourse of sodomy in which everybody was a potential sodomite, to one fundamentally about identity as not only an effect in the transformation around knowledge practices but also catalyzed by transformations in the organization of labor detailed by Lukács.

Floyd's account of reification is primarily focused on intersecting transformations in work and sexuality in the American twentieth century. Christopher Chitty and Rosemary Hennessy have demonstrated that the relationship between worker subjectivities and sexual subjectivities is spatially and temporally more extensive.[56] Hennessy charts the formation of homosexuality as an identity to the partitioning of labor under industrialization, situating it as much in industrializing Europe as in the United States. As Nancy Fraser also notes, the hardening of the divide between public and private, paid and unpaid labor, as well as the corralling of factory workers into same-sex spaces, all enabled new definitions and relationships of masculinity and femininity to emerge.[57] It also produced a separation between sexes understood as binary and a denigration of unwaged work. This in turn led to the ability for the homoerotic to find expression not only in relationship to acts but increasingly in terms of identities. Hennessy nicely complicates Foucault's narrative, which makes this shift a product of medical and juridical knowledge practices, suggesting that such practices themselves hinge on the material transformations of space, property, and labor that were central to industrialization.

Grounded in a world systems approach and using its expanded understanding of capitalism as dating from the long sixteenth century, Chitty's book, while sadly unfinished because of his untimely passing, provides a powerful rethinking of the relationship between sexuality, capitalist accumulation, and labor. His account provides a persuasive prehistory to the dynamics charted by Floyd and Hennessy. Moreover, his critique of Foucault's sexological focus is even more pointed. Positing a much longer history of popular homoeroticism, one that predates capitalism, but is also fundamentally reshaped by it, Chitty argues that a properly Marxist understanding of sexuality would chart its expression and relatively autonomy in relationship to changing class relations central to the dynamics of enclosure, agricultural capitalism (with its production of itinerant labor forces), and colonialism (with the spaces of the ship and the plantation emerging as a crucial locus of the intertwining of labor, sexuality, and rebellion). Chitty also charts the open expression of homoeroticism and general tolerance of it versus various moments of stepped up policing and sex panics to the movement between production (which is primarily about extracting productivity from labor) and financial expansion (which is about managing populations and accumulation by dispossession) that Giovanni Arrighi traces through the succeeding hegemonies of the capitalist world system.[58] Moments that emphasize productivity tend to be more tolerant of homoeroticism (if only to be able to mobilize a typically gender-separated workforce sufficient for production), while moments of financialization, which are organized around managing surplus populations and redistributing wealth, tend to be structured in relationship to sexual reaction. Indeed, one way to read the present is that we are in a moment of such reaction, although unevenly, and with a counterforce of individual identity formation that is as much about social pressures around human capital as it is about forms of micropolitics. To understand more fully the way in which gender, sex, and sexuality are formed in the present we need to turn back to Floyd's discussion of sexual reification and its relationship to the more general dynamic posited by Lukács. Given the history we have just traced, the reification of sexuality is seen as a specific structuration of the longer history traced by Chitty. The dynamic of reification emerges during the period of industrialization and the massification of work relationships that begins in the nineteenth century and reaches its apotheosis in Fordism. Nonwage work, in contrast, is not shaped by reification.

In order to understand Floyd's argument, we need to turn briefly to Lukács. Building of Marx's account of commodity fetishism, or the way in which the social relationship be people in the work of production is experienced, within the logic of capitalism, as a relationship between things, Lukács posits the reification of the lifeworld, a "phantom objectivity" produced by the relationship between money as a universal equivalent and commodities as objectified labor (83). While commodification precedes industrialization, its logic increasingly structures all forms of life beginning in the nineteenth century. Those rendered as living commodities or slaves in agricultural capitalism already have an intimate knowledge of the specific version commodification (or what Spillers describes as the production of flesh) central to the plantation economy, it does not structure the lifeworld of the so-called free laborer until the nineteenth century. "Free" labor becomes reified under industrial capitalism. Labor is commodified and it is turned into an abstract equivalent. It is quantified, and its qualitative dimensions are effaced.

Lukács builds on Marx's account of the commodification and quantification of labor, arguing that under Taylorism, which advocated scientific management practice and general rationalization of work on the factory floor, a more general social process takes place, which he terms "reification," or the hardening (literally the thingification) and fragmentation of all aspects of social life such that the relationships between these different things becomes mystified. Within this generalization of the logic of capitalist production, reification stops being about only labor (although it intensifies the fragmentation, quantification, and objectification of the labor process) and becomes descriptive of wage life as such in modern capitalism: "The transformation of the commodity relation into a thing of 'ghostly objectivity' cannot therefore content itself with the reduction of all objects for gratification of human needs to commodities. It stamps its imprint upon the whole consciousness of man; his qualities and abilities are no longer an organic part of his personality, they are things which he can own, or dispose of like the various objects of the external world" (100).

Reification, in this conception, does not just affect the realm of objects; it fundamentally transforms subjectivity. It is not just the workers' labor and consciousness that is reified but consciousness in general within industrial capitalist societies. As Fredric Jameson has argued, critical reason is deprivileged in relationship to instrumental reason.[59] The relationship between workers and their work is obscured, with the appropriation of the workers' intellect by managers and the deskilling and specialization of labor. In the intellectual world, various forms of knowledge function increasingly through specialization without any attempt to understand their relationship to the larger social whole. Even time "sheds its qualitative, variable, flowing nature" (90).

For Lukács reification functions primarily as a negative process, but he does also give it revolutionary potential. The proletariat, as the subject-object in Lukács's Hegelian conception of history, when it gains knowledge of its own objective position, can become a revolutionary agent for change. Floyd builds on this moment of dialectical reversal in Lukács's account to produce a much more fully dialectical account of reification. For Floyd reification isolates different aspects of the human lifeworld, the formation of the embodied subject itself, and the relationship between humans. If before or outside the process of enclosure, displacement, and concomitant reification, desire, sexuality, and the body were intertwined with subjectivity and experienced as continuous, with the family or the laboring collective functioning as the central ideological and social category, then under reification different aspects of desire, sexuality, and embodiment come to be experienced as objectified and separable. While, as Chitty demonstrates, the creation of same-sex labor forces produced spaces for same sex eroticism before processes of reification became dominant, by the late nineteenth century in the industrializing world when commodification and scientific management rescript social relations as measurable and quantifiable, sexuality, the body, and desire each become experienced as separate entities (primarily for white workers). The naming of sexuality that Foucault attributes to this period and the scientific focus on desire via psychoanalysis are both processes that presume the reification of sexuality as fixed in terms of different identities and desire as semiautonomous and detachable from the body. Moreover, sex itself increasingly becomes organized around reification, with desire for specific kinds of sexual bodies or objects becoming central.

For Floyd this naming of identities and desires enables a positive formation of gay male desire and community, one that is collectivist in orientation and can function both to create communities of public sex and challenge the homophobic exclusions of dominant culture. Reification here becomes productive. As he addresses its development through the twentieth century, it becomes the basis for queer community formation, one that also draws upon the critique of surplus repression in Marcuse and the unifying conception of queer as a majoritarian position articulated by Sedgwick in the 1990s. Reification is not only alienating, but it is also productive in a Foucauldian sense. It produces the very subjects that it attempts to regulate.

In our own twenty-first-century moment, this reification has taken on a neoliberal guise and is organized around the logics of niche marketing, branding, and the disaggregation of the workforce through casualization, displacement, and gig work. Its results are less massifying than atomizing. This has had an impact on our conception of sex as well. As Jordy Rosenberg argues, sexuality has become molecularized in our biocapitalist present.[60] It is presented as fundamentally desubjectified and ontological, opened up in order to be extracted, capitalized, and appropriated. Rosenberg's critique is directed toward the theoretical domains of new materialism and speculative realism, which he reads as symptomatic of the severing of subject and object in the present (with the molecularized object being the source of desubjectified agency). Yet his insights have a more general applicability. I argue in chapter 2 that new materialism has important lessons to teach us about conceptualizing the materiality of the body and sex. Still, Rosenberg's critique is an important one. As he puts it, "Consequently, the question with which we are concerned is not so much *what are the constituent parts of the molecular . . . but rather: what are the historical relationships that make possible the abstraction of the molecular as such*" (italics in original). I want to argue that one of the historical relationships is the process of atomization of sexuality (one might want to call it hyperreification) in the present, in which not only are objects dissolved into their component parts, but so is subjectivity. The subject is abstracted and atomized, becoming thoroughly separable from embodiment, collectivity, and desire. The subject becomes avatar-like and thoroughly dematerialized. It floats freely and becomes primarily about self-as-brand rather than collective identification. Within such a logic it becomes ever more difficult to produce collective forms of subjective identification and organizing. Identities, desires, and sex itself exist in various states of disconnection and individual antagonism.

It is the aim of this book to produce a theory that can help us overcome this atomization and the antinomies that it has produced. I, of course, am not proposing that we can (or necessarily always want to) simply reconcile the contradictions we engage on the level of thought, let alone praxis. Adorno quite rightly argues that a too hasty reconciliation is indeed a sure sign of ideology.[61] In what follows, I will argue for the contradictions and antagonisms that structure the relationship between subjectivity and materiality, identification and embodiment, desire and the unconscious, as well as collectivity and particularity. What I want to resist, however, is the nonrelationship into which they have fallen as a part of our atomized experience of the social in the present. This book builds toward a collectivist vision of a sexual and embodied commons, one in which subjectivity, desire, and materiality intertwine in complex and rewarding ways.

Contradiction as Methodology

In Defense of Sex attempts to think through and theorize a number of contradictions in contemporary theory and in popular discourses around sex, desire, and gender. These contradictions are not mutually exclusive. The terms of a contradiction can blur or blend into each other, while also existing in tension. One of the central contradictions explored by this book, that between sex and gender, is a perfect example of one where the central terms and the lived realities they describe are deeply interwoven with each other even as we cannot fully collapse the two terms without doing damage to crucial intellectual and political possibilities. Collapsing a problematic opposition is one of the mistakes that is often made by theoretical attempts to eradicate binary thinking. Replacing an ideological binary by merely privileging one of the terms and eradicating the other—so that nature is folded into culture or sex into gender—while having the merit of revealing an excluded middle, runs the danger of producing a singular concept that makes our understanding even less precise and more ideological. In the place of a tension between different categories, we get one that rules over the whole field. What may have been thinkable, as the source of tension or contradiction represented by the effaced category, becomes unthinkable.

Thinking through contradiction does not always lead to a desired or necessary resolution. The version of contradiction that I am using in this book, one
derived in equal parts from Theodor W. Adorno and Jacques Lacan, insists
that contradictions are never fully resolved.[62] Complete resolution is a vision
of either utopia or pure ideology from the Marxist vantage and is the domain
of death (which can be symbolic and not material) in the psychoanalytic tradition. For both thinkers there is always something that resists and escapes
dialectical movement, something stubborn, fixed, and not accounted for by
the symbolic or conceptual workings of the dialectic. The dialectic in this
context is not a synthetic one. It produces a reading of Hegel that is organized
not around the series thesis, antithesis, synthesis, but rather thesis, negation,
negation of the negation. While synthesis is possible, and sometimes necessary,
it does not resolve the contradiction or produce a straightforward positivity
(even if it is one that continues to be dialecticized). Instead, the dialectic in
this context is always organized around the negative. There is always a fundamental opposition at work in any moment of positive thought, meaning, or
social formation. As Slavoj Žižek argues, such an understanding of the dialectic
is always organized around the fundamental contradiction between the universal and the particular, the latter representing the excluded term that resists
any claim to universality.[63] There is always, then, a not-all haunting any claim
to totality. While we cannot stay fully on the level of the exception, particularly
in positing solidarity and collective praxis, we also should not ignore the disruptive conceptual work it does.

Adorno's and Lacan's understandings of contradiction are organized around
the opposition between thinking and being as well as identity and non-identity.
Adorno terms this reworking of the dialectic "negative dialectics" and theorizes
it as follows: "A rather meagre, formal definition is that it sets out to be a dialectics not of identity but of *non-identity*. We are concerned here with a philosophical project that does not presuppose the identity of being and thought,
nor does it culminate in that identity. Instead, it will attempt to articulate the
very opposite, namely the divergence of concept and thing, subject and object,
and their unreconciled state."[64] What is at stake in any contradiction, then, is
not only the formal movement of conceptual oppositions but that which eludes
or resists this movement. Any symbolic naming of a given object or being is
always a misnaming. Identity (as a conceptual category) does violence to the
very thing it names, and it is interesting to think about this formal conception
of identity in relationship to the more everyday use of the term discussed
here. At stake in both is the way in which the complexity of the contradictions
of lived experience, the unconscious, desire, materiality, and embodiment is

reduced to a singular name or reference. Adorno instead insists that we attend to what he terms the "object's preponderance," or the force and insistence that a given object or material entity exerts on the system or name that misnames it (*Negative*, 187). We should work reflexively to theorize that which eludes our systems even if we can only approach that very thing through the language that finally excludes it. Yet a materialist must insist that there is always that which constrains and disrupts our theorizing, even if we can sense it only indirectly by the way it haunts the system.

Lacan is also interested in the unresolvable contradiction between thinking and being. For him, however, it is not only about the specific contradiction between identity and nonidentity but also that which is both excluded from the system and structures it in its exclusion. In Lacan's thought this is the domain of the real. Any imaginary or symbolic opposition is always overdetermined by something that is excluded from the system and yet organizes its very structure. As Bruce Fink puts it, "the real is perhaps best understood as *that which has not yet been symbolized*, remains to be symbolized, or event resists symbolization."[65] This is the real, and it is the work of analysis to work to symbolize the real, like Adorno's insistence on working to theorize nonidentity, even as it also built around the recognition that the real necessarily eludes our grasp. Our relationship to it can only be asymptotic. We can approach it, perhaps encounter it, but it always moves elsewhere and produces new contradictions. The real in this context organizes our relationship to embodiment (Fink describes the developmental account of the real in Lacan in relationship to the uncoded or unsymbolized dimensions of the body) and to desire (for the adult subject, the real is structured in relationship to desire, which it both instantiates and eludes). Sex both as desire and as embodiment function as such a real in Lacan. They are loci of ontological negativity that exist in contradiction with our symbolic maps of gender, sex, desire, and sexuality. The contradictions I will explore over the scope of this book include gender and sex, intersex and trans, gender as a locus of nonbinary identification and gender as a binarized ideology, the repressive hypothesis and the productive hypothesis; identity as ideology and identity as part of liberatory politics; historicism and transhistorical claims; the macrological and the micrological. I will not detail them further here, but these contradictions play out in (negative) dialectical ways in what follows. The four chapters of *In Defense of Sex* can be understood to approach questions of sex, gender, flesh, and embodiment from different theoretical vantages: genealogy, psychoanalysis/new materialism, Marxist dialectical critique, and Marxist theories of the commons. Yet the chapters speak to each other and are designed to contribute to a larger, overarching argument.

Structure of the Book

Chapter 1, "The Ascent of Gender and Decline of Sex" charts the different fates of embodied sex and gender as concepts in Western culture. Drawing on the work of a range of cultural historians of sex and gender, it outlines the uneven shifts between different conceptions of sex as singular, binary, or some complex mix of the two. The chapter then attends to the way this model has been complicated more recently by feminist theorist and biologist Anne Fausto-Sterling, who initially posits the possibility of five sexes and more recently articulates a more persuasive and powerful model of sex as a continuum, one that can be binarized as a way of talking about macroformations, but one that is fundamentally not binarized in its relationship to development and lived experience.[66]

Central to the theorization of a nonbinary conception of sex is an understanding of how race, within slavery and other regimes of legal inequality and unpaid labor, is constructed in relationship to the category of flesh. As C. Riley Snorton and others have argued, both flesh and sex exist in a complicated tension with gender, which is marked as a domain of whiteness that forms in contradiction to the flesh (and implicitly with sex). In terms of gender, the book first traces sex's status as hierarchical in the ancient and early modern world. It next briefly touches on the way in which a binary understanding of sex and gender were seen as mutually enforcing in nineteenth- and early twentieth-century culture. It then accounts for gender's emergence as a central concept in the work of John Money and other psychologists and medical specialists in order to justify biomedical interventions on intersex subjects as well as enable support for reassignment surgeries for trans individuals. This concept of gender presented it as fundamentally binary and plastic. Money's concept was picked up in turn by second-wave feminism, which found its proximity to a constructivist understanding of gender generative. By the beginning of the 1990s and third-wave feminist theorizing, sex as a category had all but disappeared. While psychoanalytic critics still talked about sexual difference, many feminist and queer theorists used an expanded and constructivist conception of gender to refer to identifications, subjectivities, and embodiments. This privileging of gender and the attenuation of sex as an analytical category has intensified in the twenty-first century. With the articulation of powerful new forms of theorizing around transgender and genderqueer identities, gender has proliferated into a range of nonbinary possibilities and identifications. Sex, in turn, has become largely eclipsed as a concept, except for its reactionary use in the law and in transphobic discourse. After charting this history, the chapter will indicate that the privileging of gender

at the expense of sex comes with costs. These costs are simultaneously ideological and material.

If chapter 1 traces the larger ideological history and underpinnings of our
current concepts of gender and sex, then chapter 2, "Sex as Extimacy," is where
I articulate the specific theory of gendered and sexed embodiment that animates this book. This chapter uses psychoanalytic and new materialist theories
of embodiment, as well as theories of the flesh in Black studies, in order to
theorize the material as well as imaginary and symbolic dimensions of gender
and sex. While it theorizes the intertwining of the two, it also maps them differently in relationship to embodiment. To use a Lacanian register, while gender
tends to be more mappable on the imaginary and symbolic levels, sex tends to
function on the level of the material and often is a locus of the real. Yet this
binary division is too neat (as all binary divisions are, of course). Gender winds
up shaping the material body as well and sex is only apprehensible through
symbolic and imaginary registers. As Karen Barad argues, just because something is only accessible via the symbolic dimensions of language does not mean
it is reducible to them (25). Instead, the materiality of sex needs to be theorized
as both mappable by symbolic and imaginary means and as not reducible to
this mapping. It is both intimate and alien.

To posit this understanding of sex, I articulate it as what Jacques Lacan
terms "extimate." It is an intimate exteriority but also its inversion, an external
intimacy. Sex, like the material body of which it forms a subset, is both something that is intimate in its lived dimensions yet strange in its refusal to fully
correspond to our symbolic constructions of both embodiment and gender. Its
status as extimate means that it resists and eludes a complete symbolic or scientific mapping. Its intimate exteriority is always in tension with any attempt
to fully master it. We can work to shape it via biomedical intervention, but its
material force and agency also insist on its status as extimate to any attempt to
fully script it. The chapter also draws upon Lacan and the work of Jean
Laplanche to theorize sex as desire and drive. Sex presents itself as fundamentally oriented around a relationship to otherness in this framework. It thus
functions as a disruption to egoic and autonomous conceptions of self, disrupting the generation of human capital and foregrounding an intimate alterity
both within the subject and in relationship to the social world. Sex is disorderly,
extimate, and disruptive of one's imaginary ego constructions. Yet, if we primarily understand sex as external and negating, we have no way of building
a more affirmative and collectively oriented relationship to it. We also refuse
to take responsibility for the workings of our desire. Instead, I think we need
to return to the powerful accounts of desire and drive that were central to
psychoanalytic theorizing. The account I provide of sex as desire returns to

the psychoanalytic accounts of how sex becomes subjectified. I argue that sex may indeed initially come from the outside, as an "enigmatic signifier" in Laplanche's memorable phrase, but it is internalized and comes to constitute the drive.[67] While it is crucial to emphasize that we recognize the ways in which we subjectify sex, it is also crucial to recognize that it is fundamentally social before it becomes personal or private.

Finally, the chapter theorizes how regimes of racial violence and unpaid racialized labor also shape the flesh, which functions as a mediating concept between gender and sex. The flesh names the ways in which the collective forms of embodiment are produced by the specific forms of subjection, labor, and accumulation attaching to the regime of slavery and its aftermath in share-cropping and Jim Crow as well as the persistence of forms of poesis that were central to (primarily) West African cosmologies, as R. A. Judy demonstrates. In this sense, labor is formed very differently between official waged labor and the reifications of consciousness and the body that it produces and accumulation by dispossession which situates the body in a more collective register, parallel with Marx's idea of species being. The flesh both is distinctive in this way to the experience of slavery and other forms of nonwage labor, but also can be understood as a version of collective and trans-corporeal embodiment that connects subjects with the larger ecosystem. It thus points toward a different relationship to both labor and consciousness.

Chapter 3, "Bioaccumulation and the Dialectics of Embodiment," theorizes the way in which global capitalism intersects with biomedical technologies and practices to produce a radically uneven geography of medical intervention, appropriation, capitalization, and access. Both intersex and transgender subjectivities are structured by divisions of class, race, and geography. These divisions manifest in relationship to what David Harvey describes as accumulation by dispossession. The chapter begins with reflections on the Janus-faced quality of technology and medicine within capitalism and the Enlightenment more generally. Drawing on Walter Benjamin, Achille Mbembe, and Marx, the chapter explores the dialectics between civilization and barbarism, biopolitics and necropolitics, and freedom and necessity. It then turns to the way in which these oppositions play out in the medical accumulation by dispossession of specific bodies. The uneven medicalization of intersex and of racialized and classed bodies functions as a locus of accumulation by dispossession.

As C. Riley Snorton argues, it was often racialized subjects marked as excluded from citizenship and access to a wage who formed what were the sources of accumulation by dispossession and biomedical appropriation, ironically, for intersex and medicalized trans subjects it was typically (and continues to be) bodies that are privileged by class and race that are the primary locus of such accumulation. Historically and geographically, medical intervention into intersex has been radically uneven and mostly unnecessary. Access to medical forms of transitioning have also been radically uneven. Its medicalization as a series of conditions in the second half of the twentieth century in the Global North situates it as a site of accumulation and appropriation. The medical experimentation on Black bodies both in the Global North and the Global South has been a parallel locus of accumulation. To put it simply, intersex and trans subjects (which, when medicalized, were almost exclusively white) as well as racialized subjects functioned as test subjects for pharmacological and biomedical testing, accumulation, and innovation around the medical production and regulation of binary gender and sex. Intersex and racialized bodies (having different biopolitical statuses and subject to different levels of violence) functioned as a locus of testing and perfecting various techniques of shaping, regulating, and profiting from the medical production of sex and gender. As such, they, along with surgeries for transitioning, form the site of primitive accumulation for the emergence of what Rebekah Sheldon describes as somatic capitalism.

Medical technologies around sex and gender should be available to all who need and desire them, and the existence of such technologies have powerful utopian dimensions for trans and intersex subjects in need of or desirous of medical intervention, but it is crucial that we also theorize the very availability of these technologies as predicated on nonconsensual interventions on intersex, enslaved, and incarcerated bodies. A powerful politics of solidarity around transgender, decolonial, intersex, and feminist struggles, then, would recognize the capitalist and biomedical production of gender and sex as bound up with historical violence, even as the technologies associated with both may also promise and often offer liberatory possibilities. It would also attend to class and race divides as they structure both transgender and intersex politics and forms of identification and vice versa. We need a vision of a world in which the technologies of gender and sex are not tied to capital accumulation and to regimes of biomedicine that privilege scientific innovation over consent and intellectual property over collective forms of knowledge. It is to such a vision that I next turn.

Chapter 4, "The Sexual and Bodily Commons," is unabashedly utopian, articulating a vision for a better way of living collective life, one that affirms embodied, sexual, and subjective difference while also affirming human desire and bodily and subjective commonality. It builds upon different articulations of the commons produced by Antonio Negri and Michael Hardt, Fred Moten and Stefano Harney, and Christian Haines and Peter Hitchcock.[68] The chapter theorizes how we can build infrastructures and institutions around the flourishing of the commons, as a dimension of both the world system and what Jason Moore describes as the world-ecology.[69] I emphasize the commons rather than simply the public or state (although I think the latter two categories are absolutely crucial to the production of collective flourishing), because the state has often been involved in the violent suppression, correction, and criminalization of embodied and sexual differences. We need a productive and affirmative conception of the state, but the collective power being employed is that of the commons, which is neither state-owned nor capitalist.

While many theorists of the commons emphasize its intellectual or ecosystemic dimensions (both of which are crucial), this chapter will articulate its bodily and sexual dimensions. In short, to imagine a just world around embodiment, gender, sex, desire, and sexuality, we need to articulate a vision of collective life that affirms a range of positive embodied forms of support, access, and equality. Such a vision would include an affirmation and valuation all the work of social reproduction, access to and consensual choice around sexual practices (including the practice of not having or emphasizing sex), health care, childcare, elder care, transition technologies on demand, abortion on demand, food, clean air, and drinkable water. It would be predicated on the affirmation of embodied, identificatory, and subjective difference. It would also include a recognition and material support for bodily commonalities, including collective responses to the facticity of death, threats from illness, collective forms of embodied violence, and access to a nontraumatizing and elective relationship to sex and sexuality. It is toward such a vision that *In Defense of Sex* is written.

1

The Ascent of Gender and Decline of Sex

The ontology of gender difference developed by the architects of modern sexology is consistently in tension with the embodied experience of intersex, trans, nonbinary, and gender-nonconforming subjects.

HIL MALATINO

The two *Blade Runner* films, Ridley Scott's original (in its many versions) and its sequel directed by Denis Villeneuve, while finally conservative in the gender ideologies they advance, have much to teach us about the relationship of gender to avatar culture.[1] As one of the fetishized texts of postmodernism, the first *Blade Runner* emphasized the way in which cybernetic technology can augment reality, presenting a popular-culture version of Donna J. Haraway's theorization of the cyborg as counterhegemonic subject that combines nature and culture, technological and organic embodiment.[2] The representations of replicant life and virtual reality in *Blade Runner 2049* are much bleaker.[3] Technology does not augment reality so much as it masks and distracts from a thoroughly degraded world. While there are many scenes to choose from to demonstrate this point, this changed relationship to technology is perhaps most simply if hauntingly captured by the meal that the main character K, a replicant (and the world seems to be made up primarily of replicants at this point), is served a meal by Joi, his virtual reality companion (basically a cross between Siri and a virtual escort who has been purchased and personalized). The meal is made up of grubs that we have seen being harvested in the film's opening scene, but that appear, through virtual augmentation, as a classic mid-twentieth-century-style *steak frites* dinner, with Frank Sinatra playing appropriately in the

39

background. The turn to eating grubs is not done out of an allegiance to non-human animals or producing a more sustainable ecosystem (nonhuman animals, except for insects, have long disappeared in both films), but rather because they are the only nonhuman protein left to consume.

This vision of technology as replacement and distraction from the increasing degradation of our bodies, sensorium, and the material conditions of our existence capture part of what is at stake in what I elsewhere term avatar fetishism,[4] where our virtual selves, or avatars, are organized around "a fantasy of the transcendence of the material: most immediately the material body but also the mundane objects of the material world and the messy business of various form of material production" (22). We live in imagined and constructed selves not so much to augment who we are (superhero films not withstanding) but to mask the way in which the very embodiments and ecologies in which we operate are increasingly degraded, monetized, appropriated, and precarious. It is this dimension of avatar fetishism that I want to keep in mind as I theorize both sex and gender and articulate a vision for trans and intersex flourishing that does not merely reproduce the uneven and increasingly violent reality underwritten by this logic of ever more fetishized virtual selves and an ever more degraded material existence. It is also what I want to keep in mind as I turn to theorizing the long historical trajectory of sex, gender, and flesh in this chapter.

Before doing so, however, there is another way to read this scene from *Blade Runner 2049*. While I focused on the workings of avatar fetishism in this scene primarily in terms of the transformation of grubs into steak, the scene enacts a conventional gender fantasy to accompany is gastronomic one. Joi appears dressed in 1950s housewife apparel, sporting makeup, a string of pearls, and an elegant midcentury dress. The status of the fantasy here is complicated, since Joi is ostensibly staging it for K, yet K himself is a replicant, so the status of his fantasy is itself manufactured and implanted. The scene thus suggests the way in which our fantasies of gender are structured, in part, by fetishized images produced by a larger consumer and work culture. Gender here is not only a personal fantasy but also one that stages a generic and rather shopworn one of the larger culture. The fantasy isn't a staging of an actual past but a fantasy past, of the kinds described by Fredric Jameson in his account of the "nostalgia for the present" that informed postmodern cinema, in which a representation of the 1950s (or any other decade) with an attention to historical and ideological specificity is replaced by a "rather different thing, the 'fifties,' a shift which obligates us in addition to underscore the cultural sources of all the attributes with which we have endowed the period, many of which seem very precisely to derive from its own television programs."[5] So, we have a nostalgia not for the actual 1950s, but for a fifties that is somewhere between a national myth and a marketing concept. Here, though, the nostalgia for the present is a couple of generations further along. In *Blade Runner 2049* it is a nostalgia for a time when the nostalgia for the present still seemed seductive and pleasurable rather than desperate and degraded. Yet *Blade Runner 2049* remains fixated on the same 1950s idea of modernity that was so central to so much postmodern ideology, with its attendant conservative gender imaginary (and the 1950s locus of the film's nostalgia is confirmed in a later scene set in Vegas, with its simulated life-sized figures of Marilyn Monroe and Elvis Presley). If there is nothing but the figurations of image culture to cast back to, nostalgically, in the earlier moment of postmodernism, then in the present imagined by the film as well as the present of the film's release, these same images are clearly designed to distract from an even more degraded social and ecological world. The film replays, in a more desolate context, earlier postmodern replays of fifties culture.

Gender here is presented as something enacted and imaginary (in the Lacanian sense of the term). It is structuring on both a subjective and cultural level. It is fundamentally a performance for the Other. The Other here is not K or Joi (who would represent the small other in Lacanian terms), but the larger culture (i.e. the big Other) that keeps obsessively staging the same fantasies. And these fantasies are structured around inequality. Even as Joi and K are both products, her gendering and her professional function for which she was designed construct her as subservient to K. While he is a replicant, she is an AI commodity, part virtual assistant and part fantasy call girl. Even as gender is plastic and customizable (when she senses K isn't pleased, Joi cycles through a series of clothing styles and gendered performances, similar to the way one cycles through the customizable "skins" of avatars in video games), we recognize that she is structurally positioned as inferior to K, a replicant that can't be turned on and off, does not have freedom of movement, and lives the simulation of a full subjectivity. This inequality is brought home near the end of the movie in a scene in which K encounters an ad for Joi, in which she appears naked, stories tall, and not yet customized.

While this later scene reveals her commercial, sexual, and generic origins, I want to focus on another aspect of the scene. She appears sexed, but we do not ever see her sex organs other than so-called secondary ones, her breasts and buttocks (the film, of course, wants to keep its R rating). Instead, her body is sexed by its curves, but it also suggests that such a sexing is a mere external signification of sex. The viewer, like the 1950s obstetrician deciding the sex from what appears on the surface of a child born with an intersex condition, intuits sex from mere appearance. Yet the film suggests that Joi, like K's sexing, finally lies elsewhere, in the complex mix of codes, algorithms, and wiring that construct (in different ways and with different material statuses) both Joi and K. Such code may at first remind us of DNA and may seem to align with a binarily sexed world, but the code and the ways in which it intersects with algorithms, materiality, and other code suggests a much more complex and trans-corporeal understanding of sex in Stacy Alaimo's terms.[6] Sex may be a material substrate, but it is a complex and nonbinary one produced by multiple interacting codes, inputs, signals, and metabolic and environmental factors.

Gender's Proliferation

Gender has largely replaced sex in the progressive imaginary of the twenty-first century. Mercurial, flexible, and multiple, gender a seems of a piece with the speed and viral logic of twenty-first-century cultural life in the Global North (and in much of the Global South). Meanwhile, sex, in contrast, is clunky, sadly binary, stubborn, and thoroughly unsexy. If it does appear, it is used, as Dean Spade and Toby Beauchamp differently argue, as a category of legal regulation and state surveillance.[7] If the undoing of the sex/gender divide was central to the crucial work done by queer and trans theory in the 1990s, gender emerged as the victorious term of this dismantling. While deconstructions are not meant to have victorious terms, this is often what happens when binaries are undone within the larger culture. Thus, when the line between masculine and feminine is undone, masculine often becomes the default norm all over again. Similarly, when the sex/gender divide was rightly deconstructed by queer and trans theorists such as Judith Butler and Susan Stryker, gender emerged as the default category for sexual, embodied difference in the academy, in official discourse, and in everyday life.[8] If anything, this tendency has grown stronger in the twenty-first century. Thus, gender becomes the preferred language to talk about trans identities, many queer identities, and sexual difference more generally. This preference is everywhere visible from government and other official forms, which use gender as a euphemism for an older, binary conception of sex, to the proliferation of different nonbinary genders on sites like Tumblr and in popular culture more generally.

On one level, the replacement of sex with gender makes sense. Sex, as traditionally conceptualized, is too binary a concept. It is emphasis on male or female functions to efface queer, trans, and intersex embodiments of all sorts. Moreover, it imposes a binary logic on all bodies, doing epistemological violence to the range of possible embodiments and situating even queer embodiments within a binary template. The logic of sex as a category is often seen to be heteronormative, transphobic, and perhaps also sexist, recalling the midcentury fantasy embodied by Joi for K's pleasure.

As Judith Butler has argued, sex is tied to an essentialist framework in which the binary of sex appears as essence to which gender becomes the reflection: "If the immutable character of sex is contested, perhaps this construct called 'sex' is as culturally constructed as gender; indeed, perhaps it was always already gender, with the consequence that the distinction between sex and gender turns out to be no distinction at all" (7). In this passage, Butler not only challenges the sex/gender distinction but also finally jettisons sex in the name of gender. Sex cannot have any material force and distinction without becoming essentialist, a false limit on the possibilities of gender. Butler's insights in *Gender Trouble* and its sequel, *Bodies That Matter*, are foundational for any progressive account of gender.[9] They are right to argue, in an insight that is crucial to later trans theorizing, that the "presumption of a binary gender system implicitly retains the belief in a mimetic relationship of gender to sex whereby gender mirrors sex or is otherwise restricted by it" (*Gender Trouble*, 6). The work they do to disentangle gender from sex enables the contemporary understandings of gender as radically distinct from sex and/or nonbinary. Yet in disentangling the false mimesis between gender and sex, sex itself becomes indistinguishable from gender. What finally emerges here is a poststructuralist account of gender as entirely discursively produced. The relationship of these discourses to the material body is eradicated. While Butler goes onto theorize the relationship of discourse to the material body in *Bodies That Matter*, even here the body functions, as Stacy Alaimo and Susan Hekman put it, "a mere blank slate for cultural constructions."[10] The body is material for Butler in *Bodies That Matter*, but it is an inert materiality with no force, agency, or limits. It is a surface for discursive inscription.

The conception of the body as a blank slate is not unique to Butler. As Claire Colebrook argues, the framework has its roots in Foucault: "Butler is vigilant in maintaining this Foucaultian critique of material and normalizing life."[11] For all the emphasis on bodies and their pleasure in Foucault, the body in Foucault is indistinguishable from its shaping by and function in discourse. Foucault is a materialist. He regularly emphasizes the material body, yet this materialism gives the body no existence other than its shaping by discourse. Butler's position, as Alaimo and Hekman demonstrate, can be situated within the larger context of what they term the "linguistic turn" (6). The linguistic turn, which is also variously called the cultural turn or theoretical postmodernism, represents an antifoundationalist theoretical approach that posits all aspects of life as primarily constructed by language and/or culture. While structuralism and poststructuralism have a more complicated lineage (it is simply inaccurate to describe most of the thinkers under these rubrics as simply organized around linguistic constructivism), their focus on the structuring force of language systems combined with the emphasis on cultural construction in cultural studies, feminism, and critical race theory (to mention only three) to produce an antiessentialist conception of society in which there is no preexisting materiality or essence to the social that is not constructed by and only accessible to language. This framework did a lot of powerful work in denaturalizing cultural entities that were assumed to be natural, immutable, and foundational. As we have just discussed, within this framework, gender, like race and a whole range of other social categories, could no longer be seen as having a prediscursive meaning. Instead, the prediscursive was revealed to be a form of ideology produced by discourse itself. Yet it became almost impossible to posit any entity that exceeded or existed in tension with the workings of culture and language. Sex, the body, nature, and materiality itself were seen as fundamentally produced by the workings of discourse, or, at the very least, unable to be posited, except through the workings of language, and thus finally reducible to the same. It is as if everything became avatar-like, with no attention to what might subtend, enable, or contradict such avatars.

The emphasis on the social construction of gender and even sex has been salutary for much trans theorizing. Susan Stryker has situated the emergence of transgender theory within the context of postmodernism.[12] In *Assuming a Body*, Gayle Salamon provides a rich account of trans embodiment by drawing on both psychoanalysis and phenomenology.[13] Indeed, my own theorization of gender and sex in chapter 2 is informed by similar theoretical approaches. Yet, even as we share an archive, she also refuses to posit a material dimension of embodiment. Salamon argues that we cannot assert a materiality of embodiment (what I argue can be conceptualized as a nonbinary version of sex) because this perceived materiality is "always the precipitate of a psychic relation between body and world" (33). For her, the truth of sexual difference "arrives *only at the level of the imaginary*" (35, italics in original), even as most Lacanian accounts of sex locate it at the level of the real. Thus, Salamon's account of the gendered body finally reproduces the constructivist position that there can be no materiality outside of our linguistic or visual construction of it. Recent work by Dean Spade, Toby Beauchamp, and Paisley Currah, while providing compelling accounts of how forms of discursive and visual power construct and adjudicate the very concept of the transgender person, also remain within a Foucauldian framework in which the material is a product of the discursive and its adjudication of power.

Given the relentless ways that gender as a psychological and social binary was presented as predicated on an equally binary construction of sex, such that masculinity was normatively attached to those whose sex was male and femininity with those whose sex was female, the destabilization of both categories and their necessary relationship was crucial for trans and nonbinary subjectivities to be theorized in a nonpathologizing and affirmative register. It is understandable that trans scholars would be wary of invoking sex, given the conservative and transphobic work the concept has done. Yet we lose something when we do not theorize sex.

It is also important to recognize that Butler's deconstruction of the relationships between gender and sex, male and female, and masculine and feminine also opened up a space for intersex embodiments to become more visible and less pathologized. Yet, even as Butler's argument had this effect, its refusal to theorize matter and biology as agential, forceful, and delimiting, indeed, as anything other than discursively constructed, also threatened to render intersex invisible and untheorizable. For intersex is only secondarily about gender, it is primarily about the sexed body and its refusal to correspond to binary understandings of sex. Similarly, while trans is a different dynamic, primarily about gender and gendered identification, accounts of it lose something fundamental, as C. Jacob Hale and Jay Prosser have differently argued, when the materiality of the body is thoroughly effaced.[14]

This dematerializing dynamic was not limited to work in gender and queer theory. The turn to gender and away from sex became central to the constructedness, plasticity, and performativity of phenomena more generally under postmodernism. While both theories of performance and social construction have been reductively figured in critiques of postmodernism (neither should be understood to be voluntarist or individualist), there are also reasons for why postmodernism, both as a body of theory and as a description of everyday life in the present, has fallen out of fashion. As work within what Alaimo and Hekman describe as the material turn has demonstrated, social construction as a concept excludes as much as it enables (6). Thus, things like the resistant, agential, and insistent materiality of the body, of the world ecology, of the built environment, and of aspects of the world economic system itself tend to disappear. Everything conventionally contained under the categories of the natural, animal, or material is, if not completely negated, emptied of explanatory power and force.

Postmodernism's cultural turn, in which everything was seen as socially constructed, has given way to the material turn, which situates bodies, life, nature, and ecosystems within a materialist framework. This work has combined with recent materialist developments in Marxist theory (emphasizing the material production of social life as a whole) and ecotheory in order to produce an account of human (and nonhuman) existence as predicated on material processes that simultaneously intersect with and exceed culture. Rather than nature's being effaced in these theories, culture and nature are complexly intertwined, multiply determined, and alternately malleable and recalcitrant. It is the work of this book to present as complex and multiple an understanding of sex as has been developed around gender in contemporary gender and trans theory and activism. While gender and sex cannot be read off of each other or reduced to one being an effect of the other, the two cannot be fully severed. Nor can one be subsumed into the other.

What I do want to sever (if I can use a verb that is rather loaded in an intersex context), however, is our conception of sex from crude binaristic thinking. Instead, as I have already articulated in the introduction, the conception of sex central to this book is multiple rather than binary, organized around a spectrum of possible embodiments. Intersex and trans theorist Hil Malatino posits such a vision of embodiment in his account of what he terms the queer biology of the body: "If our collective biological bodies are constitutively queer, infinitely more complex than a dimorphic conception of corporeality allows, then it seems all of the common sense that has been made of the links between sex, gender, and sexuality are split at the root, fucked up (desirably I think) from the jump."[15] Sex, as I am theorizing it is precisely the locus of such a queer biology. Malatino has it exactly right: we need to embrace what is fucked up and queer in our understandings of embodiment. Sex within such a framework is closer to the codes, networks, and other materialities that produce Joi and K's material substrate rather than their biomorphic performance of heteronormative ideals. Yet in theorizing this more complex concept of sex, I also do not want to make the very postmodern move of complexifying my object of study to the point that it has no relationship to larger formations of ideology as well as bodily possibility and constraint. If one of the things that this book argues against is the reduction of sex to a rigid binary logic, one figured as the inverse of gender as a proliferation of individual identifications and expression, one of the other things it argues against, and this logic works in productive tension with the first, is that we need to be careful not to proliferate and individualize our objects of study so thoroughly that they stop functioning as sites of power, constraint, ideology, and collective world-making. Thus, while we can look at the categories female and male and see in fact a spectrum of sexual embodiments that include intersex bodies and bodies with or without certain sexed capacities or developments, we also do not want to erase the ways in which certain issues, like reproductive rights or the vulnerability to certain diseases, are statistically tied primarily to bodies that we still name female and male.

It is crucial that we do not deconstruct sex and gender to such a degree that the ideological and material force of certain embodiments and identifications are effaced without being undone. I think we need to theorize the reason that the material body has become such a flashpoint of reactionary political struggle, from the transphobic insistence that trans people be defined by their ostensible "birth sex," understood as a binary, to the ways in which reproductive rights for women and transmen are being systematically dismantled. For this reason, this book proposes a different, queer understanding of the material body. While it is important that we complicate certain feminist visions and understandings of both sex and gender, it is also crucial that we do not abandon the politics of feminism or the critique of dominant masculinities. Two recent books on masculinity, K. Allison Hammer's *Masculinity in Transition* and Cynthia Barounis's *Vulnerable Constitutions*, nicely attend to the way in which hegemonic masculinity can continue to signify is ostensibly counterhegemonic and queer contexts.[16] Womanhood and manhood are powerfully legible and embodied categories for many people, ones that shape life chances, actions, and possibilities in large, structural ways. Such an insight is even more important globally than it is nationally. Thus, as with all my work, in this book I am attempting to both think the micrological and the macrological, the subjective and the collective together, teasing out both their contradictions and their congruences.

Recognizing this larger context does not negate the necessity of affirming gender identifications for trans and intersex folks, but it does suggest that the enemy of a radical gender politics is not sex or the material body but a specific reading of that body and its relationship to gender. As Malatino argues, intersex and trans need to be theorized together: "there could be no resistance that would ameliorate the maltreatment of intersex individuals without coalition made with trans and queer folks, particularly those that have been deeply affected by the administrative violence that attends to the process of gender regulation" (24). Gender regulation and regulation of sex need to be thought together. Moreover, as Pidgeon Pagonis and other intersex activists assert, given the overlap between the two, intersex and trans should be powerfully joined in struggle.[17] To do so, however, we need to produce an account of sex as well as gender that can enable an adequate theorization of intersex as well as trans forms of identification and embodiment. Such a conception would recognize way in which trans and genderqueer subjectivities, as Paul B. Preciado has theorized, are often also about bodily modification or transformation within what he terms the "pharmacopornographic regime" of contemporary capitalism.[18] Such conception would avoid what David A. Rubin describes as "intersex exceptionalism" (64).[19] It would also avoid a similar trans exceptionalism. Instead, trans and intersex both as lived experiences and as categories of theoretical analysis would be understood as thoroughly bound together and with the functioning of the rest of the gender, sex, in what Rebekah Sheldon terms "somatic capitalism," or the mode of capitalism that mines, exploits, and re-shapes bodies.[20]

Gender's Limits

Gender understood as a constructed category might be suspect in our own more materialist moment, if only because it seems to participate in the same thoroughgoing logic of linguistic or cultural construction in which so much of postmodernism participated. There are other reasons to be suspicious of the proliferation of gender and the effacement of sex in our present moment.

For example, the concept of gender as flexible, individualized, and open to self-expression echoes much of the logic of subjectification in contemporary neoliberalism. While Dan Irving has argued persuasively that transgendered rights claims often unconsciously rely on the self-entrepreneurial rhetoric of neoliberalism, I want to make a stronger claim here that contemporary ideas of gender echo neoliberal conceptions of subjectification as such.[21] As Michel Foucault argues, subjectivity in neoliberalism is organized around the logic of human capital, in which a person is supposed to function as a self-entrepreneur through investing in themselves and tailoring their skills, affect, and personality to market demand.[22] It is no longer the society that has the responsibility to train workers and provide for citizens; rather, it is the individual citizen who must shape themselves for the market or risk being left behind. This demand for the performance of human capital becomes ever more pressing as industrial jobs in the Global North and certain parts of the Global South are replaced by positions in affect, intellectual, communication, and service labor (when they are not becoming automated). Moreover, as David Harvey notes, such a notion of flexibility is applied to both production (as a way of keeping costs down by hiring and firing workers and moving production locations) and the worker themselves (holding down multiple jobs via the gig economy, retraining and educating oneself at will, maintaining one's health and competitive advantage, and so on).[23]

The current conception of gender as plastic, individualized, performance based, and often postideological echoes this logic all too well. By postideological I am describing current conceptions of gender that proliferate the category so much that it stops being understood as a category of ideological socialization at all. A conception of gender as a locus of ideological socialization is precisely what was at stake in earlier feminist critiques of the category. While I do not want to rebinarize gender, I do want to interrogate what happens when it be-comes so plural, so individually determined, so micropolitical that it seems to elude larger ideological structures and formations. On one level, maybe it has begun to outstrip the grip of ideology, and certainly I want to affirm the utopian currents at work in various redefinitions, appropriations, and rearticulations of gender. Marquis Bey has articulated some of these positive currents in arguing for the abolition of gender.[24] While I want to affirm utopian possibilities attaching to rethinking or thinking beyond gender, and I share Bey's desire to move beyond identitarian logics, it also strikes me as idealist (or voluntarist) to imagine we can simply abolish gender or shatter it in relationship to a conception of Deleuzian becomings. Abstractions, particularly the ones we use for designating forms of difference and hierarchy, need to be undone on material levels and not just on the level of language or identification. As Louis Althusser has taught us, it is precisely when something seems outside of ideology that we need to interrogate its ideological coordinates.[25]

The atomization of gender categories is too congruent with the atomization of social life and larger forms of solidarity that characterize existence under neoliberalism to remain uninterrogated. In advancing such an interrogation, I am thinking as much about the commonsense logic of how gender is lived, signified, commodified, and talked about in our contemporary moment as I am about the articulated positions of contemporary gender theory within feminism, queer, trans, and intersex theory. Yet, I want to interrogate theory too for its recurring language of performativity and malleability in thinking about gender, which, as we will see, echoes the definitions of sex and gender as "plastic," and thus open to endless surgical shaping, as Jules Gill-Peterson and Iain Morland have differently demonstrated.[26] While I recognize the genesis of the account of gender as performativity in speech act theory and performance studies, the metaphor also echoes in a striking way the emphasis on performance in the logic of neoliberal capitalism. Here gender is not only a performative iteration as Judith Butler has argued, but also potentially a maximization of human capital in the logic of neoliberalism (*Gender Trouble*, 128–41). As one example of how this logic works, I would point to the way in which the most visible trans bodies are presented as hyperglamorous and seamlessly transformable, Caitlyn Jenner being only the most obvious example. While on one level we want to affirm the powerful ability of trans bodies to signify as sexy and natural, this hypervisibility also has its costs. It is tied to the affective dimensions of the contemporary political economy and to the generation and distribution of what Dana Kaplan and Eva Illouz term "sexual capital," or the accumulation of sexual attractiveness for the generation of profit or the maximization of human capital. [27] In such a political economy, hypervisibility situates the glamorous trans body as capitalizable and thus exploitable (particularly within the frameworks of entertainment and sex work), at the same time many less glamorous and ordinary trans and intersex lives, lives situated unequally in terms of race, class, and nationality as well as gender and sexuality, become rendered, as Erin L. Durban argues, less visible.[28]

As this last comment suggests, the last thing I want to do is reduce gendered or transgendered subjectivity to an effect of neoliberalism. Quite the opposite. I want to disentangle the logic of gender and sex from neoliberalism in order to enable a gendered and transgendered politics that will be more fully resistant to the depredations and subjectifications of the current heteronormative and biopolitical capitalist order. There has been much written lately about whether, with the rise of the totalitarian, ethnonationalist version of capitalism represented by Trump, Modi, and their ilk on the one hand and the emergence of genuine left alternatives on the other, we are exiting the era of neoliberalism. While I want to hold open the possibility that we might be in a historical moment of transition, one that can hopefully produce an inclusive, collective politics of economic, racial, sexual, and gendered justice, I also think forty years of neoliberalism (not to mention centuries of capitalist transformation) has left a deep (although not inalterable) imprint on how we think about our relationship to the social, to embodiment, and to our own subjectivities. Moreover, late neoliberalism has placed an even greater emphasis on the production of walled identities and avatar culture. As I discussed in the introduction, the emphasis on avatar culture in social media, in media culture more generally, and increasingly in various aspects of job performance, from working in various forms of online chat and help services to operating drones or functioning as a monetized YouTube personality, has also had the effect of severing our sense of selves from our embodiment even as our material conditions become ever more degraded (although most of us haven't resorted to eating grubs yet) and various aspects of our embodiment become ever more central to accumulation and biomedical appropriation.

In order to better theorize both gender and sex in the present, we need to have a sense of the meanings both terms have accrued historically. Such a historical account is what I provide next. While these histories are necessarily reductive and schematic, they will help us understand the complex web of meanings, many of them contradictory, that accrue to both concepts in our current moment.

Historicizing Sex

In *Making Sex*, first published in 1990, Thomas Laqueur argues that our current conception of two sexes only emerged as dominant in the nineteenth century.[29] Before this period a one-sex model prevailed. Central to the assumption of a two-sex model is the idea that male and female anatomy are fundamentally different. The one-sex model, on the other hand, posited that women were physical inversions of men, and thus lesser, but possessed the same fundamental anatomy. Ovaries were seen as internalized testicles and the vagina as an inverted penis. It is only at the end of the eighteenth century, according to Laqueur, that the notion that female and male productive anatomy became seen as radically different. Laqueur interestingly posits this shift in relationship to the questions of women's rights and citizenship that emerged in the postrevolutionary era. As Joan Wallach Scott has argued, debates around gender and the inclusion of women in the public sphere and in the conception of nation became newly pressing with the emergence of the modern nation-state.[30] Laqueur reads the emergence of the two-sex model as part of an attempt to produce a biological grounding for sexual difference that would limit women's access to the universal rights claims that were otherwise part of revolutionary and national discourse in the late eighteenth and early nineteenth centuries. Binary sex, then, has long been employed to naturalize or ground ideology.

Laqueur's argument about the strong dividing line between the one-sex and two-sex models has been persuasively challenged by Helen King.[31] His notion that a two-sex model prevails in the present has also been complicated by Jules Gill-Peterson in her groundbreaking *History of the Transgender Child*. King addresses Laqueur's arguments directly, demonstrating that his evidence privileges certain figures, Galen and Aristotle, at the expense of others, Vesalius and Hippocrates, and that both one-sex and two-sex models were present in ancient world and continued to be so in the Renaissance. The shift, if there is one, from early modern to modern conceptions of sex is one of one model becoming more dominant rather than wholesale replacement. Laqueur in his more careful moments admits as much. He argues that the shift to the two-sex model "did not happen all at once, nor did it happen everywhere at the same time, nor was it a more permanent shift" (150).

In rehearsing my accounts of the historical understanding of sex, I am less interested in whether Laqueur is historically correct. I am persuaded by King's critique and Gill-Peterson's alternate history. Like Foucault's arguments about sexuality, what is most interesting in Laqueur is not whether he is historically accurate but rather his framing of the concept of sex as fundamentally unstable and changeable over time. What emerges from both Laqueur and King is a recognition that our understanding of the body's sex is constructed and shaped not only by scientific advances but also by larger political and social factors. Fundamentally different understandings of sex run concurrently throughout much of Western history.

Medical research into sex was done within a colonial context in both Europe and the United States, in which race determined not only citizenship status but one's status as human, as Sylvia Wynter demonstrates.[32] Given this context, it is perhaps not surprising, as Sander Gilman argues, that conceptions of race and histories of racial violence are bound up with the generation of knowledge about sex.[33] The Black body functioned as both a foil against which the white body was understood and as an acceptable locus of medical experimentation. If discourses of nineteenth-century womanhood in the United States severely limited the viewability of female anatomy, no such moral compunction applied to Black slaves and second-class citizens under Jim Crow. African Americans regularly served as test subjects who were subjected to nonconsensual forms of biomedical testing and experimentation. The infamous Tuskegee syphilis experiments are only the tip of the iceberg of a long history of violent and non-consensual medical experiment on people of African descent. C. Riley Snorton demonstrates how Black women's bodies formed the raw material upon which modern gynecology developed.[34] As I will detail at greater length in chapter 3, this violent appropriation and exploitation of Black bodies points toward the similar use of intersex and trans bodies as raw material for the development of contemporary urology and concepts of gender as surgically alterable. While I do not want to equate the experience of Black subjects within regimes of what Achille Mbembe has theorized as the necropolitical violence that is central to slavery and settler colonialism with the position (such as my own) of largely white intersex children in the postwar moment, who benefited from anesthesia, being seen as fully human and other forms of racial privilege, the structural parallel here should also not be dismissed.[35] In both cases nonconsenting in-dividuals formed the embodied material upon which medical techniques and regimes of knowledge were shaped.

Central to Snorton's formulation of medical violence in the emergence of gynecology is his use of Hortense Spillers's concept of "flesh."[36] In her founda-tional essay "Mama's Baby, Papa's Maybe: An American Grammar Book," Spillers argues that slavery, in its violent commodification and objectification of Black bodies, reduced the Black body to flesh, "that zero degree of social conceptualization that does not escape concealment under the brush of dis-course" (67). Key to her theorization of flesh is its degendering in which the "the male body and the female body become a territory of cultural and political maneuver, not at all gender-related, gender-specific" (67). Spillers marks the way in which gender designation itself is bound up with whiteness and the Lockean Enlightenment discourse of owning one's own body (which, of course, was denied to enslaved people). Without such a position, the Black body in slavery was rendered (in Snorton's terms) "fungible," a commodity without recognized subjectivity and endlessly exchangeable. R. A. Judy and Marquis Bey argue for affirmative dimensions of the idea of flesh, one that is more collective, derived from Yoruba practices according to Judy, and opens out to ecosystemic materialities.[37] Yet, while I explore these affirmative dimensions more fully in chapter 2, here I want to emphasize the violence that produced it. Within this logic, gender stops signifying even as bodies become the object of violence, extraction, sexual exploitation, and experimentation. To wit, Black subjects are rendered commodities. While Spillers still emphasizes a binary concept of sex, what is most striking in this argument is that gender functions as an index of whiteness. Sex and gender are disarticulated here in a way that suggests that they can form in contradiction with each other as much as in congruence. To be gendered in this context is to be white. However discursively and materially constraining, gender is an indication that one is not fully reduced to the fleshly body. Of course, forms of gendered violence such as rape work to produce just such a reduction. So one's position, depending on gender, class, age, and sexuality, in such a structure of gendered whiteness can be uneasy and precarious.

This racial imaginary haunts the conception of both sex and gender in the postslavery era as well. As Jules Gill-Peterson argues, it is central to the discourse around the plasticity of first sex and then gender. Such a concept of plasticity was racialized via eugenicist discourse in the early and mid-twentieth century, justifying surgical and hormonal intervention into and modification of white intersex and later trans individuals and refusing the same to trans and intersex individuals of color, consigning them instead often to the mental ward or the prison. The argument underpinning this divide was that "birth defects" were fixable because white children were sufficiently plastic. There was no need for marking defective white children as eugenically inferior; they could be transformed instead. This understanding of the plasticity of sex and gender put pressure on the two-sex model, indicating the stubborn persistence of the one-sex model within an ostensibly two-sex framework.

Central to much sexological discourse in the early twentieth century was the notion of a constitutive "bisexuality," which was a modernization of the one-sex model. In this context, bisexuality did not merely carry its present-day meaning of attraction to people of both sexes; it also had a physiological meaning. The child was made up of the stuff of both sexes and had the potential to develop as an adult toward either sex. Children were both plastic and unruly. They represented a queer amalgam of a range of different desires and possibilities. While this understanding preserved a binary conception of sex as its endpoint, it reinstated the one-sex model for childhood, which allowed (white) children to be conceptualized as sufficiently plastic in order to justify medical and psychological intervention. While popular accounts of Freud often associate him with a strong conception of the two-sex model, Freud's theorization of sex privileges the one sex model in a range of contexts. In Freud, too, bisexuality and what he terms hermaphroditism are central to childhood sexuality. In *Three Essays on Sexuality* he asserts a fundamental "psychic hermaphroditism" and a latent disposition toward "polymorphous perversity" in all subjects, and especially children (144, 191).[38] The liniments of the one-sex model are also visible in Freud's infamous account of the castration complex (which is all about how desire gets routed to a proper object, but only with great effort and often incompletely) as well as his understanding of a singular libido and set of drives.

The psychoanalytic and sexological emphasis on bisexuality dovetailed with work on intersex and trans subjects at Johns Hopkins (which specialized in intersex and trans medicine, beginning with the urology clinic and Harriet Lane Home and continuing later with the Gender Identity Clinic) returning the one-sex model to prominence. As Gill-Peterson puts it: "If all children were naturally intersex or inverted to a certain degree, as doctors and psychiatrists at Hopkins had begun to speculate, then the rationality of binary sex itself was put in question. Perhaps trans childhood and trans life were important but not pathological or even exceptional forms of humanity" (95–96). Either trans and intersex life needed to be de-exceptionalized and depathologized or some new concept needed to emerge to stabilize the binary understanding of sex. This concept was gender: "This looming epistemological crisis of sex was acute enough as the midcentury approached that it would motivate two of the psychologists who conducted interviews with trans people at Hopkins in the 1950s, John Money and John Hampson, to craft a new category of embodiment and psychology called 'gender' that they hoped might finally achieve a level of control over plasticity, cementing the sex binary once and for all" (96). Before we get to gender, however, we should track the further developments of sex as a concept. It is noteworthy here, though, that gender replaces sex as an even more plastic entity, one that hopefully would respond more forthrightly to medical and psychological intervention.

The two-sex model was central to most forms of second-wave feminism, particularly materialist and separatist feminisms. Sex as a category was crucial to the materialist critiques made by feminism, particularly around reproductive rights and the differential medical treatment of men and women. Yet also central to second-wave feminist theorization was an emphasis on the inessential connection between sex and gender. While both were understood to be dualistic, gender was thoroughly social and did not have a necessary connection to the sex binary. As I have already described, this understanding of gender as radically distinct becomes even more developed, indeed radicalized, in third-wave feminism and in some trans discourse, where sex as a material substrate is seen as a discursive production of the discourse of gender itself. Finally, the emergence of more attention to intersex by scholars such as Anne Fausto-Sterling, Hil Malatino, and David A. Rubin and by activists like Bo Laurent and Pidgeon Pagonis renders the very debate between one- and two-sex models potentially incoherent.[39]

What emerges from my very swift and reductive historical account of scientific and social definitions of sex, then, is how unstable an object of analysis it is. There are at least two ways to approach this instability. One is to provide a strong constructivist account that posits sex as nothing other than what it is produced as through discourse. This is a version of Judith Butler's genealogical critique; what masquerades as a prediscursive material foundation is in fact the discursive construction of an ostensibly pre- and extradiscursive entity. Like both Nietzsche's and Foucault's different uses of critical genealogy, the one provided by Butler demonstrates that what we think are causes (material sex) are actually effects of our discursive constructions (which we misread as the effects produced by the original cause).[40] Such a strong constructivist account enables Butler to fundamentally deconstruct the opposition between sex and gender, demonstrating that sex, the ostensible foundational category, is actually produced by gender, which in turn goes from being dependent on sex to discursively producing the very concept of sex as a foundational category. Sex is an "ideal construct which is forcibly materialized through time" (1). While this version of strong constructionism has done a lot of powerful work, enabling scholars of sex and gender to denaturalize a lot of the claims that have been made about the essential differences between men and women and opening up a discursive space for the visibility of transgender and intersex subjects, it also runs the danger of effacing the force, limits, and agency of the biological and material body. Such an effacement is particularly loaded for intersex subjects, given that the fundamental dimension of the difference of our experience, for many of us, is about the material sexed body (this of course also has gendered ramifications, but reducing sex to gender erases a crucial dimension of our experience).

Instead of the strong constructionism that was so much in vogue during the linguistic turn, I want to pair a soft constructionism with a materialist attention to the biological dimensions of sexed embodiment. Such an approach asserts that we all have material bodies and that such bodies have definable properties (what we term various organs, systems, and the like). Some bodies have uteruses, some do not. Some bodies have external testes, some have internal "undescended" testes, some do not have either. Some bodies have specific genital organs and configurations, others have other ones. There is often variation within these categories as well as indistinctions. How these categories (the unity they designate itself a construction) are then turned into a model of or an account of the general category called "sex" that refers to the material reproductive and sexual system is a matter of social construction. This construction always works in a complex relationship with the body's materiality. Language does not construct this materiality, but instead describes how we conceptualize it. Yet how we describe aspects of the biological body can have a powerful impact on what we see and what we don't.

Historicizing Gender

If the concept of sex has a long history, stretching back to antiquity, the history of the concept of gender appears much shorter. While the *Oxford English Dictionary* situates the first English usage of the term in relationship to "males and females as a group" in 1474, most scholars of gender agree that the term didn't take on its recent usage as a set of psychological and physiological behaviors and norms tied to a biomorphic conception of sex until the 1950s, with the work of sexologist and advocate of surgeries on intersex and trans people, John Money. Money is a complicated figure. Founder of the Gender Identity Clinic at Johns Hopkins, he is at once progressive in aspects of his engagement with transgender and nonnormative sexual behaviors and also deeply misguided in his regularizing of nonconsensual genital surgery on intersex folks. For better or worse, though, his concept of gender becomes foundational for the way in which the concept is elaborated not only in scientific and social-scientific discourse but also for feminist, gender, and queer theory.

Before turning to Money's understanding of gender, I want to suggest that the concept of gender informs thinking about sex before it became codified in Money's diagnostics. Gill-Peterson argues that "Money's historiographical role in [gender's] invention has been given too much weight" (99). She goes on to argue, "I think we should locate the emergence of gender in work with intersex children with adrenal conditions before Money arrived at Hopkins" (99). So, while I will focus on Money as the person who did the most to codify the postwar conception of gender, it is important to understand the larger material and institutional context of the definition's genesis. Gender also haunts historiographical work on earlier periods. For example, while Laqueur's argument is primarily focused on sex, his claims for how the one sex model differentiates between men and women depends on a conception of gender: "I want to propose instead that these pre-Enlightenment texts, and even some later ones, sex, or the body, must be understood as the epiphenomenon, while gender, what we would take to be the cultural category, was primary or 'real'" (8). What this concept of gender is and designates is not quite clear. The primary usage of the term in English in the pre-Enlightenment period was in reference to language. It also was used to designate kind. So, for a historical text, Laqueur's claims seem to be rather ahistorical in applying a relatively modern, culturalist understanding of gender to texts that predate the existence of such a concept.

Yet, as classicists have noted, there was a concept of gender in ancient Greece, for example, although it was tied to notions of "virtue" or "natural kind."[41] So gender in relationship to sex floats in the linguistic and cultural ether for a long time before it is scientifically codified by Money and his compatriots. While I will primarily focus on the definitions of the term that follow from Money's codification of it, it is productive to keep in mind the chiasmus that Laqueur posits between sex and gender, what is real and what is malleable. Sex and gender are never fully disambiguated, even in the present. While my argument is that we need to distinguish them if only to posit their intersections, entanglements, tensions, and remainders, it is important to keep in mind their mutual implication and historical slipperiness.

As Nikki Sullivan argues, Money's conception of gender is often misunderstood as thoroughly constructionist.[42] His conception, which he termed gender identity/role (GI/R), was "interactionist" in recognizing "the generative effects of both biology and culture" (19). The concept of gender as both identity and a role has shaped much thinking about gender that has come later. Jennifer Germon has demonstrated the way in which Money drew upon Talcott Parsons's sociology in developing the concept of it as a role.[43] The idea of gender as a role has been not only central to sociological and psychological accounts of the category but also feels closest to the fantasy of midcentury gender that we saw animating *Blade Runner 2049*. The idea of gender role is both social and often implicitly functionalist. Men and women have contrasting, yet complimentary, performances of masculinity and femininity that together create a social whole. Social role theory feels like the most dated aspect of the midcentury conception of gender, very much like those fourth- or fifth-generation 1950s images that we see in the film. Yet, before we dismiss gender as a social role completely, it can also function as an account of lived ideology, or what Pierre Bourdieu would term habitus.[44] This latter account of gender is collective in orientation and can enable the theorization of gender-based oppression (at least some aspects of it). It can also function as a capacious category for political organizing. So I don't want to reject the idea of gender as a larger social formation and set of social scripts that can (although don't need to) attach to certain kinds of sexed bodies, even as I work to produce accounts of gender

and sex that are more adequate to the complexities and multiplicities of identification, embodiment, and social struggle.

The other category central to Money's account, identity, is one that does
not feel dated at all. Indeed, if anything, it has proliferated and flourished in
the twenty-first century. Gender as identity has functioned as an effective and
precise designation in a world in which the concept has broken with the binary
and functionalist logic that structured it in the midcentury moment and has
come to describe a range of different identifications, including those of trans,
intersex, and nonbinary subjects. Gender as identity, then, seems to be the
least dated and unfortunate of Money's frameworks for the concept. Certainly,
gender as identity, especially when identity is imagined in macrosocial modes
(as it is, for example, in much feminist and antiracist critique), can function
powerfully as a concept that both names collective forms of oppression and
exploitation and offers a position for positive identification. Even modes, such
as Marxist and queer analysis, which have a more ambivalent relationship to
identity (for the first generation of queer theorists, a minoritarian conception
of identity was an object of their critique, and Marxist theory has long emphasized that class is primarily not an identity but a structural relationship), there
is still the ghost of an identitarian logic at work. The majoritarian position
articulated by Eve Kosofsky Sedgwick and other early queer theorists and
Marxist understanding of class rely on a notion of who is queer and who represents the proletariat.[45]

Yet, while identity does important work in the present and offers itself as
both more flexible and more attentive to power than the gender role tradition,
there are a number of problems with it as a concept too. I have already rehearsed
some of this in the introduction, including its relationship, especially in the
contemporary moment, to branding, human capital, and atomization, but I
will focus here merely on the way in which identity, when seen primarily as
personal, produces a flattening of the complexity and contradictions of subjectivity and can work to erase the material context in which it functions. When
not a sociological or macro-concept, identity functions primarily as egoic. It is
a site of identification, a concept by which we articulate a unified concept of
self. Ego identifications are important and can indeed structure subjectivity
and political action in important ways. They are also not always positive (with
Lacan's notion of an ideal ego, we often experience ourselves as lacking or
inadequate in relationship to this ideal), and there is a strong political value in
articulating commonality and alliances with others who have experienced
identity-based oppression, exclusion, or exploitation.[46] Yet there is a reason why
Lacan framed his radical reinterpretation of psychoanalysis against its post-
Freudian domestication as ego psychology. The emphasis on the egoic excludes

the contradictions represented by the unconscious and the drives. It also privileges the imaginary register, in Lacanian terms, over the workings of the symbolic and the real. As Anna Kornbluh argues, subjectivity becomes organized primarily around the imaginary, which is central to the production of "immediacy" in contemporary capitalist culture. Mediation disappears, circulation intensifies, and we are "drowning in a deluge of images without context."[47] Immediacy's emphasis on the imaginary generates antagonisms or intense identifications over symbolic mediation. Some of the antagonisms and "borderwars," to use Jack Halberstam's term, we see in the present between different identity groups, suggests that too many of our political struggles on the left (the sexual left and otherwise) are organized around imaginary transference and projection, the workings of identification and disidentification (144). Imaginary politics produce an investment in border policing as well as rendering large the narcissism of minor differences. It is hard to understand the infighting between transmen and butch lesbians, which Halberstam describes at an earlier moment, without a conception of imaginary formation.[48] If you accept a psychoanalytic framework, one of its core insights is that self-knowledge is inevitably limited. There are aspects of ourselves that exist in tension and contradiction with our conscious understandings of ourselves, and those aspects are often projected onto those with whom we imagine ourselves in immediate opposition.

The Copernican revolution that Lacan (and later Jean Laplanche) attributed to Freud is founded on the contradictory relationship of the ego (or the cogito) to the rest of the psyche and particularly to the unconscious.[49] I will explore this psychoanalytic framework more fully in chapter 2, but here I merely want to note that identity seen as a singular and self-identical concept (and this is true even when it is conceptualized in terms of intersectionality and multiple identities) is necessarily in tension with aspects of the psychoanalytic conception of the psyche. The latter emphasizes that there are aspects of ourselves and our relationship to the social of which we are not only not aware but about which we are in denial or which we consciously repudiate or repress. Such an understanding of subjectivity, including sexual and gendered subjectivity, not only emphasizes that identity can perhaps best be understood as identifications (which can function as agential and conscious acts as much as something over which you don't have fully conscious or political power) but also recognizes that we are creatures structured in contradiction, whose relationship to sex, gender, subjectivity, and political struggle is often complex and split. For Money, gender as an identity exists in contradiction with neither the sexed body nor other abandoned, subterranean, or repressed identifications. It is instead a binaristic and regulative ideal, one that he used to buttress his justification for medical intervention into intersex children. In this context, the singularity of gender identity became a way of effacing the contradictions that the sexed body and that other gender identifications, experiences, and desires might produce, thereby complicating the ostensibly clear directive for surgery.

Building on Sullivan's account of Money's conception of gender as interactionist (combining both biology and culture), Iain Morland persuasively argues that Money conceptualized his neologism of gender specifically as plastic, drawing upon the earlier understanding of sex as plastic. Money also used a model derived from cybernetics in order to account for this plasticity: "Compellingly for Money, cybernetics theorized the adaptive consequences of plasticity: it combined the study of homologous adaptations in organisms and machines with a humanist discourse about the exceptional plasticity of people."[50] As Gill-Peterson notes, it was not just any body that was plastic. This was a conception tied to whiteness. Within this framework, gender as plastic, when nurtured along the proper developmental path, enfolds the sexed body and, once the latter is surgically shaped to fit the former, works by constructing a feedback loop. Gender and sex, both always understood as binary, reinforce each other through the workings of the feedback loop that is developed between them. Yet, as Morland argues, the cybernetic model here, while invoked, is not actually followed. Rather than a genuine feedback loop between sex and gender, gender became the only actant and sex became a passive surface (once properly sculpted) upon which gender does its work. Money also eschews causality for a cybernetic model of prediction, thus giving the material body and biological sex no causal force at all. Gender is thoroughly binarized and unmoored from material constraint or contradiction. It is a regulative ideal that becomes its own causal justification. Since it is conceptualized as flexible, its proper realization also functions as a biopolitical, cultural, pedagogical, and political ideal, one that prefigures later ideals of human capital production and branding.

As David A. Rubin and Jennifer Germon have argued, drawing on the foundational work of Suzanne Kessler, Money's conception of gender as plastic and socially determined shaped second- and third-wave feminist theorizing about the category.[51] Germon and Ara Wilson persuasively demonstrate that gender moved from clinical uses in intersex case management, psychology, and the ego-based, clinical psychoanalysis of the 1960s and 1970s to an initially uneven uptake withing feminism. Wilson nicely historicizes this shift: "Gender first appeared in 1970s feminist discourse in the form of explicit citations of clinical psychological works. In the academy, these clinical accounts of gender appeared as references in social psychology, feminist sociology, and non-clinical writing about homosexuality and transsexuality. Feminist intellectuals began to refer to the medical-psychological works on gender identity from Johns Hopkins University and UCLA, particularly [psychiatrist Robert J.] Stoller's work."[52]

Wilson goes on to argue that gender identity, rather than gender or sex role, became the term of choice, instituting a psychological understanding of the term. Yet, at its most visionary, gender in feminist theory became a central organizing category, one that replaced (or supplemented) a dimorphic understanding of biological sex with an understanding of gender as thoroughly cultural and psychological. For Gayle Rubin, gender provided a crucial emphasis on the social shaping of biological sex.[53] In her celebrated essay "The Traffic in Women" she articulates the workings of the oppression of women historically and in the present in relationship to the "sex-gender system," which she defines as a "set of arrangements by which a society transforms a biological sex into products of human activity" (34). Given the essay's focus on producing a structural account of women's oppression along the lines of Marx's account of the structural exploitation of the proletariat, her emphasis on gender as a labor done on bodies to socialize them (gender transforms the raw material of sex into a socially regulated and exploited substance) is persuasive in its macrosocial reach. Yet, even as Rubin provides a persuasive account of the production of gender, her thinking, in this early essay, echoes Money's account of gender as plastic and binary. While the emphasis on the labor of gender nicely denatures it, revealing it to be a product of culture, this transformation of sex into gender functions to both abolish sex as socially meaningful and reifies it as a binary. As with Money, sex imposes no limitations on gender and its structuration other than as the binary substrate upon which parallel understandings of gender as binary are produced.

Gayle Rubin's theorization, along with other early feminist formulations, became central to second-wave understandings of sex and gender. Sex, understood as male or female, becomes the substrate upon which gender is organized. Yet there is no necessary relationship, other than an ideological one, between masculinity and maleness or femininity and femaleness. The critique of second-wave theorists such as Rubin was crucial in denaturalizing gender as a social construct, one that could deviate from the sex to which it was conventionally tied. Her framework undoes the ways in which normative understandings of gender as the social facing yet biological expression of sex were used to naturalize and normalize male domination. It also provides the possibility of male femininity and what Jack Halberstam has termed female masculinity.[54] In all these ways, this second-wave understanding of gender undertook necessary cultural work. Yet its concept of gender inherited some of the problems of Money's account as well. It may seem more thoroughly constructionist than Money's account of gender as plasticity, but Rubin deemphasizes sex in relationship to a more dynamic and complex account of gender. Sex is acknowledged, but it has no causal or material force. Like the raw materials of capitalism, sex functions as a raw material, but its contribution and influence on the finished product of gender is thoroughly obscured. It is only with recent work in eco-Marxism, such as Jason W. Moore's *Capitalism in the Web of Life*, that we have learned to attend to the ecological contributions to production, what Moore calls "cheap nature" along with various forms of gendered and racialized unwaged labor, such as that produced under slavery and as part of the work of social reproduction.[55] Part of the work of my argument, then, is precisely to attend to sex as a nonbinary part of gender's ecology—the material that intersects with and is in a complex dialectical tension and interaction with gender.

If sex still had a place in second-wave theorizing, by the time we get to the work of Judith Butler as a paradigmatic third-wave theorist, sex becomes nothing more than an ideological effect of gender, a projection backward as a foundation or essence for gender's expression but that is just a contingent effect of the latter. While Butler has recently revised their earlier formulations, nicely recognizing the importance of "trans and materialist criticisms" of their earlier account of gender, it was her work in the 1990s that became particularly influential.[56] As I have argued, Butler's work crucially separates gender fully from being bound to any binary notion of sex. Instead, gender here appears radically contingent and potentially nonbinary. As with Money's insistence on proper binary rearing and a body that is shaped to "conform" to this rearing, gender is malleable. This is a performative constructionism thoroughly unmoored from material limitation or interaction. The complex sex of intersex bodies does not matter. We become fundamentally gendered subjects, whether normative or queer.

The recent work that has been done under the rubric of the material turn promises to be more productive for giving both sex and gender their due. Emphasizing "definitions of the human corporeality that can account for how the discursive and the material interact in the constitution of bodies,"[57] the thinkers of the material turn attend to the force and agency of the material body. Within such an account sex would be seen as material, productive of both possibilities and limits, and yet not foundational or determining in any straightforward way. Yet, even in the new materialisms, we can see a plastic conception of gender and sex still present in Donna J. Haraway's conception of "natureculture" or

Samantha Frost's account of the "biocultural," which, I should note, does theorize the force and agency of the body as semiporous.[58] Moreover, there is often an implicit whiteness to the bodies theorized by new materialism, one that echoes the implicit whiteness of gender. Mel Y. Chen describes the way in which racial and queer mattering are often situated further down on an ideological set of sliding scales that runs from live to dead, human to animal, animate to inanimate.[59] Which bodies count as both human and animate echoes the concept of who gets to occupy normative conceptions of gender.

While Money used his concept in much more rigid, and at times, incoherent ways in order to justify all sorts of medical surveillance and intervention, his model, which prefigures recent work in epigenetics as well, emphasizes the intermixing of the material and the cultural, the biological and the behavioral. This framework has proven productive in recent feminist and scientific arguments (including those made by feminist science studies) in order to combat a reductive biological and evolutionary determinism on the one hand and strong constructionism on the other. Even as we want to move beyond Money, his work, as Sullivan notes, "has been hugely influential and that rather than being confined to the worlds of scientific research and or clinical practice, its influence has shaped us all" (20). Not only did his concept of gender migrate unevenly to second-wave feminism where it became central to articulations of the sex/gender binary, it informs recent work that has tried to deconstruct or blur the distinctions between nature and culture, gender and sex, suggesting that these attempts too may not be as radical or as new as we would like to suppose. For example, while such a natureculture perspective provides a more complicated account of the interaction of the material and the conceptual, the biological and the cultural, Money employed his similar conception of the plasticity of gender to suggest that culture could instantiate a gender identity and role where sex was more ambiguous or even opposed the ostensible identity. Money's fraught use of his model was attached to his investment in an absolutely binarized framework for both sex and gender. Later biocultural models have properly rejected this binarism. Yet the emphasis on the porosity and flow in much new materialist work, especially of the Deleuzian orientation, frames all of gender and sex as potentially malleable and fluid. This too seems to privilege plasticity over that which may resist or exist in tension with gender's malleability, notably sex and the flesh. I want to suggest that it is crucial to think about how aspects of both sex and gender can exceed any attempt to fully synchronize the two terms. I also want to suggest that we need to think about the agency, force, and resistance of sex that does not use the metaphor or logic of plasticity.

Gender over Sex

What emerges from these two long histories of sex and gender is the increasing emphasis on the latter and the attenuation of the former in academic and professional discourse. Part of the promise of both science and the Enlightenment is the ability to transform the world, especially the natural world, into forms and entities that please, affirm, and aid human endeavor. While there is a utopian kernel at work here, and science and medicine contribute positively to contemporary life in myriad ways (I write this while admiring the work that the coronavirus vaccines have done and wishing that people could distinguish more effectively between institutional critiques of science and medicine and paranoid or macho rejections of them), it is also crucial to recognize that the materials and entities we transform through science, whether petrochemical, geological, plant-based, or animal (including humans as animals), also exert force, resistance, and agency in the broadest sense, as feminist new materialism has taught us. Moreover, there are often unexpected consequences to such transformations, as the climate emergency demonstrates.

We need an account of both sex and gender that is not thoroughly plastic, manipulable, customizable, and what C. Riley Snorton terms "fungible" (and it is crucial to remember here that such a conception of gender is shaped not only by neoliberal capitalism but also by a long history of specifically racialized capitalism and the conversion of those of African descent into living commodities under slavery). Certainly we want to affirm the way in which technologies enable effective and affirmative bodily transitions for trans and genderqueer folks who desire them, whether it is through surgeries or the use of hormone therapies. Similarly, the technologies of surrogacy carry the utopian possibility (and reality) of divorcing birth from specific bodies and enabling a more collective and nonheteronormative relationship to childbirth, rearing, and care, as Sophie Lewis argues.[60] I want to affirm the ways in which technology enables various kinds of human and nonhuman flourishing more generally. This dialectical approach to technology will be central to my reflections on the relationship of surgery and medicalization to both intersex and trans in chapter 3. I think we need to be neither accelerationist nor Luddite about technologies. Instead, a properly eco-Marxist and queer approach to technology would analyze both what it enables and aids and at what costs and through what forms of violence.

Paul B. Preciado's engagement with the material and embodied transformations produced by testosterone and the way in which he reveals some of the affirmatively erotic dimensions of transitioning has much to recommend it, yet his account of the virtues of the pharmapornographical regime is at once too sanguine (as in optimistic) and not sanguine enough (as in bloody). It does not detail the material costs on which the extraction and testing of such technologies took place. On the other hand, Silvia Federici's account of surrogacy and transitioning technologies as only a negative development of biocapitalism is too anti-Enlightenment and negating of biomedical intervention.[61] Even as we affirm the possibilities that technology poses for noncapitalist flourishing, both Preciado and Federici, despite their profound differences, are right to emphasize the ways in which technology in the present is profoundly intertwined with biopolitical capitalism. If there is a promise to the ascent and plasticity of gender as it is currently conceived, it would finally have to be fully realized outside of the dictates of the market and the kinds of neoliberal branding, inequalities, and flexibility that it promotes. It would also have to be seen as not the final word in relationship to questions of embodiment and difference.

Sex, as an account of the bodily remainder, as a version of the Lacanian real that exists in tension with the symbolic and imaginary, or as embodied sexual organization that exists in tension with gender conceived as fully plastic, is crucial for further theorization. As my earlier, brief history of sex as a concept demonstrates, it, like gender, is far from a settled or uniform notion. Even as gender helped prop up the collapsing two-sex model, sex emerged in the twentieth century as a much stranger entity than many thought. If this queering of sex has been obscured by gender and its productive queering, it is time we return a queer conception of sex to the forefront of theorizing embodiment and desire. Psychoanalytic accounts of both sex and desire complicate any simple notion of sex as about opposites. In a similar way, theories of intersex embodiment radically complicate any conception of embodied sex as binary.

It is important, employing the materialism mixed with soft constructionism I am advocating, that we neither reify sex into a fixed entity of positivist science nor theorize it away by pointing to the malleability of its various discursive meanings. Recognizing the partial constructedness of sex as a category does not mean that we need to treat it as flexibly as gender. It does not mean that strong constructionism was right all along and that we should see sex, like gender, as a product of discourse and, as such, open to radical historical contingency and performative resignification. This is one road to take in approaching sex, but there is another one. It is the materialist road, which posits sex, like flesh, as that which exists in tension with human cultural scripts and refuses plasticity, encodes wounds, and exists where gendered ideologies come undone and racialized and sexed ones become exacted. Like Hedwig's angry inch in the play and film of the same name, sex is what remains from the manipulations and transformations of biomedicalized gender. It insists angrily on a reckoning.

We have to theorize sex not only as such an angry inch but as also having parallels to the code that shapes Joi's endlessly fungible existence. It is a version of bodily infrastructure that makes our avatar fantasies possible. We need to attend to gender in all of its complexity as a locus of identification, transformation, ideology, and possibility, but we also need to theorize sex as the extimate dimension upon which gender constructs its meanings. It is to such a theorization that I turn to in chapter 2.

2

Sex as Extimacy

It's extimacy when you lay down next to me

SOMETHING BARRY WHITE SHOULD HAVE SUNG

So, what is sex? It may seem strange to be asking this question about a book's central topic at the beginning of chapter 2. If I have not articulated what sex is yet, maybe I never will. Perhaps there is no point in reading further. It is not so much that I have not provided definitions of sex but that such definitions are always at best partial and necessarily catachrestic. I have noted both in the introduction and chapter 1 that sex is as elusive as it is multiply defined. It functions in contradiction to our symbolic logics and thus refuses simple positive definitions.

Having traced out the logic of how it has been defined historically in chapter 1, this chapter advances a materialist account of sex as both embodiment and desire. Like all nonreductive materialisms, this account theorizes how the symbolic (as both a much more malleable form of materiality—that is, the materiality of the signifier—and as something that carries immaterial messages that can become materially embodied as symptoms) and more obdurate, though still partially manipulable, materialities (in this case the somatic materiality of the body) intertwine. In the mature Lacan, the real functions as a locus of the impossible or the excluded yet determining.[1] It is that which refuses meaning and exists as a form of intimate nonbeing that disrupts any account of being and self. In contrast, in Lacan's early developmentalist accounts, such as the famous mirror stage essay, he also uses real to discuss materiality, including the materiality of the body in continuity with other forms of materiality. Gilles Deleuze and Félix Guattari, in *Anti-Oedipus*, draw upon this early association in articulating the "body without organs," which is a figuration for the uncoded materiality of the body before or in tension with symbolic inscription.[2] In what follows, I will draw on each of these resonances, but I will generally use the language of the "real" when talking about that which is excluded yet determining and I will use the phrase "material body" when I am referencing the materiality of the body. Yet the logic of Lacan's real will always inform my discussion of materiality. There is always what Slavoj Žižek describes as a *not-all*, an intimate otherness, at work in any positive account of the materiality of the body, sex, and desire.[3] There are always elements of what exists that resists translation into our symbolic frameworks, imaginary figurations, and discursive constructions.

It is also crucial to provide such frameworks and constructions in accounting for the materiality of the body. It is crucial to theorize the body as material, substantive, and active. Lacan also provides a powerful framework to think about the contradictions that structure our relationship to embodiment, particularly his late theory of the Borromean knot. Drawing on this theory, I will argue that the body is both here, present to us, and also elsewhere, an intimate alterity. In doing so, I will also draw on the pathbreaking work of new materialists such as Samantha Frost, Karen Barad, Mel Y. Chen, and Stacy Alaimo to theorize the body as permeable yet constrained (part of a "constrained self-relation"), in which "the embodied human does not simply move in a field of action but absorbs manifold substances from its habitat and responds perceptually, biochemically, and viscerally to the threats and promises that the social and material world present."[4] The body is at once part of an ecosystem, a biological entity, an imaginary edifice that intersects with its materiality, and a symbolic construction. We subjectify it, but always in incomplete ways.

In theorizing the body in this manner, I should be drawing more fully on the work of Gilles Deleuze rather than Lacan, it might seem, since the former renders everything material and imagines a much more entangled relationship between language and other systems and forms of materiality. Moreover, Deleuze has been a significant influence on both posthumanism and new materialism. The reason I draw on Lacan as well as Laplanche and other psychoanalytic thinkers in complicated relationship with new materialism is that, as I argue in the introduction, I am interested in thinking through contradiction rather than merely providing an additive model in which everything operates on a plain of immanence. While Deleuze has much to recommend him, I am invested in Lacan's theorization of the incommensurability of the different registers (symbolic, imaginary, and real) as well as their entanglement.

If my theorization of embodiment willfully mixes Lacan and new materialism, my account of sex as desire mixes Laplanche and Lacan. What both psychoanalytic theorists emphasize is that desire is an intimate alien, something
implanted by and routed through the other (the parental other, initially, and
then for Lacan, the Other in the domain of the symbolic as well). Following
Lacan's lead, Laplanche's work breaks with the emphasis on endogeny in parts
of Freud, later ego psychologists, and most theorists of the object relations school.
Laplanche proposes what Gila Ashtor describes as an "enlarged sexuality," which
she describes in the following way:

1. A sexuality that absolutely goes beyond genitality, and even beyond
   sexual difference;
2. A sexuality that is related to fantasy;
3. A sexuality that is extremely mobile as to its aim and object . . .
4. A sexuality that has its own "economic" regime in the Freudian
   sense of the term, its own principle of functioning, which is not systematic tendency toward discharge, but a specific tendency toward
   the increase of tension and the pursuit of excitation.[5]

This conception of sexuality is valuable for several reasons. More than any
other psychoanalytic model, this understanding is not dependent on a binarized
conception of sex. If I am arguing that sex as embodiment is not binary, then
our theories of sex as desire and act cannot be structured within a binary
framework. Laplanche's conception of sexuality is also mobile in ways that
open it up to all kinds of queer desires, embodiments, and theorizations. It
crucially engages fantasy as a complicated production of the relationship of
self to otherness, and specifically the sexuality of the other, which provokes it.
This understanding of sexuality as mobile is also captured by Marquis Bey,
whose conception of the flesh will also be important to this chapter: "Sexuality
is not some innate thing, with its parameters all in place beforehand. That is
not to say that one can choose to be gay or straight or bi or pan; rather it is to
say that straightness and gayness and bi-ness are predicated on historically and
culturally delimited understandings and requisites for where one locates both
one's sexuality as well as where one locates the operative endogenous hotspots
on one's desired object."[6]
Sexuality is shaped by cultural and historical meanings as they become
encoded on bodies. Sex as desire here is thoroughly nonbinary, and while Bey
importantly emphasizes its cultural and historical codings, I want also to emphasize the way in which it becomes central to both the unconscious and fantasy.
It does not have to be innate to become structuring and extimate (it is not a

choice, as Bey notes), but those structures themselves are shaped by historical and cultural meanings. Flesh, as Bey and others have theorized, is another example of a structuring form of embodiment that has been produced by culture and history. I will turn to theorizing it more fully at the end of this chapter, but it is important to note that it provides a model for thinking about the mutual imbrication of historicism and the more structural accounts of psychoanalysis. While I will generally use the seemingly static categories of psychoanalysis in what follows, it is important to recognize that they too describe a historically sedimented set of dynamics and formations. They become what Theodor W. Adorno theorizes as second nature (what he also terms "natural history" or a reified state of being that is experienced as natural).[7] But second natures can be changed and do change. While I primarily present a psychoanalytic account of sex in which historicism is bracketed in this chapter, it is important to remember that what I am theorizing finally also is historically shaped and can be reshaped.

Even more fully than Laplanche, Lacan theorizes sex as about our fundamental relationship to otherness and the social. Otherness is central to Lacan's conception of desire. As Patricia Gherovici and Tim Dean have differently argued, Lacan too can be used in ways that go beyond sexual binaries and the logic of the phallus.[8] As Dean argues, the *objet petit a* in Lacan functions, in contrast to the phallic signifier, by a fetish logic which emphasizes the "radical impersonality of desire" (17). As with Bey, the psychoanalytic understanding of desire is about understanding the "operative endogenous hotspots" of oneself and the one's object. Yet it is crucial to emphasize that such endogeny is actually produced initially via exogamy. It begins outside the subject and becomes an extimate encystment. The structure of desire is thus organized around a fantasized object that is fundamentally detached from fixed gender and sexual schemas within the symbolic. It also works by continuous displacement. It is the "in you, more than you" that both is linked to the other but necessarily exceeds them (*Four Fundamental Concepts*, 263). It is the phantasmatic trace of the real, or the "little piece of the real" in the domain of the other. Similarly, Alenka Zupančič has argued that sexual difference in Lacan is not about a sexed binary but an ontological split or fault that structures all subjectivities.[9]

There is a scene in the first season of *The L Word: Generation Q* in which Micah Lee, a trans man played by trans actor Leo Sheng, hooks up with José Garcia, played by Freddy Miyares. In the scene in which they fuck, José moves behind Micha and then hesitates. He says that he does not know what to do here. Micha reaches behind and indicates that he will take care of it. They then begin to fuck. The show nicely does not show us or indicate how they do so (anally, vaginally, or some other way). The scene divorces sex from any kind of binary logic, presenting instead a range of pleasures related to different body parts, fantasies, and desires. This scene captures the polymorphous conception of sex as desire that I am articulating in this book.

Sex is both embodiment and desire. Central to my argument is Lacan's account of extimacy, as that which exists in an intimate exteriority. Sex, in both senses, is extimate to the conscious subject. In addition to sex being extimate, I will also theorize it as material, drawing on both the work of Anne Fausto-Sterling, other scholars of intersex, and feminist new materialists.[10] Drawing both on the work of the Black studies scholars (Spillers, Snorton, Judy, Weheliye, and Bey) I have been in dialogue with throughout this book and on Maurice Merleau-Ponty's and Herbert Marcuse's rethinking of the flesh and eros in a collective register, I connect the flesh to Marx's idea of species being and think about how the flesh can become a model for a different kind of embodiment and a different relationship to the social and the ecosystemic.[11]

What should also emerge from this chapter is a conception of sex, sexuality, and gender that is both materialist and affirmative of a whole range of different embodiments and desires, including trans and intersex embodiments and trans and intersex folks as subjects of desire (both desiring subjects, shaped by the desire of the other, and as objects of desire). Before developing this argument, I want to turn to Lacan's late theorization of the Borromean knot, because it suggests, for all of its notorious difficulty, a model for understanding how the real, symbolic, and imaginary are both intertwined and exist in contradiction. It is perhaps his most complex and complete version of extimacy. The subject is structured by and in relationship an intimate otherness. Our symbolic and imaginary constructions of ourselves are always disrupted and deformed by the real.

Knotted Subjects

The Borromean knot is one of Lacan's final frameworks for understanding the work of analysis and the constitution of the subject. It is a principal reference for his seminars of the mid-1970s, becoming his final account of the relationship between the symbolic, imaginary, and real, each braid of the knot representing one of them as they intersect with the others. Key to the knot is its topological dimension. It is an entity that is mathematically thinkable yet not representable in a two-dimensional way (thus it cannot be understood in imaginary terms). Nor is it a metaphor or signifier; it resists symbolic formulation. Its status, then, is, as Luke Thurston posits, "a form of 'showing' which aimed beyond the logical limits of speech."[12] Conceptually, the "knot" consists of a three-dimensional intertwined set of rings (the three representing the symbolic, imaginary, and real). The removal of any one ring means that the whole formation falls apart. As Lacan puts it in Seminar XXIII, "the Borromean knot consists in this relationship which what is *enveloped* with respect to the circles finds itself *enveloping* with respect to the other one."[13] The three are thus mutually enveloping and determining, in an Escher-like fashion. Each ring is braided with the others, yet it also exists in contradiction with the others, such that the negation it represents (its removal from the whole) means the collapse of the structure. In mathematical terms, it can only be understood and produced within three-dimensional space. Such a topological understanding indicates that the knot ex-sists (it is situated beyond meaning), and thus is not representable in its true form. As Lacan puts it, the knot is "constituted by a geometry that may be said to be forbidden to the imaginary, because it can only be imagined through all kinds of resistances and indeed difficulties" (*The Sinthome*, 21). It thus functions like a version of the real, even as it also refuses the fixity of any account of the real, since it is equally made up of the other two registers of the symbolic and imaginary. Indeed, the real cannot be apprehended separately from the other two without the whole collapsing. If this sounds contradictory, it is intentionally so. It suggests the fundamental contradictions at the heart of the subject.

Lacan uses this formulation to stage various metaphysical problems and contradictions. He is an antiphilosopher, as Alain Badiou argues: someone who is invested in simultaneously thinking through and undoing metaphysical edifices by pushing their logic to the point of contradiction.[14] While it is important to keep this antiphilosophical position in mind, I am more interested here in how this framework shifts his privileging of the symbolic and complicates dynamic yet discontinuous relationship among the three registers (symbolic, imaginary, and real), positions that were central to much of his theorizing in the 1950s and 1960s.

Thurston argues that in Lacan's late conception of the Borromean knot the subject becomes more substantial, although in ways that still privileged its overdetermination by the complex intertwining (and discontinuities) of the three registers: "In the topology of the Borromean knot, Lacanian theory no longer offered an account centered on an insubstantial subject, whose coherence derived from its position as a speaking being (*parlêtre*). It constituted in itself—as writing embodying a certain real—a 'subversion of the subject,' a quasi-ontological (or 'onto-graphic') substance, which seemed incommensurable with a notion of the subject as a linguistic instance of pure negativity (153)." Thurston posits Lacan's conception of the real as a form of writing (it is "onto-graphic"), by which he means a kind of nonhuman code or automatic writing (and is interesting to think about in terms of sex as code, as we discussed in chapter 1). This notion of the real as a kind of writing not only echoes Lacan's earlier account of the unconscious as structured "like a language" but also suggests parallels with Laplanche's conception of the unconscious as formed by the waste products of enigmatic signifiers. There is a writing here, but it is one not comprehensible to the conscious subject and their position within the symbolic. It may have its source in what is initially external to the subject, but it becomes both intimate and alien. It is what ex-sists in the subject, and often takes form as nonsymbolizable jouissance, what Lacan calls the sinthome (as opposed to symptom) in his late work. The subject is theorized in terms of substance, but a substance that is decentering of the subject itself. The real and the symbolic are not so much in nonrelationship, which was central to his accounts of the two in the 1960s. Instead, they are in an intimate, intertwined position, between continuity and discontinuity, relation and nonrelation. Along with the imaginary, their entanglement produces a complex, contradictory, Escher-like construction of the subject, becoming the basis for a Lacanian understanding of the subject as embodied but not in any straightforward, empirical way. Instead, the subject and its relationship to substance is extimate. It is this concept of extimacy that is central to my theorization of sex in relationship to both embodiment and drive.

Extimacies

Lacan first introduces the concept of extimacy in *Seminar VII*, where it is part of his account of the Freudian notion of *Das Ding*, or the object in the domain of the real (as opposed to symbolic objects, or objects which can be symbolized). Lacan goes on to describe it as "that dumb reality which is Das Ding."[15] It is the foundational object or mute materiality that refuses to be dialecticized but instead becomes that around which the symbolic is constructed and for which it cannot account effectively. For Lacan, this becomes the basis for his theory of the drive, which he elaborates more fully in the seminar as well as later ones. What I am most interested in here, however, is how it articulates a fundamental contradiction between knowing and being, the symbolic and the real.

It is precisely as an extension of this discussion of the Thing that Lacan formulates extimacy, which he describes as an "intimate exteriority or 'extimacy' that is the Thing."[16] There is something in us more than us (and that we often perceive in the domain of the other). It is both intimate and alien. It is the thing that is foundational to our existence as subjects and yet it comes from elsewhere. Part of the work of analysis is to take responsibility for our relationship to this extimate thing. If we domesticate it too much, thinking we have simple control or agency over it, we miss any genuine engagement with it. The same is true if we locate it thoroughly outside of ourselves. We need to make space for it as the intimate other, the thing that lives inside and alternately nourishes and haunts us.

While Lacan merely invokes the extimate in *Seminar VII* without defining or discussing it further, it has been taken up by later commentators, most notably by Lacan's nephew and the executor of his estate, Jacques-Alain Miller. Miller is a controversial figure and has made several unfortunate statements over the years, including transphobic ones. Despite this history, I think the theory of extimacy can be used productively to provide a materialist account of sex and gender, one that can affirm the specificity of trans and intersex subjectivities and embodiments. Miller glosses extimacy as "a term used by Lacan to designate, in a problematic manner, the real in the symbolic."[17] The extimate is a way of accounting for the real in symbolic terms. Hence its problematic nature. The real can be invoked or pointed at in symbolic terms but its status is not symbolic (even if its genesis in part may be produced by inscription). The real is that which intimately determines our subjectivity and yet is experienced as alien or other. It is the otherness at the core of our being. So it is at once intimate and other, in a word extimate. The other crucial insight that Miller adds to the concept is that it troubles concepts of interiority and exteriority, disrupting the idea that psychoanalysis is a discourse about subjective interiority, à la psychology. The real may be at the core of our being but it is also external, and its genesis is as much social as it is psychological. The drives and the unconscious are extimate in exactly this way. I also want to extend extimacy it to the material body as it exists in tension with as well as is braided with our symbolic and imaginary constructions of it. In doing so, I am articulating an understanding of embodiment as fundamentally Borromean, a product of the complex intertwining of the symbolic, imaginary, and real.

The Body as Extimate

I theorize sex as embodiment not only in relationship to the Borromean knot but also in terms of the notion of extimacy. The two concepts provide overlapping frameworks for understanding the intimate otherness or alienness of our experience not only of subjecthood but embodiment. Embodiment considered in relationship to the Borromean knot is made up of the following: (1) imaginary mapping of the body in terms of the body ego, its gendering, and its relationship to morphology, fantasy, and identification; (2) the symbolic encoding of the body in terms of signifiers, forms of biofeedback, various kinds of measurement, and the linguistic construction of subjectivity, via the shifter "I"; (3) the real as aspects of the body and the subject that exceed and resist both symbolic and imaginary coding and that form in contradiction with any positive totalization. None of these registers can be understood without apprehending their intertwined and knotted relationship. Thus, while I have argued that gender is primarily a dynamic of the imaginary as it is overdetermined by the real and sex is shaped complex intertwining of the symbolic and the real and can be most fully associated with the latter, both sex and gender (as well as subjectivity) are products of the complex and distinctive braiding of all three. Thus, when we think about trans subjectivity and intersex subjectivity, each emphasize one dimension of Lacan's schema more fully, but each also are shaped by the sum of their braidings.

In terms of thinking about sex as embodiment in relationship to the real, I theorize the extimate body in relationship to the material dimensions of our body that we have not fully symbolized or constructed an imaginary embodiment around or that exist in tension with such symbolizations and bodily mappings. And of course, the material body is always in partial tension with our symbolic and imaginary framings of it, given that language and image are never coincident with what they reference. So the real dimensions of the material body exist as extimate. Our bodies are intimate yet strange. We can be carrying diseases without realizing it. We rarely think about our internal organs unless we become more conscious of them due to illness, biomedical feedback, or cultural symbolization. And while the growth of biofeedback as part of the larger framework of what Adele Clarke and colleagues describe as biomedicalization, or the neoliberal paradigm of individual responsibility for wellness, there is still a tension (and disjunction) between how we symbolize this feedback and what this feedback is representing.[18]

Body horror, both in films like those of David Cronenberg (and now those of his son Brandon too) and video games like the *Resident Evil* franchise (when its campiness or desire to become an action game does not destroy the survival horror elements), captures the uncanny extimacy of the body as real. Central to most of them are moments when aspects of the body emerge or transform that fundamentally break with our imaginary and symbolic mappings of the body. What should remain internal all of a sudden becomes external. You capture a glimpse of yourself in a broken mirror, and you do not recognize the thing you have become. As I have written at greater length elsewhere, I absolutely identified with the "monster" Lisa Trevor in the reboot of the first *Resident Evil* game.[19] Her disfigurement and debility, in Jasbir K. Puar's terms, are the product of medical experiments overseen by her father (in my case it was my doctors who occupied the paternal position).[20] The resonances with my own surgical history were too obvious to ignore. I did not want to kill her. I wanted to hug her and tell her everything would somehow be okay.

To return to sex and its relationship to the real body, while we signify sex in terms of sex organs obsessively in our culture (how many crude drawings have we seen in library books or restroom stalls?), this overrepresents one dimension of what Anne Fausto-Sterling terms genital sex at the expense of others (gonadal sex, hormonal sex, genetic sex, morphological sex, organ sex other than the visible sex organs, and so forth).[21] I had a particularly vivid experience of this distortion during a department meeting at my institution that was designed to teach faculty how to be trans-affirmative in their teaching. It was an otherwise excellent presentation and one for which I advocated, but the presenter, who was articulate about differences in gendered embodiment and identification, referred to sex as the stuff "between your legs." From the point of view of intersex theory and embodiment this is finally an inadequate (although not unusual) account of sex.

To use another intersex example, the intersex body often refuses to conform to the surgical interventions made upon it. (One hopes that Lisa Trevor's embodiment was not intended, either.) An ideal body is imagined, one conforming to John Money's binary account of gender, which we discussed in chapter 1, and to the symbolic constructions of the medical textbooks. The body is inscribed by the surgical knife, but the real of the body intervenes, often in the form of scar tissue, in the attempt to produce a binary and properly sexed body. Even when many of us wanted the surgery to be successful (just to end the string of surgeries) the body asserted its own will. We can theorize this resistance (or insistence) of the material in relationship to the Lacanian account of embodiment as both extimate and Borromean. There exists an irreducible tension between how we conceptualize the body as we signify it or alter it and the body's ex-sistence. The body or aspects of the body (in this case the workings of scar tissue) can be understood as agential in Karen Barad's account of materiality as having agency.[22]

New Materialism and Embodiment

In invoking Barad, I am turning to the more positive account of materiality of the body that I derive from new materialism. In elucidating my account of embodiment that borrows from both new materialism and psychoanalysis, I am working to avoid two contrasting models. The first is what is rightly critiqued as a Cartesian mind/body duality by much work in new materialism and feminist science studies. This model thoroughly separates the mind or psyche from the body, typically privileging the former at the expense of attending to the latter. There are all sorts of problems with this framework, from not thinking about the material basis, limits, and possibilities that structure human existence and enable human thought, and the treating of the body as purely instrumental and inert, to dismissing the ways in which the mind and body are intertwined, including the nervous system, the endocrine system, and the neurobiology of the brain. The second model is one that collapses human thought, writing, representation, and symbolization into the material body, making no distinction between the materialities of writing and representation and the functioning of the body as it intersects with other ecosystemic materialities. This model reads everything as material and looks to science as the final arbiter of this materiality. Certainly we need to pay attention to scientific advances, but this does not mean we should read everything as similarly material. Not only are different materialities defined by different forms of porosity, temporality, and permeability, as Samantha Frost argues, but not everything is material, although many things have a material basis or are in a dialectical or dynamic relationship with their material underpinnings.[23]

For example, while money as a signifier is material (it is a piece of paper or electronic digits on a computer screen), it is its nonmaterial function as a guarantor of (relative) value that makes high-frequency trading so profitable and enriches or devastates economic actors all around the globe. Money is what Marx terms a "real abstraction," and any materialism worth its salt, or carbon, takes into consideration real abstractions, which set limits and enable possibilities just as much, and often more, than the table in front of us or the floor upon which we stand. While the concepts of psychoanalysis seem less clearly forms of real abstraction, I think this is precisely what Lacan and Laplanche differently propose with their emphasis on signifiers as central to the construction of the symbolic (Lacan), the unconscious (Lacan and Laplanche), and the drive (again both). Like the value of money (money's signified), these are not material in the sense of physically present (I leave to the side the ways in which what humans perceive as material can be perceived in other ways at different scales and by different entities), but they carry a kind of material force and weight.

I thus theorize both a positive materialism, one linked to the biological body as it has been theorized by new materialism, and a psychoanalytic materialism that is structured not only in terms of the material body but also in terms of real abstractions such as Lacan's three registers. My approach also combines the positive and the negative, presenting both a positive account of the body as situated within various other materialities and material systems, and an emphasis on negativity that we find in psychoanalysis; there is always a negative dimension to any positive account. This negativity exists in tension with our positive accounts of the body and the psyche. We typically call this negativity the unconscious, but the drives also exist in tension with any positive account of subjectivity, as does Lacan's real.

While psychoanalysis and new materialism have typically theorized in opposition to each other, there is more common ground between the theoretical approaches than is commonly presumed. For example, both work to decenter the egoic or Cartesian subject. Both suggest that agency or action is shaped by more than conscious thought or choice. Both suggest the importance and limits of language. Both also theorize what exceeds language. Finally, both are built around critiques of mastery. They unthink mastery, in Julietta Singh's terms.[24]

To the degree that there remains a tension between the two approaches, I want to read this tension itself as productive, as forestalling of any simple framing of the material as positive and active on the one side, or as apprehensible by the subject in only negative and phantasmatic terms, on the other. I want to insist on the importance of thinking both accounts of embodiment in their very contradiction. Emerging out of the critique of what Stacy Alaimo and Susan Hekman term the "linguistic turn" and the pervasiveness of social construction, feminist new materialism argued that the materiality of the body, the earth, and the ecosystem (as well as other forms of materiality) was all but thoroughly effaced by the emphasis on language as constitutive in poststructuralism and postmodernism.[25] Moreover, in feminism, a concept of linguistic performativity, associated with the early work of Judith Butler, became dominant.[26] In contrast, feminist new materialism argues for an understanding of materiality as co-constitutive with language, even as Barad maintains a performative account of language, matter, and the apparatus. For them, these categories name intra-active constituting phenomena produced through their very performative transactions. As Barad puts it, "Matter is neither fixed and given nor the mere end result of different processes. Matter is produced and productive, generated and generative. Matter is agentive, not a fixed essence or property of things" (137). Matter is the focus of Barad's new materialism, but it is matter as active and agential, constitutive as well as constituted by the intra-activity of various phenomena, including language. The body, the ecosystem, the climate, infrastructure, and viruses (to name only a few of the entities analyzed by new materialists) cannot be reduced to their construction through language, nor can they be rendered as part of a simply inert objectivity. Instead, new materialism posits the force and agency of various forms of materiality that act in a productive, dynamic relationship with language and subjective or scientific apprehension. Where I disagree with Barad is with their insistence on all language being primarily performative. For me the representational dimensions of language are crucial. Certainly, there is an agential or performative dimension to representation (how we construct meaning always shapes what we perceive as meaning's content), but I think we dismiss the representational dimensions of language and the work of symbolic mediation (and the way it can produce understandings that are scaled up and are not limited to one's immediate situation) only at our peril. A purely performative understanding of language edges it too close to privileging the Lacanian imaginary and its egoic and often Manichaean understanding of the world. The mediations of the symbolic are crucial to maintain even as it itself is traversed by the imaginary and exists in fundamental tension with the real. Still, I think we can attend to representation and its value while still maintaining Barad's core insight about the co-constitution of the agencies of language (as a different form of materiality) and matter.

The materiality in new materialism with which I am fundamentally concerned in this chapter is that of the body. For new materialists, the body is not inert matter but rather a complex, ever-changing system that exerts not only resistance and force but also various forms of agency. It is fundamentally dynamic and manifests "intra-actively," as Barad theorizes it. It is produced by the braided workings of linguistic, perceptual (or that which is produced by specific "apparatuses," a term they borrow from physicist Niels Bohr), and material (148). Moreover, it is not a closed, homeostatic system, but one that opens simultaneously outward and inward, exchanging all kinds of material with the larger ecosystem in which it exists. Echoing Lacan's notion of extimacy, Barad describes the relationship of the cultural and the natural as "a relation of 'exteriority within'" (135). Thus, like the Borromean knot, the natural and the cultural are complexly braided and intertwined. Our experience of the combinations of both are intimate and strange. (In this sense, they are uncanny, involving a trace of the strange in the familiar and vice versa.)[27]

In emphasizing the liminal and permeable qualities of bodies, new materialism tends to echo the concept of extimacy on a more materialist level. Our bodies are not simply our own but are in what Stacy Alaimo has termed a "trans-corporeal" relationship with the natural and cultural systems and materialities in which they are embedded:

Bracketing the biological body, and thereby severing its evolutionary, historical, and ongoing interconnections with the material world, may not be ethically, politically, or theoretically desirable. Trans-corporeality offers an alternative. Trans-corporeality, as a theoretical site, is where corporeal theories, environmental theories, and science studies meet and mingle in productive ways. Furthermore, the movement across human corporeality and nonhuman nature necessitates rich, complex modes of analysis that travel through the entangled territories of material and discursive, natural and cultural, biological and textual.[28]

Alaimo nicely emphasizes the need to not only theorize biological embodiment but also the way in which embodiment, far from being sealed within an impermeable corporeality, opens outward and inward, producing "ongoing interconnections" with the ecosystem in which it functions. While this may initially seem far from our discussions of sex, some biological accounts of the production of intersex (primarily in fish) emphasize toxic environmental actants. Such accounts can of course run the danger of repathologizing intersex embodiments, yet they also point toward the trans-corporeal genesis of sex. Sex is not just a complex nonbinary product of a range of different internal actants (including hormonal, chromosomal, gonadal, morphological, and the like) but external ones as well. The body and sex are thus extimate in this way as well. They are not just ours. They are part of the ecosystem and materialities in which we live. They are the expression of an intimate exteriority as well as exteriorized intimacy. We may want to theorize trans and nonbinary embodiments and identifications in a similar way. They are not merely shaped by internal necessities (as is often posited by theories of gender dysmorphia) but are a product of complexly chiasmatic (or extimate) and biocultural drives, identifications, agencies, forms of social reproduction, and biosocial transformations.[29] As Anja Heisler Weiser Flower, drawing on an eco-Marxist framework, articulates it, trans liberation "requires a view from full ecological concreteness" in which culture and nature, materialities and abstractions all function within the shaping of trans possibility.[30]

Samantha Frost is the new materialist who most extensively theorizes human embodiment. Echoing Barad's braided understanding of the relationship among culture and nature as well as Alaimo's understanding of trans-corporeality, Frost posits humans as "biocultural creatures." We are products of the intersections of biology (again not understood as inert, but dynamic and intra-active as well as interactive with other biological entities) and culture (4). For Frost, the biological dimensions of humans means that we "are creatures who are embedded in various ecologies and networks of relations and who can integrate their acknowledgement of their embodiment, animality, physicality, dependence, and vulnerability into their self-conception and their orientation toward modes of being in the world" (3). Frost emphasizes the materiality of embodiment and the ways it intertwines with both nature and culture, ecosystems and socioeconomic systems. Similarly, in emphasizing the cultural side of the biocultural dyad, Frost not only emphasizes the complex web of cultural productions and meanings that the cultural materialism of Raymond Williams and other cultural studies practitioners theorize but also culture in the sense of cultivation (which Williams, of course, presents as one of the earliest meanings of the word). In other words, "to think of culture in terms of cultivation

enables us to incorporate in our thinking simultaneously and sometimes variously aesthetic, arboreal, commodified, composed, cruciferous, disruptive,
economic, embodied, fermented, fractured, institutional, linguistic, meta-
phoric, normative, oceanic, organic, patterned, political, representational,
subjected, trashed, treasured, violent . . . in short, the material, social, and
symbolic worlds we inhabit."[31] While this description runs the danger of many
post-Latourian lists of becoming meaningless in its disconnected seriality, what
I take from Frost's argument is that the biocultural needs to finally be considered as a holistic and generative concept, one that cannot be reduced to its
definitional parts (the biological and the cultural).

Instead, material composition and decomposition are a product of the intra-
active relationship of the biocultural as a complexly unified dynamic. Also
crucial to Frost's account is that the human body is not purely defined by relationality. It does not disappear into pure flows and becomings. Instead, it
must be understood that "energy takes form as matter through its constrained
self-relation" (26). The body, for Frost, is semipermeable and organized around
distinct temporalities that complicate its interactions with other forms of matter.
Thus, while her model, like other new materialists, emphasizes the way in
which our biological bodies are dependent upon and open outward and inward
in relationship to the ecosystem and other dimensions of the material world,
she also articulates an understanding of the body as a semiautonomous system.
This understanding feels crucial if we are not going to strangely dematerialize
the body into pure flows just as soon as we properly materialized it. Still, the
body is also a dynamic, porous, and active entity in this theory. We can understand trans, nonbinary, and intersex relationships to the body as dynamic and
as a form of (partially constrained) becoming. Culture and identification, along
with the ecosystem, the political-economic system, and other forms of materiality shape the material body. It is not just gender that is a site of transformation, but the materiality of the body and its sex too, even as these latter function
as extimate in relationship to our conscious selves.

Desire as Extimate

It is not just sex and embodiment that are extimate. Desire is as well. In theorizing desire as extimate, the work of Jean Laplanche will be as central, if
not more so, as that of Lacan. Laplanche's project of producing a new foundation for psychoanalysis returns to a number of Freudian concepts to tease
out their most radical and exogenous dimensions. He is particularly invested
in disentangling exogenous and social dimensions of the unconscious, the drives,
and sexuality from their more innate, endogenous, and biological theorizations,

which became central in Freud's late work and in much of establishment psychoanalysis to follow, including the object-relations school. He does not reject embodiment, instinct, or biology in doing this, but he does specify that there is a radically social and exogenous dimension to Freud's key discoveries that often gets erased when they are reduced to innate instincts or biologisms. Part of the problem here is not so much the biological as such but rather the version of biology, which is fixed rather than interactive and transformable in relationship to social and ecological contexts. Laplanche's understanding of embodiment echoes its theorization in new materialism. Like the forms of embodiment posted by Frost and Alaimo, desire is shaped by external dynamics as much as internal ones. Central to Laplanche's theoretical account is an account of drives as embodied but originally coming from outside the subject. The body is not effaced but central: "I have never left the body and I have never opposed the body to the mind. By placing drive and instinct in opposition I am not opposing the psychical to the somatic. . . . Drive is not more psychical than instinct. The difference is not between the somatic and the psychical but between, on the one hand, something that is innate, atavistic, and endogenous and, on the other hand something that is acquired and epigenetic but is by no means less anchored in the body for all that."[32]

This distinction between instinct as endogenous and drive as acquired and epigenetic is central to the opposition Laplanche creates between the Ptolemaic and the Copernican in psychoanalysis. He situates the true Copernican revolution enacted by Freud as the scandal of infantile sexuality and the social formation of the unconscious. His account of infantile sexuality as the central and most disturbing insight of psychoanalysis becomes the basis of an enlarged conception of sexuality. Laplanche reads much of later Freud as a Ptolemaic retreat from the radical, Copernican decentering produced by the revelation of infantile sexuality, its structuration in and of the unconscious, and the understanding of the latter as socially shaped.

For Laplanche, sex and desire exceed any relationship to biology they might have. Central to this understanding is that both are structured in relationship to a socially oriented understanding of the drives: "Infantile sexuality is Freud's great discovery. It is the 'sexual' enlarged beyond the limits of the difference between the sexes and beyond sexual reproduction. It is the sexuality of the component drives, connected to erogenous zones and functioning on the model of Vorlust—a term in which we again encounter the word Lust as meaning pleasure and desire simultaneously."[33]

In making this argument in *Freud and the Sexual*, Laplanche cuts a diagonal path through one of the core debates between those primarily influenced by Freud's account of sexual trauma in his earliest writings and those influenced by his later renunciation of it in the name of fantasy and a constitutive infantile sexuality. Drawing upon Judith L. Herman's foundational work, trauma theory has long held psychoanalysis responsible for turning away from sexual abuse.[34] In contrast, later Freudian and post-Freudian psychoanalysis generally emphasizes fantasy and the sexual instinct. It also tends to figure trauma (as Lacan does in *Seminar XI*) as more of a universal condition of subjectivity than a specific effect of violent events that overwhelm defense mechanisms and exceed the ability of language to make initial sense of them (53–65). For Laplanche these are false oppositions. For him, infantile sexuality is a fundamental reality, yet it is not endogenous. Its genesis is external, specifically deriving from the adult caregiver. This sexuality can be implanted unintentionally by routine care and touching (what he terms "implantation"), or it can be the result of violence and abuse (what he terms "intromission").[35] In either case, it is mediated by fantasy and in either case the unconscious sexuality of the adult is translated to and by the child, the untranslated remains or noise of which becomes the basis of the unconscious. In short, Laplanche proposes that the unconscious is produced by an enigmatic signifier which is the unconscious sexuality of the adult, which itself was probably produced in infancy and is experienced as a message in need of translation by the child. Yet the child, because it does not yet have a language for sexuality, is unable to translate aspects of the message. This untranslated noise becomes the kernel of the unconscious and is only activated via the workings of what Freud termed *nachträglichkeit*, variously translated as belatedness, deferred action, or retroactive meaning.[36] For Freud, *nachträglichkeit* describes the temporal logic of trauma, in which something traumatic is implanted but does not produce symptoms or effects until it is later recalled by an experience which echoes (however distantly) the first. For Laplanche, sexuality, whether produced by a traumatic event or by regular care (which the caregiver cannot help but unconsciously sexualize) remains encysted and dormant, forming the basis of the unconscious, until later sexual understanding disturbs the message and suggests its significance.

Laplanche's understanding of sexuality as initially exogamous and yet encysted posits it as fundamentally extimate. It is, as Avgi Saketopoulou puts it, "our own forgiveness to ourselves."[37] While such an otherness, in its opacity, may seem apolitical, another version of the undecidability central to much poststructuralist thinking, Saketopoulou argues just the opposite. Desire, in its opacity and its exogamous origin, is structured in relationship to the social. Our egoic selves are about fortifying "functional stability" that is often "reliant on problematic social values" (9). In contrast, desire, precisely because of its extimate and unconscious dimension, has the "radical potential for self- and world-making that arises when we meet the other without trying to exercise our will over them and when we surrender to our own foreignness to ourselves" (7). For Saketopoulou, desire is fundamentally bound up with the social. Because it is a foreignness within us, it opens both outward and inward in ways that disrupt egoic mastery and structures social encounters around libidinal possibility.

While desire itself can certainly have sadistic as well as masochistic dimensions, how we structure our relationship to it is, as I argued in the introduction, about how we subjectify it. We cannot master it on an egoic level. Indeed, such forms of mastery—egoic rather than phantasmatic—are where nonconsensual violence can find its home. As Saketopoulou argues, "the ego's investments lie in the direction of resisting the foreign—in the other but also the internal foreignness in ourselves that originates from the other's effraction into us—by appropriating it into its structure" (9). For her, the ego and fantasies of egoic mastery are where forms of structural violence like racism, sexual violence, economic violence, and more are reproduced. Instead, Saketopoulou, quoting Laplanche, argues "the unconscious is never 'ours,' in that its force is not under our command, it is also *of* us, which means that we are responsible for its effects in the world" (16, italics in original). Responsibility without mastery is fundamental building block of the social. It recognizes both our own desire in its opacity and the other's desire without trying to master either.

This critique of mastery or control is central to the conception of embodiment that we discussed in relationship to new materialism. Rather than trying to dominate the ecosystem or our own embodiment, we instead need to recognize is intimate otherness and be responsible for our relationship to it. In arguing this, of course, I do not want to suggest that we are fully in control of either. Such a position becomes an idealism that can very easily become not only a fantasy of mastery but also one in which people are blamed for their illnesses or the immediate environment in which they live. Instead, being responsible to both is about recognizing the power of both self and other (including the nonhuman other) in their otherness. In Marxist terms, it also recognizes that all of our actions take place in a "world not of our choosing" and are the product of many different forces and forms of mediation.[38] The responsibility that I am theorizing here is not the neoliberal version that blames the person for their own suffering. Such a position is about what Saketopoulou describes as the nonconsensual "sheer violence" of bending the other's will to one's own (here the social super ego's or "big Other's" own). For her, consensual BDSM is about bending one's own will in response to the intersubjective structuration of desire. The responsibility I am describing here is thus one grounded in attending to the otherness both within and without.

A critique of mastery is present in psychoanalysis at its most radical. Any regular reader of Lacan's seminars will recognize the ways in which he attempts to forestall egoic knowledge and mastery among his students and even in relationship to his own too easy moments of comprehension. He regularly scolds his listeners for thinking that they too quickly understand what he is teaching. Instead, his discourse, with its puns, wild shifts in registers, moments of obscene humor, lexical density, syntactical jumps and ambiguities, and ever-evolving terms, is designed to disorient the conscious self and speak to the unconscious, including his own. Such a challenge to mastery is central to Lacan's psychoanalytic praxis. It is designed to produce a knowledge that resists fixity and propels the subject toward transformation. It aims for the full speech that speaks to the split subject rather than the empty speech that is easily mastered by the ego.

In theorizing desire in its insistently social dimensions, we will turn from Laplanche, who still tends to focus on the individual subject, back to Lacan, who, as Samo Tomšič and Slavoj Žižek have differently demonstrated, produces a thoroughly social account of the workings of desire, fantasy, and lack.[39] Central to Lacan's disruption of egoic mastery is the recognition that desire is the desire of the Other. While such a position seems, at first glance, to ally with Laplanche's understanding of desire as encysted otherness (and such is hardly a surprise, given that Laplanche was one of Lacan's students), it has a fundamentally more social orientation. Desire is routed through the social as such, what Lacan describes as the big Other (which is a purely phantasmatic construction), a fantasy figure that functions as that which guarantee's meaning. Yet there is no big Other, finally. Instead, we have the circulations of desire and language around an absent center. Thus, while the *objet petit a* is about the fetishistic logic of the little piece of the real and is oriented toward the small or intimate other, the fantasy of the big Other organizes the social as such. As with the *objet petit a*, however, desire in its fundamentally social dimension always exceeds its object. It is precisely what exceeds demand and satisfaction. The social is traversed by restless and often recursive fantasies. It is to the work of such fantasies that we turn to next.

The Stuff of Fantasy

So how do we situate the drive and desire in relationship to the material and social worlds in which the subject operates? Moreover, how do we produce a concept parallel to the one that we typically call identity that is neither fully self-consistent nor a form of personal property? Fantasy becomes the crucial ligature in psychoanalysis that situates both desire and subjectification (particularly via the logic of identification rather than identity) in relationship to the world in which the subject moves.

The relationship between fantasy and the desire of the other is captured in Wong Kar-wai's celebrated film *In the Mood for Love*. In the film the two main characters, Su Li-zhen and Chow Mo-wan, wind up forming a romantic relationship with each other because they both realize their two absent spouses are having an affair elsewhere. The moment where they fall in love takes place when each character embodies the gestures and quirks of the absent spouse for the other, thus giving each access to the fantasy other that their spouse was only a stand-in for. By marking the incompleteness and artificiality of the position of stand-in, they are able to experience a fantasy of fullness for the moment, an experience that would not be replicable by their actual spouses. They have a moment of gaining a connection to the in-you-more-than-you that their spouses represent. It is a radical gift of love in both directions, one that may not be able to last, but one that marks that fantasy is structured by a promise of access to an otherness that always recedes. It is precisely when the *objet petit a* of fantasy becomes evident for a moment (the fixation on a gaze or the movement of a hand) that its structuring dimension of one's relationship to the social becomes visible. Fantasy, like love, becomes the oscillation between absence and imagined fullness, gesture and meaning.

Fantasy thus forms the fundamental logic by which the subject is sutured to otherness and the social. While the idea of fantasy as a logic may initially seem contradictory (isn't fantasy precisely about the fanciful and free-associational?), Lacan, in his seminar of the same name, insists on "the logic of fantasy."[40] It is not that fantasy is constituted as a logical discourse as such (although it does have a relationship to the symbolic). Instead, for Lacan fantasy serves a structural function of orienting the drives and desire in relationship to the constitution of reality:

> How, subsequently, we will define reality, what I called earlier the
> *ready-to-wear the phantasy (le prêt á porter le fantasm)*, namely what
> constitutes its frame and we will then see that reality, the whole of
> human reality, is nothing other than a montage of the symbolic and
> the imaginary—that desire, at the centre of this apparatus, of this
> frame, that we call reality, is moreover, properly speaking, what covers—
> as I have always articulated—what must be distinguished from human
> reality, and which is properly speaking the *real*, which is never more
> that glimpsed. Glimpsed when the mask, which is that of phantasy,
> vacillates, namely, the same thing as Spinoza grasped when he said:
> desire is the essence of man (6, italics in original).

Lacan's language here is striking. First of all, his use of film language to describe the constitution of reality (which needs to be thoroughly distinguished from the real) suggests that what we experience as reality is akin to being immersed in a film to the point of forgetting the theater, the apparatus (which in this passage suggests the logic of fantasy itself), the screen, and our position as a viewing subject. Reality is fictional. It is structured by the workings of language and desire as they manifest in fantasy. It is thus also fundamentally a projection, both in the psychoanalytic sense and filmic sense (think of the ways projection works in the scene I just described from *In the Mood for Love*). Reality is constituted via the "montage" of the symbolic and the imaginary. Thus, while, a typical psychoanalytic understanding of projection would articulate itself in relationship to the binary discourse of the imaginary (what I find distasteful and disavow in myself can be located in what is most distasteful about the other; on the other hand, I identify with that which I desire to be), Lacan also suggests that the filmic understanding of projection draws on the triadic or "mediated" logic of the symbolic, to use a phrase reworked by Anna Kornbluh in a Lacanian Marxist register.[41] The world in which we move, speak, write, and interact is a "montage" constituted not only by imaginary projections, but symbolic frameworks, and the narrative, or metonymic, movement of desire.

Montage is a striking word, given that, in its Eisensteinian formulation, it involves a dialectical engagement with the narrative desire and symbolic knowledge of the viewers to properly function as a coherent filmic sequence. Explicitly temporal, montage situates the subject in a reality that is dynamic, one made coherent not only by the logic of the signifier, but also the logic of fantasy, and the workings of desire. Our accounts of reality are saturated with desire, traversed by imaginary investments, and mediated by symbolic logics. All of this exists in contradiction with the real, which, as Lacan puts it in this passage, can be glimpsed when the mask slips as fantasy vacillates. At the risk of sounding too much like the *Screen* theory appropriation of Lacan, which was partial and shaped by the very incomplete understanding of Lacan in the Anglophone academy of the 1970s, only every now and then, at a particularly reflexive or avant-garde cinematic moment or even just the banal disturbance of someone accidentally spilling a soda in your lap, you are thrown out of the world of the film and become conscious of the apparatus of the camera, the structured space of the movie theater, and the materiality of your embodiment. It is only in such moments that the real, as that which structures and determines, even as it exists in contradiction with, the reality that is constituted by the montage of the symbolic and the imaginary, is glimpsed.[42] In elaborating this account of fantasy, I want to articulate what it means for gender and its relationship to sex and what it means for discourse, especially political discourse. I will first turn to gender.

Lacan describes desire as located at the center of the frame that is fantasy and that constitutes reality. As a frame, fantasy is also a mask, a precise image for the way in which our position in the social is structured by both the holes in the mask which frame what we can perceive and the surface of the mask that frames ourselves to others. This understanding of fantasy dovetails with the other metaphor that Lacan uses for understanding the structure of fantasy: fantasies are ready-to-wear. They are the ready-made outfits in which we clothe ourselves as we structure our relationship to the social. Fantasy thus has a relationship to the imaginary and the way in which it shapes the ideal ego and our understanding of gender. Gender, in using Lacan's nicely queer and trans-affirmative metaphor, is what we wear in terms of both clothing and what Anzieu describes as our skin ego in order to appear as character in the phantasmatic film in which we find ourselves.[43] Gender in this framework, to recall Judith Butler's *Gender Trouble*, is fundamentally drag (134–41). It becomes that which we wear and clothe ourselves in order to appear in the reality film which is constituted by desire. It is thus finally about identification, as well as what exceeds and forms in tension with identification, including sex and other domains of the real. Yet it is not all imaginary. It is both imaginary and symbolic and structured in relationship to the real. Such an understanding of gender thus makes it a complex formation, one that is not merely about visible appearance and identification, but also how both are read within symbolic systems and form in contradiction to a real which can only be glimpsed in everyday life. Gender, in this framework, is primarily a montage of the imaginary identification and the symbolic structuration of gendered discourses. It has a complex and intertwined relationship to sex as extimate. Similarly, sex as desire is what motivates the whole domain of fantasy. As we articulated it above in relationship to the Borromean knot, gender, sex, and desire are finally products of the intertwining of all three registers, so my different articulations of them here are about their local knotting and the specific form taken by the three strands of the knot. To say that each is made up of all three is not to say that each has the same relationship to all three.

Several insights flow from this framework for thinking about gender, fantasy, and identification. One is that identities are not forms of personal property or straightforwardly chosen but are produced through dynamics of egoic identification and, just as important, disidentification. Another one is that they are constituted in relationship to fantasy, one that is shaped in terms of the other as much as the self. While it is important to recognize that we are not in control of our identities from the outside, that we are inscribed by all sorts of social meanings, it is also crucial to recognize that we are also not control of them from within our subjectivities and embodiments.

A recognition of identification would enable a politics around embodiment that would refuse the forms of mastery that Julietta Singh has rightly critiqued.[44] Identifications are not ours in the sense that a form of private property is ours within the logic of capitalism (and private property itself is organized around a fundamental amnesia about the conditions of its production, as Marx demonstrates). They are instead complex, fantasy-based bonds and internalizations that originate from the other as much as the self. Identifications are neither as malleable as discourse nor as resistant to straightforward human scripting as biology, which itself is, as Samantha Frost puts it, more about "different zones of activity" than "different substances" (27). Similarly, fantasies are always partial and involve conscious and unconscious disidentifications as much as identifications. These disidentifications come to haunt the subject as much as identifications help shape their ego. Thus, it is not just our identifications that shape us, but also what we disavow, reject, and project. Judith Butler argues as much in *Bodies That Matter* when they theorize a melancholic relationship to homosexuality as central to the constitution of heteronormativity.[45] As Kadji Amin has recently argued, this passage in Butler suggests that the status of being "nonbinary" is not tied to specific identities but is part of the formation of contradictory gendered (and sexed) identities as such.[46] In arguing this, I do think it is important to note the political risks and subversions some enact in challenging normative gender in their nonbinary ways of being in the world, but the fundamental insight that our relationship to gender is contradictory and not tied to identity as property remains cogent. Part of what such an understanding of the contradictory workings of identification and disidentification would enable is a recognition that we do not start with identities, but instead are split subjects situated in a field of meaning and desire that begins outside of ourselves. Fantasy enables us to situate ourselves in its ready-to-wear qualities. It also allows us to accessorize them, if I can extend the metaphor. Choice is present in this domain, but it is choice within a field of identification and fantasy. Moreover, we have an intimate relationship to that which we reject. Such an understanding of fantasy and identity might help short-circuit the endless splitting of political and identity positions in the present moment.

Within such a framework, what we call identity is an egoic construction, one that has its own materiality and temporality. This materiality is structured by fantasy and bound in complicated ways to what Lacan describes as the imaginary body, what Freud alternately termed the body ego.[47] Our egos are mapped onto our material bodies, and this mapping involves an intertwining of the body's surface, its materiality, the extimate domain of sex, and our phantasmatic conception of an embodied self, which is often distorted in greater or lesser ways and becomes intertwined with the materiality of the body and our mental maps of it. It is not merely linguistic or mental but embodied and lived.

To argue as much is to suggest that fantasy has its own temporality, one neither as flexible as some contemporary conceptions that figure gender as choice, nor as fixed, binarized or immutable as social role theory used to posit it. Instead, fantasy is something that is structured as a lived relationship to the body and to the field of the Other. As such it has a complicated temporal persistence. It can neither be simply reworked in relationship to representation, nor is it thoroughly fixed. Instead, it can be worked through (in the Freudian sense), but such a working through often involves repetition and a complex and often difficult engagement with unconscious investments and resistances.[48] Gender is on some level a set of phantasmatic repetitions through which we live an imaginary relationship to embodiment and desire. These repetitions are not primarily voluntary, although the choice to inhabit an identification that challenges cultural norms is a powerful assertion of political will, one that often involves both bodily risk and a sense of affirmation. The repetitions are often formed by the social and ideological coordinates of the society in which they occur. Yet fantasy is also a privileged ligature between the social and the subjective, the discursive and the material. Gender as fantasy can have many different embodiments, yet those embodiments are neither voluntarist nor unrelated to larger forms of social ideology and power. Gender can be a site of liberation, particularly in the ways in which it has been redefined by contemporary trans, intersex, and nonbinary activists and subjects but it is also rarely out of ideology's ambit. Gender as fantasy also becomes one of the privileged ways of imagining the body's materiality. Our body egos become part of our somatic mappings of our body. We live our imaginary body as it becomes woven, perhaps stitched, to our material bodies. The two are intertwined in all sorts of ways. Yet, as I argued earlier, they are not coincident. The imaginary body often varies from the material body. Moreover, there are many aspects of the material body that are not regularly part of our imaginary body.

If fantasy works to structure gender and embodiment, it also plays a crucial and underrecognized role in shaping social and political discourse. As the Lacanian maxim has it, fantasy is on the side of reality. As such, it also forms in opposition to the real. Reality (in opposition to the real) is a montage, as Lacan theorizes, of the symbolic and the imaginary. Yet it is not always made up of equal parts of both. As Anna Kornbluh argues, the present is defined by a waning of the symbolic and an intensification of the imaginary.[49] This imbalance is particularly evident online, where structural issues such as economic inequality or structural racism and sexism are reduced to ideas of personal privilege or individual failure, while the purported solutions, either getting individual people fired, canceling them or, in cases where the law is broken, incarcerating them in a penal system that does nothing but perpetuate (particularly racial and class) inequality and violence, are equally individualized and do nothing to alter the structures that produce and reproduce inequality. Indeed, when the solution is getting people fired—and certainly in the case of sexual violence in the workplace this is necessary but not finally sufficient—it does the work of neoliberalism for it, rendering all economic positions more disposable.

To the degree that we experience social antagonisms as individualized via the lens of a Manichaean moral discourse organized around scapegoating, we are dwelling too much in the imaginary, with none of the mediation promised by the symbolic. It is hard to imagine a capacious left that can address and transform the structural dimensions of inequality, oppression, and exploitation in a context in which collectivity is undone by individualized antagonisms and the inability to think beyond immediate imaginary investments. Certainly dwelling entirely in the symbolic can become its own limitation, replacing righteous anger with dry abstraction and the endless metonymic chain of signification. We need our metaphors, where metonymic slippage stops and the structural enemy becomes clear, but it is crucial that we metaphorize wisely and not in ways that just strengthen current structural inequalities. Of course, the symbolic finally functions, on its own without the provocations of the imaginary or the insistences of the real, as a fantasy of perfectly mediated liberalism. This vision is not the goal of any leftism worth its name.

Instead, we need an integration of the imaginary and the symbolic in order to collectively produce a different relationship to the real (and eventually alter the real's coordinates) and thus a genuinely different reality. We also need a reflexive practice in which we employ the symbolic to interrogate our own imaginary transferences and attempt to engage the real as a way of reorienting the current symbolic. The imaginary is also the axis of desire and desire is crucial to world building. As such, the imaginary is also a domain of the sexual. In arguing for the importance of sex as desire in this book, I am arguing for the importance of social desire, the workings of the imaginary in relationship to the symbolic and the real, as informing our relationships to others to the social world, to our world-building visions and to the work of building a better future.

To produce an imaginary that can respond to symbolic mediation and critique while not losing its political force or edge, we need to imagine it in a more collectivist vein rather than the thoroughly personal register in the present, in which, as Lauren Berlant puts it, the political has become personal rather than the other way around.[50] As Kornbluh has also argued, within such a reduced imaginary the exception becomes the rule. We need to theorize collective norms and rules, ones that are pro-queer, socialist, antiracist, and just around gender and sex. Chapter 4 proposes just such a vision in its articulation of a sexual and embodied commons, but in the present moment I want at least to gesture to how we can build (and discipline) an imaginary that is collective rather than individualized. I also want to similarly gesture toward how the symbolic and imaginary can transform the real and transform in relationship to a new event that emerges in the real.

Jodi Dean provides a blueprint for creating a leftist montage of the imaginary and the symbolic.[51] Central to her reworking of the imaginary and symbolic via the logic of both comradeship and the party is a collective articulation of the ideal ego and the ego ideal. In terms of the former, comradeship functions to provide a collective site of imaginary identification, although one that is not substantialized as a body ego but instead is symbolically reworked to function as an imaginary point of collective identification. Unlike identities, which are often organized around affective affinities and embodiments, comradeship is a thoroughly abstract conception of shared identification. Comradeship is not about liking or resembling other comrades. Instead, it is about the collective desire and shared (individual as well as collective) responsibilities to each other in realizing that desire. The party functions in a similar way as a collective point, or ego ideal (what Freud would term the superego), around which a collective politics can be structured.[52] Political struggles necessarily have to be multiple, addressing a complex array of different issues and transformations, yet they also need a unifying structure around which to organize. Such a structure has been absent on the left for too long. A new articulation of party and the forms of collective judgment around which it should be organized would enable such a unified front. Given that various right wings around the globe are presenting an increasingly unified front via a revitalized fascism, the left needs forms of collective organization that enable it to present an equally united front.

The other theorist who provides a template for understanding the political framework of Lacan's categories is, of course, Alain Badiou. While I will in not be able to come close doing justice to Badiou's exceedingly complex philosophical system in the space of a paragraph, I at least want to indicate the way in which he rethinks Lacan's categories of the symbolic and the real in relationship to his opposition between the state and the event.[53] The state, for Badiou, is both the symbolic state of a given society or world and the material state apparatus as that which reinforces symbolic stability (and thus structured inequalities). The event, on the other hand, is a manifestation of the real that erupts outside of and against the symbolic constituted by the state. Radical thought and political struggle emerge in the attempt to force the state to recognize that which it excludes, forcing an event. It also works to transform the symbolic (and invest the desire of the imaginary) to recognize the event and force the production of a new symbolic order or state, one that is transformed by the event itself. Of course, this new symbolic order produces a new real and will have to account for new events, but in Badiou's revolutionary political vision the event can and often does represent the position of those who are excluded within the current state. It thus produces a radical new social order, one that can incorporate for the first time those who were previously excluded. It also generates a new social symbolic and a new understanding of reality. Badiou's vision, finally, articulates perhaps the most radical version of what is at stake in Lacan's tripartite schema. It is a blueprint for revolution itself.

While I will return to what a collective politics of embodiment and sex might look like in chapter 4, to conclude this chapter, I want to turn to how we can transform the social symbolic to produce not only a different social system but also a fundamentally different relationship to embodiment (particularly what I termed above as the real of the body), which also necessarily and crucially is about imagining a different relationship to the global political economy (or world system) and political ecology (or world ecology). In doing so, the chapter draws upon the category of the flesh in recent Black thought. It also turns to Marx's early concept of species being. Both of these categories will reappear in chapters 3 and 4. For now, though, let us turn to the generative category of the flesh and how it relates to histories of imperialism, racialization, and the reification and commodification of the human body.

The Dialectics of the Flesh

In theorizing a positive account of the materiality of the body, as I did in our above discussion of new materialism, I also want to attend to the way in which the category of the flesh has been invoked, by Hortense Spillers, Alexander G. Weheliye, R. A. Judy, Marquis Bey, and C. Riley Snorton, to account for the specifics of the forms of embodiment that accompany racialization within imperialism, settler colonialism, and slavery and its aftermath. I also want to think about the relationship of this concept of the flesh with the different one posited by Maurice Merleau-Ponty in the unfinished book, *The Visible and Invisible*. Finally, I will articulate these different understandings of the flesh in relationship to Marx's account of species being and a renewed understanding of sensuality articulated by Marcuse, one that can emerge, in part, from the legacy of enfleshment associated with slavery and its aftermath.[54] If the previous section developed the political dimensions of the psychoanalytic framework I have been employing, this section addresses the political dimensions of the new materialist argument I posited earlier. I dialectically juxtapose these arguments rather than working to fully synthesize them. Yet I also think they speak to each other and need to be conceptualized in relationship to each other.

The flesh is a mediating term between embodied interiority (as semipermeable, in Frost's terms) and the sociocultural, political-economic, ecosystemic, and other material exteriorities in which humans exist. While earlier I referenced Didier Anzieu's concept of the "skin ego" in relationship to gender and forms of gendered identification, flesh is a parallel concept but suggests something less tied to our egoic (or imaginary) mapping of the body and more of a somatic locus of inscription from the outside and registration by the nervous system from within.

Of course, the concept of the flesh predates these modern uses, functioning as a central term in early Christian doctrine. Within this context the flesh, as the locus of worldly experience and desire, is contrasted with the soul. It is a locus of sexuality and potential corruption but also the locus of penitence and the elicitation of truth. Foucault, in the posthumously published *History of Sexuality Volume Four*, articulates it as a mode of embodied experience: "The 'flesh' should be understood as a mode of experience, that is as a mode of knowledge and transformation of oneself by oneself, depending on a certain relationship between a nullification of evil and a manifestation of truth."[55] Such a regime represents a shift in the understanding of sex and desire where "instead of having a regimen of sexual relations, or *aphrodisia*, that blends into the general rule of a righteous life, one will have a fundamental relationship with the flesh that runs through one's whole life and serves as a ground for the rules that are imposed on it" (36, italics in original). The conception of flesh in the early Church, then, was a form of embodied desire that was a locus of self-discipline as well as institutional discipline. It was also a locus of embodied truth.

The violence implicit in this disciplinary relationship not only indicates the way in which such pastoral practices became translated into secular institutional ones, suggesting the link between Foucault's long project on sexuality, where he initially articulates his concept of biopolitics, and his seemingly different one on carceral discipline in *Discipline and Punish*.[56] Central to Foucault's account of disciplinary power is the ways in which he theorizes a disciplinary regime that was taken up by early industrial capitalism. Whether the disciplinary regime shaped the structure of industrial capitalism, as Foucault argues, or whether it emerged out of transformations produced by capitalist production, I leave to one side. Another way to articulate this is that civil society and the political economy shape each other in a symbiotic, one might say productively dialectical, manner.

The relationship of capitalism to concepts of the fleshly discipline becomes even more stark if we accept the argument articulated by world-systems analysts Immanuel Wallerstein and Aníbal Quijano that capitalism begins in the Americas, with the plantation functioning as the first modern factory and in which agricultural production was organized around the generation of capital.[57] Within this framework, modern slavery is not a holdover or a mere continuation of feudal and ancient practices of slavery or serfdom. If modern slavery is the locus of the emergence of capitalism (what Jason W. Moore describes as the centrality of agriculture to the "rise of capitalism"), then it is here where the most violent and thorough forms of disciplining of the flesh took place.[58] This is, in fact, the insight proffered by Hortense Spillers and elaborated by a number of thinkers within Black studies and de/postcolonial theory.[59] Spillers powerfully argues that the body in slavery is reduced to flesh. In so doing, the body becomes degendered, although not desexed. Such a process produces a different set of familial relations (which were always subject to destruction and disruption) under slavery and as a postslavery legacy in which the family structure was more collective and the maternal lineage is privileged (as it was in the slave code). Gender in this context is a privilege of whiteness. As Russ Castronovo has argued, the idea of the abstract disembodied subject of liberal law emerges in the United States against the forms of excessive embodiment attributed to Black subjects.[60] Black subjects were represented as too fully embodied, defined by a materiality which is adjacent to (or often constructed as equivalent to) animality. Within this framework, as Hazel Carby demonstrates, gender and proper gendered relations were seen as the province of white, middle-class subjects and a locus of antiracist contestation for Black ones.[61] Whereas gender was social, sex was material and bodily. Moreover, this body was marked as Black and abjected. The violent disciplining of the flesh under slavery, then, not only had a political-economic motive but also drew upon a set of meanings that were derived from the Christian construction of the flesh as the locus of sex and desire. These meanings were reworked into framework of liberal law but continue to haunt the racial divide perpetrated by the slave economy. As Arianne Cruz, Elizabeth Freeman, Kirin Wachter-Grene, and others have argued, there is a violent, erotic economy to race relations in the antebellum United States (and probably in other locations in the Americas where modern slavery was practiced).[62] Indeed, contemporary kink and psychoanalytic conceptions of sadism and masochism need to be understood within this larger racialized history, as an aside that Freud makes about beating fantasies derived from *Uncle Tom's Cabin* in "A Child Is Being Beaten" suggests.[63] Freud's essay is also central to Laplanche's understanding of fantasy and the implantation of sexuality, suggesting that race, as well as gender and sex, needs to be understood as central to the formation of sexuality and embodiment in the context of modernity.[64]

Drawing on the work of Spillers, Sylvia Wynter, and Giorgio Agamben, Alexander G. Weheliye argues that the reduction of racialized subjects to flesh under slavery can be understood in relationship to Euro-American discourses of humanism (the slave forming the other to privileged discourses of "man") and Agamben's conception of bare life. Within this framework, the slave is reduced to bare life, which becomes another way of talking about the reduction to flesh. As Achille Mbembe argues, such a dynamic is part of the necropolitics that form as the dialectical flipside to the biopolitics shaping the formation and governance of liberal democracies: "the violence of democracies was forthwith exteriorized onto the colonies."[65] The colonies, in turn, become the locus of necropolitics. In elaborating the necropolitics of slavery and its relationship to the production of gender, C. Riley Snorton, as I discussed in chapter 1, theorizes the flesh as it is produced in regimes of bioaccumulation and medicalization, regimes that inform not only contemporary structures of racialization but also the frameworks by which we understand transgender and intersex as well. Working from this framework, Marquis Bey theorizes what they call "tranniflesh" as a basis for Black transgender embodiment, one organized around an opaque excess that refuses the identitarian workings of normative gender (82). Thus flesh, as we will see more fully, is dialectical, a space for the possibility of becoming as well as a site of negation.

Slavery, as a particularly violent form of the disciplining of the flesh, transforms the body as a whole into a commodity and a locus of appropriation and labor. It is crucial to differentiate this dynamic of the commodification of the body from the selling of labor power as a commodity by the wage worker. They are not only organized around different forms of labor (unwaged, violent extraction or accumulation by dispossession, in terms of the former and exploitation via the production of surplus value in case of the latter), but they also produce a different relationship to the body, to ecosystems (what Marx calls "nature"), and to nonhuman forms of materiality which are part of them.[66] While we need to theorize the relationship of race to class formation and vice versa, this different set of relationships to work suggests the ways in which class has been segmented along racial lines, not only in terms of the status of labor but in terms of embodiment. The wage worker's body is reified, as Lukács describes, and the worker themselves are alienated from the products of their labor and from their sensuous relationship to nature.[67] This sensuous relationship to nature, what Marx describes as species being, is not negated in the commodification of the slave's body, instead the slave is made part and parcel of nature itself, which is also in the process of commodification (75). Thus, while the reduction of the slave to a commodity is a form of necropolitical violence par excellence, it does not sever the relationship of the slave to other slaves or to the ecosystem in which they toil.

This doubleness is captured by R. A. Judy's rearticulation of the flesh as not only a locus of violence and desubjectification but also as the site in which a different conception of the relationship of human embodiment to sensuality, poesis, and the ecosystem are articulated. It also echoes Mel Y. Chen's theorization of the interconnection and racialization of different forms of animateness, in which those who are racialized are often figured as closer to animals and the environment. This form of mattering derives from racist hierarchies, yet it also suggests a different position from which to understand one's relationship to the world. Judy posits a collective consciousness of the flesh that is similar to Chen's theorization of different kinds of animacy.[68] I will not be able to do full justice to Judy's complex rethinking of the category of the flesh in the magisterial *Sentient Flesh*, but I want to trace its implications for reconceptualizing embodiment. The positive valence of the flesh derives in part from the different understanding of the relationship between subject and world and subject and community that was central to Yoruban belief systems in West Africa. Such beliefs became syncretically mixed during slavery, articulated as an enacted poesis via Black expressive forms such as the Buzzard Lope, and echoed all the way up through the work of Max Roach, Albert Ayler, James Brown, and beyond, as Judy argues (236). These beliefs and practices are not merely the remnants of older forms, but they are active forms of poesis, one that enacts a specific relationship between subjectivity and the world: "We do not fall into the world, we exist in the world; which is to say we exist in common" (19). He goes on to argue that this being in and of the world can be understood through the trope of sentient flesh: "Perhaps the way forward is something like 'fleshly thinking' in contrast to the personal embodiment—to think with the world and the earth both in view and not situate thinking somewhere outside of the flesh" (19). This fleshly thinking and the artistic forms (such as Juba beating and dancing) that flow from them "are indeed contradictory, in the sense that they operate a discourse of being-in-common contesting with the depersonalizing practices of slavery" (216). It produces a semiosis in which humans are part of the ecosystem and the collective rather than cut off from it.

While Judy only gestures at this, this concept of sentient flesh echoes Marx's account of species being, in which humans, before the alienation produced by wage labor, experience themselves in a sensuous relationship to nature that not only allows the human to appropriate and transform nature but also enables his "relations to the world—seeing, hearing, smelling, tasting, feeling, thinking, being aware, sensing, wanting, acting, loving" (87). In contrast to the alienated form of being produced by wage labor and the reification of the working body, Marx's account of the sensuousness of species being emphasizes all the senses as they constitute and are constituted by the ecosystem and the political economy in which humans exist. This becomes a historically produced version of Stacy Alaimo's trans-corporeality, one that also echoes the relationship between humans and other fleshly entities articulated by Judy's concept of sensuous flesh.

While it is important not to fully conflate these different concepts, with their very different provenances, it is equally important to suggest that they can speak to each other. Each represents an attempt to reorient human perception, labor, and poesis around a recognition and valuation of the ecosystems and collectivities in which they exist and which they transform. Each also speaks to the damage done by capitalism, the history of slavery, ecological violence, and individualizing and disembodying systems of perception. While there has been much work recently on the specificity of racialized experiences and the dangers of appropriation, I think we can emphasize specificity without effacing human commonalities. Judy's book is notable for the way in which it argues for a very specific mode of being that is inherited from African religious practices and transformed by the violence of dispossession and slavery into a poesis that is at once a protest and a form of world-making. Yet it also situates this experience within the larger intellectual history of Black, Euro-American, and Arabic thought. He finally underscores human commonality within historical differences and vice versa. Within this framework I think we can follow Judy's lead in thinking about how his double conception of flesh can point (along with Marx's understandings of species being and new materialist conceptions of embodiment and trans-corporeality) to an understanding of sensuality as a form of fleshly embodiment that, like sexual desire, opens out to otherness, to the human and nonhuman collectivities we are part of, and allows and recognizes forms of otherness within.

Flesh and Sensuality

If the workings of fantasy become one of the ways we conceptualize our relationship to the social (the montage of the imaginary and the symbolic), sensuality becomes another (a reconceptualizing of the relationship of both the symbolic and imaginary to the real). While as Marx and Judy differently underscore, forms of consciousness are shaped by changes in political, economic, ecological, and ideological systems, they also suggest the ability of consciousness to reflexively constitute itself against the forms of violence that characterize the present. For Marx, this is the proleptic work done by theory itself in imagining existence outside of capitalism. For Judy, it is the powerful reconstitution of a lifeworld and poesis over against the necropolitical violence of slavery and its aftermath. While we will not be able to fully transform human relations and human consciousness without transforming the political-economic and ecological conditions of everyday life, we can imagine and strive toward new modes of being that can only be fully realized as part of larger material transformations. If the forms of political organizing articulated by Dean and Badiou produce a politics around desire, a new understanding of sensuality can produce a new politics around embodiment.

Capitalism, as Marx argues, works not only to alienate humans from what they produce but also causes them to instrumentalize the material world (including animals, plants, and other humans) as inputs or means for producing profit. This rendering of the world as so much dead or degraded matter expresses itself not only in the reification and degradation of the worker's body, the de-privileging of critical thought in relationship to instrumental rationality, and the sheer instrumentality of industrial food production, but also in the obsessive logic of consumption in which the commodity as fetish functions to render its sensuous dimensions thoroughly secondary. Similarly, capitalism, with its booms and busts, its orgies of speculative investment and cycles of austerity (for the poor and working classes only, of course), creates a relationship to the world of everyday provision that is shaped fundamentally by dynamics of excess and asceticism, delirious consumption and unproductive guilt and renunciation, as Melinda Cooper has argued.[69]

A reorienting of our relationship to embodiment, what I want to call a new (or renewed) sensuality, would redefine our relationship to the lifeworld in which we take our sustenance. Such a reorientation would involve what Herbert Marcuse described as sensuous reason, which works to "reconcile the two spheres of the human existence [i.e., reason and sensuality] that were torn apart by the repressive reality principle."[70] For Marcuse, the repressive reality principle is none other than the forms of sensuous renunciation that are produced by the capitalist work ethic. While I have suggested there are other aspects of contemporary capitalism that insist on a similar ascetic dimension of contemporary economic life (even overconsumption is a kind of panicked inversion of asceticism), Marcuse's emphasis on imagining a different relationship to reality, one that integrates reason and sensuality is instructive. In contrast to such forms of renunciation and instrumentality (with the latter's detached, "mastering," and "domineering" approach to the material world),

Marcuse's sensuous reason would reintroduce qualities of receptivity and openness to materiality (186). It would thus mix the active and receptive, but in a way in which the sensuousness, vulnerability, and power of the material world, including our own material being or fleshliness, would be newly affirmed and valued.

Maurice Merleau-Ponty posits an affirmative conception of the flesh that functions as a utopian beacon for what the experience of the world might be like when we fully embrace sensuous rationality and produced a nonalienated or atomized relationship to the life world and the ecosystem. Importantly, this vision dovetails with the affirmative versions of Alaimo's trans-corporeality and Judy's sentient flesh. Merleau-Ponty imagines a conception of the flesh that moves beyond the monadic subject posited by much Western philosophy, including his own earlier versions of phenomenology (even as they were crucial for theorizing such a subject as embodied). Merleau-Ponty's flesh opens outward to a world that is also fleshly and inward to a subject who thinks and perceives in embodied ways: "If we can show that flesh . . . is not the union or compound of two substances, but thinkable by itself, if there is a relation of the visible with itself that traverses me and constitutes me as a seer, this circle which I do not form, which forms me, this coiling over of the visible upon the visible, can traverse, animate other bodies as well as my own" (141).

Here flesh becomes the medium where one is seen as well as seeing, touched as well as touching (touch coiling over onto itself), and in which bodies co-constitute each other. This is a vision of the unalienated and sentient flesh that Judy also posits, in which being is collective, a being with other enfleshed beings both human and nonhuman. It is a sensory and sensuous relationship in which otherness is incorporated both within and without (and the two bleed into each other). While this vision may feel thoroughly utopian, it is a glimpse of something to strive toward (a moment where the real is glimpsed otherwise). If earlier in this chapter I articulated the need to produce collective dynamics of identification and desire, here I try to imagine a collective relationship of embodiment, production (of which poesis is one version), and ecological becoming. Chapter 4 will return to this utopian vein in working toward an embodied and sexual commons, but before turning to this we need to explore the more conflictual and exploitative realm of bioaccumulation, where the body becomes a crucial site of appropriation and commodification in both historical and contemporary capitalism. With the history of violent dispossessions of the body still fresh in our minds, we turn next to the dynamics of bioaccumulation.

3

Bioaccumulation and the Dialectics of Embodiment

One day we may come after you. Taking back what's ours. Even it out.
Even it out. And then we cut, cut, cut.

NONBINARY ARTIST FEVER RAY

How do we theorize medical possibility and medical violence together? How
do we theorize the genuine promise of medical technologies to enable consensual flourishing, as with various technologies of transition, while also maintaining an attention to forms of nonconsensual violence, such those done on
intersex, trans, underclass, working-class, and Black subjects in the name of
advancing and perfecting medical techniques? How do we theorize the uneven
and complexly situated global capitalist enterprise that is biomedicine in relationship to the forms of flourishing and suffering it produces? How do we
theorize the divides around class, race, gender, sexuality, and embodiment that
structure biomedicine's ambit within the capitalist world system?

This chapter theorizes the way in which global capitalism intersects with
biomedical technologies and practices in order to produce a radically uneven
geography of medical intervention, appropriation, capitalization, and access.
Both intersex and transgender subjectivities are structured in relationship to
divisions of class, race, and geography. These divisions emerge in relationship
to what David Harvey describes as accumulation by dispossession.[1] Harvey
theorizes accumulation by dispossession as the capitalist appropriation and
privatization of that which is held in common. In theorizing this concept,
Harvey reworks Marx's account of primitive accumulation in *Capital*, where
the latter theorizes accumulation as the initial violent appropriation of private
property from common property at the onset of capitalism.[2] In renaming it

accumulation by dispossession, Harvey rearticulates primitive accumulation as a recurrent dynamic, one that is central to the workings of capitalism in general and can be distinguished from the exploitation of wage labor. Eco-Marxists like Jason W. Moore, theorists working in and around social reproduction such as Tithi Bhattacharya and Maya Gonzalez and Jeanne Neton, and decolonial theorists such as Aníbal Quijano further the application of this concept, arguing that the exploitation of wage labor is necessarily accompanied by the unpaid appropriation of nature, unpaid and often forced labor marked by divisions of race and gender, the workings of financialization via debt, and other forms of extraction.[3]

In what follows, I will theorize the ways in which accumulation by dispossession, extraction, and the logic of commodification intersect with dynamics of biomedicalization. In doing so, I work to attend to the long history of what Macarena Gómez-Barris has termed "extractive capitalism," in which ecosystemic resources and forms of racialized unwaged labor are not only appropriated, but also the body, typically racialized and/or class abjected, becomes a crucial site of accumulation by dispossession.[4] Biomedical advances depend on extraction from and the nonconsensual or exploitative "Guinea pigging" of bodies that are marked as outside the formal structures of citizenship, biopolitical normativity, and/or the formal political economy. This is not only a long history that was present at the intersections, detailed by Pratik Chakrabarti, of biomedicine and Euro-American imperialism, but also as a part of the specific history of slavery in the Americas and the exploitation of animal test subjects. These practices continue in the present, with trials that offer "free" untested medicine to the uninsured in exchange for becoming test subjects.[5] It is also present, in uneven ways in bodies marked by disability (including intersex bodies and the bodies of trans folk, which were often defined by their status as defective) and by deviations from the norm. To momentarily take the example of my own body, I was taught that my intersex condition was a birth defect, one that needed to be fixed by what was sometimes presented as explicitly experimental medicine.

While it is important to understand the different economic, racialized, and citizenship positions of these differently embodied subjects, bodies as sites of accumulation by dispossession become what Jasbir Puar theorizes as debilitated, as limited and abjected in their subsequent incapacity and as defined by a political-economic and biopolitical "right to maim."[6] These embodied sites of extraction and debilitation, in turn, produce new economies of biopolitical commodification, in which certain technologies become available as enhancements or affirmations for a price and for those who have access to health care. In terms of access to transitioning, this produces a radically uneven field, in which who has access to transitioning and under what conditions is structured by inequalities around race, gender, geography, and even historical trajectories. As Erin L. Durban reminds us, we need to theorize the very different global positions and forms of access in which transitioning occurs.[7] As I will explore more fully, the divide between appropriation and commodification also shapes the larger workings of desire within global capitalism, marking which bodies are seen as debilitated and which are idealized as enhanced. While most of this chapter focuses on how embodied sex intersects with the accumulation by dispossession of bodies, it is also crucial to think about how it also shapes sex as desire and who and what counts as desirable, at least in a hegemonic sense.

Turning the Angel of History to Face Forward

In theorizing the Janus-faced dimensions of modern medicine, I want to link it to the longer and more general history of the Enlightenment and the imperial development of the capitalist world system. In what may at first seem like an excursus, I turn to dialectical formulations of Walter Benjamin, Achille Mbembe, and Marx himself to provide the larger theoretical framework for this chapter. It may seem strange to situate a chapter on sex, gender, sexuality, race, and embodiment with Walter Benjamin's much picked-over "Theses on the Philosophy of History."[8] Yet Benjamin's dictum in Thesis VII that there "is no document of civilization which is not the same time a document of barbarism" is one of the guiding principles in the argument I advance in this chapter (256). Benjamin's dictum captures the complex, dialectical production of both possibility and violence, sustenance and suffering that lies at the heart of Western medicine, and behind it the larger and similarly contradictory legacy of the Enlightenment.

Given the violence of the climate emergency and the long history of (neo) colonial and capitalist exploitation, appropriation, and destruction, it may seem easy, in the present conjuncture, to toss the Enlightenment and its heritage into the already overflowing dustbin of history. Yet to do so would be a mistake, for a number of intertwining reasons. First, we need to attend to all that the Enlightenment has enabled as well as what it destroyed. Throwing both away together is to undo the genuine forms of collective freedom that it enabled along with its bloody history of conquest and exploitation. We need to attend to all the work done by decolonial, postcolonial, and Marxist theory to theorize the trail of dead left in modernity's wake, yet we also need to embrace the possibilities and freedoms, as Marxist theory also argues, that modernity has won as well. Second, given the scale of human life in the present, we need solutions that can work at the scale of contemporary science, political-economy, and medicine. While anarchist theory has contributed much to critiques of the state, its model of direct democracy and its privileging of localism does not scale up effectively. Yet collective solutions to things such as the climate emergency, resource depletion, and ever-growing inequality need to function at a global scale if we are going to be able to produce a genuine transformation in the crises of the present. We need to theorize at the global level; yet we also need to not feel paralyzed by the global. Struggles for social equality can start in various localities, but we need to find ways to link up with and recognize movements around the globe, since our enemies, like capitalism, are already global. We also need to find democratic socialist governing structures that can orient a collective response to global economic, social, and climatological dynamics (and such structures can be put into place while respecting the internal autonomy of smaller governing and cultural units).

The problem with accounts of the dialectical or contradictory dimensions of the Enlightenment is that they can seem to reify the very contradictions that they are designed to theorize. At first, Benjamin's adage, with its absolutist language, seems to do just this. If there is *no* document of civilization that is also not a document of barbarism, then we should just throw up our hands and recognize the fundamentally contradictory dimensions of human existence. While such an approach can be one of the dangers of dialectical thinking, flattening out history into a metaphysical set of contradictions that remain forever unchanging, such a reading of Benjamin would be a fundamental misreading. In attending to Benjamin's thesis, it is crucial to remember its historiographical focus. Benjamin is not arguing that there is no possible civilization or, to use a less loaded term, society that does not produce barbarism (which I take here as systematic and unnecessary violence) as its dialectical flip side. He is instead insisting that, within class societies and the long history of economic and social inequality, there is no historical or present society that has avoided this contradiction. Yet his very argument imagines that such a just society is possible. At the beginning of Thesis VII he asserts, "To historians who wish to relive an era, Fustel de Coulanges recommends that they blot out everything they know about the larger course of history. There is no better way of characterizing the method with which historical materialism has broken" (156). His point here is that the past needs to be measured against the future. While he is concerned with the legacy of violence that might be read in the past's future, his focus on historical materialism itself emphasizes the promises of justice and possibility that have eluded the historical record so far.

The pathos of Benjamin's argument only makes sense if there is possibility beyond the ruins of history. While many commentators, borrowing from

Benjamin's own language, have categorized this future possibility as messianic, it need not be so. He is asking us to refuse to clean up the past. Instead, we should "brush history against the grain" and chronicle to those on its losing side to imagine a more just future. What would be the point of such an exercise if we could not learn from it? To borrow an image from Thesis IX, if the angel of history has its face "turned toward the past" even as it rushes forward, it must at some point turn its gaze forward again (257). We may not want to call it the "angel of history," in this formulation but rather an "angel of prolepsis"—looking forward to divine the possibilities of a more just future. This, at least, is the promise of Marxism (what Benjamin calls "historical materialism"): to imagine a way forward from the contradictions that structure both the past and the immediate present.

Before taking leave of Benjamin, I want to suggest one more way in which we can read his dialectic of civilization and barbarism, this one perhaps slightly against the grain of Benjamin's own framework. The language of civilization and barbarism of course has its resonance in the long history of imperialism, in which barbarism is not only a description of a society organized around economic or political violence, but also one that is considered "backward" in comparison to the advances of civilization. This latter definition functions, of course, as a form of orientalist discourse, in Edward W. Said's terms, constructing spaces of racial and civilizational otherness as fundamentally backwards and in need of rule (appropriation and exploitation) by the metropole.[9] Before we suggest that Benjamin himself is complicit with these orientalist meanings, it is crucial to recognize that his dialectic is based on the production of barbarism, not its discovery. Civilization, in its contradictions and inadequacies, produces barbarism as its other. For every moment of aesthetic or civilizational achievement lies a history of toil and blood on another scene. This other scene can be class-based, geopolitical, or both, but for someone to be able to pursue the "higher arts" in a divided economic or political system, others must do the dirty work that ensures survival. Similarly, geocultural formations in the so-called periphery must provide the raw materials for accumulation to happen in the metropole. Barbarism is produced not discovered. It is the necessary flip side to civilization in an unjust political economy. Yet we can also read Benjamin in one final way, in which civilization and barbarism are descriptive terms of formations that are not only conjoined but equally fraught. Rather than the first term being positive and the other negative, we can read positive and negatives within each. Thus, to refer to our discussion of the flesh in chapter 2, it is the persistence of nonmodern ("barbarian") conceptions of embodiment, what R. A. Judy defines as "the flesh" and Marx defines as species being, into the truncated world of the senses produced by modernity ("civilization") that becomes a crucial site of potential renewal. The very terms of the dialectic, and not just their valence, can be flipped.

In developing his concept of necropolitics in the book of the same name, Achille Mbembe develops a similar opposition that is central to the relationship between the metropole and the (post)colony.[10] He posits the opposition between biopolitics, which in Foucault's foundational account shapes the life of the metropole and Western democracies, and necropolitics, which produce regimes of death and terror in the names of accumulation and autoimmunity (which has also been theorized in relationship to the parallel concept of thanatopolitics by Roberto Esposito).[11] If for Foucault and others who follow him biopolitics is a form of positive and ostensibly soft power that shapes life and life chances in the aggregate, necropolitics is its negative correlate, which can be found in neocolonial spaces and states of exception (which Mbembe defines in relationship to actual spaces, such as extra-state spaces like occupied Palestine, or those of economic offshoring rather than a metaphysical state). The plantation becomes the iconic historical location of necropolitics:

> If, in the name of the plantation system, the relations between life and death, the politics of cruelty, and the symbolism of profanity, get blurred, what comes into being in the colony and under apartheid is a peculiar formation of terror, to which I now turn. The most original feature of this terror formation is its concatenation of biopower, the state of exception, and the state of siege. Race is, once again, crucial to this concatenation. In most instances, racial selection, prohibiting of mixed marriages, forced sterilization, and indeed exterminating vanquished people found their first testing ground in the colonial world. The first syntheses arise here between massacre and bureaucracy— that incarnation of Western rationality. (76)

The concatenation to which Mbembe refers is necropolitics, biopolitics' negative double. In my discussion of the underside of Western medical regimes which follows, it will be crucial to attend to the ways in which, as Mbembe argues, race and geography structure the domains of necropolitical violence. The practices of sterilization and antimiscegenation laws, along with bureaucratization of mass violence, are central to the formation of modern dynamics of race, class, sex, and bioaccumulation. The split between biopolitics and necropolitics and their relationship to the geopolitics of imperialism as well as capitalist development structure medical regimes in the modern period. In theorizing the latter, we need to read the dialectic of civilization and barbarism, and that of biopolitics and necropolitics, as at work in the organization of modern medicine as such.

There is one further opposition I want to draw on in theorizing the double-ness of modernity and modern medicine: Marx's own between freedom and necessity. Marx articulates this opposition in the third volume of *Capital*:

> The realm of freedom really begins only where labor determined by necessity and external expediency ends; it lies by its very nature be-yond the sphere of material production proper. . . . Freedom in this sphere, can consist in only this, that socialized man, the associated producers, govern the human metabolism with nature in a rational way, bringing it under their collective control instead of being domi-nated by it as a blind power; accomplishing it with the least expendi-ture of energy and in conditions most worthy and appropriate for their human nature. But this always remains a realm of necessity. The true realm of freedom, the development of human powers as an end in itself begins beyond it, though it can only flourish with this realm of necessity as its basis.[12]

This articulation of the hard-won achievement of freedom out of necessity is a central postulate of Marxist materialism. (As an aside, I would also argue that it is central to psychoanalytic materialism too: it is only by working through repressed materials that the subject or a society can gain freedom from the compulsion to repeat. One does not start in a realm of freedom; one only achieves it through the process of "working through" psychic materials.) In contrast to liberal theories of the free or autonomous subject, Marx argues that human societies are in thrall to forces and powers that exceed their con-trol. We find ourselves in thrall to various forms of necessity (the necessities of food, shelter, drinkable water, and breathable air being the most basic). Freedom is instead achieved by labor and the transformation of the human and nonhuman environment into something that can enable human flour-ishing. Yet this is not achieved all at once. Within class divided and hierarchical societies, freedom is achieved by the privileged class or caste via the systematic production of unfreedom of the subordinated classes. This unfreedom can take the form of explicit enslavement and appropriation (as in the necropolit-ical spaces Mbembe describes), or it can take the form of the necessity of selling one's labor power to survive and exploitation (where biopolitics and the market determine winners and losers). Benjamin's dialectic of civilization and barbarism flows from Marx's opposition between freedom and necessity. For civilizational achievements to be produced in a class divided society, barbarism must be enacted on another scene.

Marx does articulate a solution to the repetition of this opposition: the socialization of labor and its relationship to the "human metabolism" and "nature." Metabolism is a key term in this passage. While Marx only makes glancing reference to it here, the concept is central to Marx's work (mostly in notes) on the maintenance or destruction of ecosystems. As Kohei Saito and John Bellamy Foster have demonstrated, the concept of "metabolic rift" is central to Marx's ecological thinking.[13] Marx articulates this notion to theorize how ecosystems can either be reproduced or devastated by human economic activity. Whenever a metabolic rift occurs, the reproduction of the ecosystem is threatened or destroyed. The fixes within capitalism to such destruction usually involve spatial or resource-based fixes, such as expansion of agribusiness into newly appropriated lands or the use of various chemical fertilizers or petrochemically altered seeds. The rift is thus never healed but merely displaced. While I finally prefer Jason W. Moore's language of "metabolic shift" rather than "rift" because it suggests regularly stabilized regimes of ecological maintenance and accumulation within a larger decimation of the capitalist world ecology, the idea of necessity returning in the form of ecosystemic limits and possibilities is a crucial one not only for eco-Marxist theorizing but also for more general theorizing within a Marxist frame.[14] It will be crucial to our thinking about sex and accumulation as well. What such a model finally suggests, as in my reading of Benjamin, is that the terms "freedom" and "necessity" can be relativized or even reversed. In the name of producing a just and sustainable world ecology, we may need to recognize the forms of necessity hidden behind our rhetorics of liberal and consumerist freedom. Rather than only wrestling freedom from necessity, we also need to wrestle necessity from its guise as freedom, acknowledging the forms of necessity that structure our present and possible futures (ones that hopefully do not end in human extinction or unchecked ecocidal violence on a world scale). There are certain freedoms that we may want and need to achieve to maximize just and desirable living. There are also certain necessities, such as biological ones—death being the most forceful—that need to be part of our social calculus of embodied existence.

In the theorization of bioaccumulation that follows, it will be important to keep in mind the three different oppositions that I have just articulated: those between civilization and barbarism, freedom and necessity, and biopolitics and necropolitics. These oppositions are crucial to theorizing new technologies, medical procedures, ecosystemic arrangements, and forms of political economic organization. They enable us to attend to both what technologies and social systems enable, such as successful transitioning, sustainable ecosystems, economic equality, and what forms of violence they underwrite in the name of advancement, such as the experimentation on specific, often abjected, bodies, the degradation of specific ecosystemic elements, entities (including nonhuman flora and fauna), or whole ecosystems, and the production of economic immis-eration, unsustainability, and inequality. The goal of any just social organization is, of course, to maximize the positive outcomes, while minimizing or elimi-nating the negative ones. In articulating such a vision below, I want to avoid two different rhetorics that are common around social contradictions. The first rhetoric is a classic capitalist one that has taken on even greater social specificity under neoliberalism: inequalities are inevitable in systems, and it is up to individual actors to negotiate these contradictions. The second rhet-oric is a voluntarist one (as such it is merely the flip side of the first): it just takes the right set of ethical commitments and orientations to produce a just world. Certainly, ethical commitments are part of affirmative political trans-formation. Yet producing just systems involves more than just individual or political will. It also involves a collective and complex engagement with the contradictions produced by systems and by the different organizations of life within the present.

One of the most powerful recent representations in recent cinema of the doubleness I have been theorizing is Jordan Peele's *Us*.[15] While *Get Out* has gotten more attention as a compelling critique of racism and racial capitalism as they function in the contemporary United States (one in which Black vitality is literally appropriated and accumulated by a wealthy white family), *Us* is just as interesting and even more oriented toward collective politics. Perhaps the best description of the film is that it is a communist fantasy for our profoundly divided economic present, one that is also informed by the long history of racialized labor and accumulation by dispossession. As a horror movie with just the right dose of comedy, a genre Peele excels at, *Us* tells the story of the "tethered," a group of doubles who live underground in bunkers, which echo modernist institutional settings, and feed on rabbits (largely white ones that echo the use of inbred rabbits in commodity testing) and develop their own language based on gestures. Each person in the aboveground world has a sub-terranean double of which they are not aware.

A more precise representation of Marx's understanding of freedom and necessity is hardly imaginable. Like the worker whose work is occluded by the workings of commodity fetishism, the tethered represent those who do the necessary labor so that those above can enjoy the commodified freedoms and pleasures of contemporary life. The divide between the tethered and the abo-veground people also directly references the violence of slavery and contem-porary incarceration not only in the name (the tethered), but also in the shackle with which Red, the leader of the tethered who was forced to switch places with her double as a kid, enchains her aboveground double, Adelaide (both roles are played brilliantly by Lupita Nyong'o). While the film alludes to slavery and the disproportionate incarceration of people of color, class is just as central as race in structuring the divide between the tethered and the folks above ground. In this way, the film also feels like a reflexive critique of the Black bourgeoisie (represented most humorously by the Howard University sweatshirt–wearing Dad of the main family, Gabe, played by Winston Duke). Among other things, Peele uses the film to critique his own class position.

It is also striking, as Johanna Isaacson has pointed out, that the film is set in Santa Cruz, California, which has a sizable homeless population and is one of the most expensive places to live in the country, even as it markets itself as a seaside paradise.[16] The film tells the story of the revolution that the Tethered lead, in which they kill their doubles and reproduce a radical version of hands across America (which they learn about from the child Adelaide, who becomes Red, when she is abducted). The film stages a full-on communist revolution, the tethered wrestling freedom from the necessity and suffering they experience. The question the film ends with (a question that this chapter is also interested in) is what do they do once they gain this freedom? What do they build next? Thus, the horror is only horrible from the point of view of the bourgeoisie. In relationship to the tethered it is a black comedy (and this tonal split suggests one of the reasons that Peele employs a mix of the two genres). While the film critiques an understanding of race without class, it also suggests the impossibility of theorizing class without race (and I might add sex, gender, and sexuality). The tethered are an underclass (literally in terms of the spatiality of the film) who produce without wages, thus suggesting the long history of accumulation by dispossession that happened under slavery and colonialism. This representation of capitalism without wages leads to our discussion of Marxism beyond the reach of the wage.

Marxism beyond Wage-Based Exploitation

Revisionist work in Marxist theory has lately expanded its theorization of social contradictions to address not only the political-economic dimensions of class but also those of race, sex, gender, and sexuality. This new Marxist work theorizes accumulation by dispossession (what Marx called "primitive accumulation") as a regular occurrence within capitalism, one that emerges alongside of and in contradiction to wage-based exploitation. Within this framework, these new Marxist approaches attend to unwaged and informal work as much as waged work.

These changes in Marxist theory have been happening for a while, but, as I mentioned in the introduction, their prominence is perhaps best captured by the work done by two edited collections, *Totality Inside Out*, edited by Jen

Hedler Phillis, Sarika Chandra, and the late Kevin Floyd, and *After Marx*, edited by Colleen Lye and Christopher Nealon. While arguing that these transformations in Marxism have their first articulation in Althusser's notion of overdetermination and the radically open dimensions of his account of Marxist historicism, Lye and Nealon assert that they have gained new force in the specific political-economic context of the twenty-first century:

> But the declining profitability of twenty-first-century capitalism put the question to both the presentist model of base and superstructure and to the linear timeline of all-subsuming accumulation. Capital, while more productive of material goods than ever before, has proven incapable of maintaining a rate of surplus value that would enable other great expansions of accumulation along the lines of the postwar years. This contrary situation—expanded production and declining profitability—calls for a theoretical vocabulary that imagines capitalist accumulation not only in terms of its ability to reproduce the working class, or subsume social relations, but in terms of the capitalist impera- tive to overcome a tendency toward diminished profits, which has produced both the deindustrialization of the global north and the slumification of the south. The situation demands a vocabulary that contends with the incorporation of ever more people into the ranks of what Marx called "surplus populations"—those who are not worth incorporating into waged work on a regular basis.[17]

While Lye and Nealon argue that this shedding of labor, the shift from industrial to partially postindustrial production, and the alternate modes sub- jectification produced by these dynamics are all part of a long downturn in terms of capitalist profitability (typically dated from the early 1970s), I think we can be agnostic about whether capitalism will find yet new ways to exploit labor, savage ecosystems, and appropriate wealth in the future. Our Marxist critique does not depend on affirming such a timeline, especially because it is finally the kind of linear one that Lye and Nealon are correct to critique. Moreover, while they see the model of base and superstructure as a product, if I am reading them correctly, of the privileging of industrial production in the moment of high Fordism, I think we can see various kinds of nonwage and extractive labor (labor that is often marked by race, gender, sex, and sexuality as much as class, if not more) as also part of an expanded conception of the base, or what I prefer to call infrastructure.[18]

Where I am in full agreement with Lye and Nealon, however, is in their argument that other locations of capitalist violence and forms of unwaged work have come to prominence in our present moment. What Michael Denning terms "wageless life" has always been part of capitalism, often figured under forms of nonwage appropriation such as slavery, the exploitation of the incarcerated, social reproduction, and the money derived from shadow and unofficial economies, such as the drug trade, the sex trade, piece work, black market economies, and so on.[19] While the exploitation of the industrial proletariat was the central focus of nineteenth- and twentieth-century Marxism, different social actors and laborers have emerged as newly visible within the leading forms of capitalism in the present, which privilege the appropriative, the extractive, and the financialized (the latter depending on capital derived from either exploitation or accumulation). Such a recognition also comes from the changed epistemologies of work and activism inside and outside the academy, where race, gender, and sexuality have been crucial sites of struggle and knowledge generation. What the present conjecture has enabled us to see is the ways in which waged work, typically defined by class, forms in tandem and depends on unwaged work, which is typically racialized, gendered, and sexualized.

Such a shift in focus is central to the argument put forward by Kevin Floyd, Brent Ryan Bellamy, Sarah Brouillette, Sarika Chandra, Chris Chen, and Jen Hedler Phillis in the introduction to *Totality Inside Out*. For them, the crucial Marxist category is totality, which they employ to map the forms of appropriation, oppression, and exclusion that go along with waged labor and form undertheorized sites of accumulation. For them, as for Fredric Jameson, totality is not an existing entity but a heuristic. It represents the interpretive imperative, to theorize what has been excluded or left out but is determining from narrower interpretive frameworks. They argue:

> The essays in the collection engage with recent Marxist work such as social reproduction theory, class composition approaches, and materialist energy critique, new approaches that possess the potential to reorient and dramatically expand older orthodox Marxist accounts of race, gender, sexuality, and class itself as social locations and principles of social organization. . . . Recognizing that political economy and subject formation, economics and identity, accumulation and climate catastrophe are co-constituting can help us to avoid reproducing deadlocked debates over causal primacy, or culture and political economy, and instead explore how capitalist imperatives might knit together racist, misogynistic, heteronormative, ableist, imperialist, and environmentally destructive social relations.[20]

What Floyd and colleagues propose is a new understanding of the totality of capitalist relations, in which sites of contradiction, appropriation, and exploitation are understood to not only be informed by class but also by other axes of difference and subjectification, including race, gender, and sexuality as well as a new understanding of class that attends to the centrality of the underclass and the unwaged (what Marx termed, in an unfortunate phrase, the lumpenproletariat). While I prefer, as I have argued throughout this book, the language of subjectivity to their use of identity, I think that they are theorizing the ways in which identities are inscribed with in these logics of accumulation rather than their function as sites of individual self-definition. We are inscribed into identities, yet, as I argued in chapter 2, such identities and identifications exist in a complex formation with conscious apprehensions, unconscious drives, desires, alternative identifications, and traumas as well as nonconscious forms of embodiment and subjectification.

What is crucial to both their argument and that of Lye and Nealon is the emphasis that waged labor needs to be understood as one node, a privileged one under Fordism, of the forms of subjectification and labor produced by capitalism as both an economic world system and a world ecology. Central to modern Marxist theorization are the various forms of appropriation that precede and accompany the exploitation of wage labor in order to produce surplus value. If the production of surplus value is measured by the amount of value produced by workers in excess of the amount they are paid (which typically goes toward the reproduction of the workers as workers), accumulation by dispossession functions by forms of appropriation that happen either as a supplement to waged exploitation or before the worker sells their work on the market. They are the forms of accumulation that produce the initial dispossession of subjects and ecosystems that in turn force the workers to sell their labor and ensure that the wage relation will be profitable for the capitalists. From the vantage of the capitalist, they are cheap or free forms of accumulation, including the appropriations of land that went along with the histories of enclosure and imperialism, the appropriation of unpaid labor that is often gendered (as in social reproduction) and racialized (as in slavery, but also in terms of things like subprime mortgage lending), forms of accumulation via debt (student loans, mortgages, credit card debt, and the like) that are central to the financial economy, and what Jason W. Moore describes as the "Four Cheaps," which are appropriated in order to maintain the profitability of wage labor, "low-cost food, labor-power, energy, and raw materials."[21]

In describing the original forms of "primitive accumulation," which he situates in the early modern period, Marx describes it as being defined by "conquest, enslavement, robbery, murder, in short, force."[22] We can read the whole history of imperialism, with its appropriations of land, raw materials, and unpaid labor in relationship to this version of accumulation by dispossession. Yet Harvey also coined the term (perhaps differentiating it from the "primitive" version) to describe seemingly more quotidian forms of appropriation. The whole debt economy in the present works by transferring wealth from the proletariat and underclass and those precariously of the middle class to the financial classes. Forms of what Tithi Bhattacharya and others have called social reproduction, which has been reframed by Maya Gonzalez and Jeanne Neton as indirectly market-mediated labor, are also crucial forms of accumulation by dispossession. In this case, the labor is typically gendered and consists of unpaid and very cheaply paid domestic labor that functions to reproduce the conditions of production, both from day to day and through multiple generations of workers. Similarly, Petrus Liu has theorized the global segmentation of the labor force around both gender and sexuality, indicating the ways in which sex work functions in spaces defined by the casualization of labor and the logic accumulation by dispossession.[23]

This understanding of accumulation by dispossession in relationship to wage labor can be theorized as a dialectic that accompanies the ones we discussed above. Thus, violent forms of accumulation by dispossession such as slavery, ecological devastation, and the settler colonial theft of land form the barbarism or necessity in relationship to the "civilized" logic of wage labor, in which one gets to "freely" sell one's labor for a wage (of course, the very forms of dispossession that I discussed insure that "free" workers need to sell their labor for wages). Similarly, in the name of democratic freedom and the enhancement of life via biopolitics, both of which form in spaces that are centered on wage labor, there is the concomitant production of necropolitical spaces that are about the exhaustion of unpaid labor, genocide (as a part of imperial conquest), and ecocide. To really understand the violence of capitalism, we need to comprehend its necropolitical and barbarous flipside along with its exploitative and biopolitical official guise. Given the history of modernity so far, both sides of capitalism (and it is crucial to remember that wage exploitation is also a form of profound violence, one that also limits life chances and renders whole populations precarious) have been bound together.

Theorizing Bioaccumulation

In turning to the biomedical shaping and production of sex, we should maintain this understanding of the doubleness of capitalism. The history of medical science as it intersects with the sexed body and the production of desire manifests precisely such a doubleness. On the one hand, the achievements of modern medicine are manifold. There are all sorts of ways in which medicine has extended life chances, if unevenly and in capitalized ways, made certain lives more livable or livable at all, and provided powerful techniques, including surgeries, pharmaceuticals, and vaccines to produce collective forms of health and longevity. If the biological body, before the middle of the twentieth century, was largely seen as a product of nature and confined by nature's limits, in the twenty-first century, biology itself, as Nikolas Rose has argued, "is no longer destiny."[24] On the other hand, medicine has been a relentless site of experimentation, uneven care, commodification, all organized around what disability theorist Eli Clare describes as the ideology of cure which "rides on the back of *normal* and *natural*."[25] Much violence is done in the name of these three totems (cure, normal, and natural).

The contemporary understanding of biology as a locus of medical intervention and transformation represents not its eclipse, but rather a rethinking of it as a culturally and medically manipulable variable. In being open to intervention, biology becomes one of the central sites of political-economic investment and commodification, part of a "new political economy of life" in late modernity, or what Rebekah Sheldon calls somatic capitalism.[26] Biology/nature and culture are not opposed here. Instead, biology becomes a medium by which culture functions. In making this argument, I am not arguing that biological and natural limits have been abolished by contemporary biomedicine. Biological limits, the materiality of the body, and the status of sex (as we discussed it in chapter 2) all have limits, although ones that change historically with the growth of biomedicine. Aspects of the material body, as theorized by new materialists and by Lacan's account of the relationship of the real to embodiment (figured most complexly in the Borromean knot), still set limits on and produce contradictions around the biomedical, symbolic, and imaginary transformations of the body.[27] It is just that nature and biology no longer represent externalities to the workings of culture. Instead, they, along with their historical and material limits, are immanent to its workings. They become a version of natureculture, in Donna J. Haraway's terms (although, I would argue, one still riven by internal contradictions and tensions between what we figure as the cultural and the natural).[28]

Dynamics of bioaccumulation function precisely to transform biology into the capital. It is a way of capitalizing life itself. While Rose situates the political economy of life as a twenty-first-century phenomenon, and it certainly has its greatest expression in our present, bioaccumulation has a much longer history. The long history of modern medicine can be understood as a recurring, always growing, and uneven attempt to bring the domain of biology not only into culture but also into the capitalist world economy and forms of governmentality that structure modern life (and it is crucial to remember that Michel Foucault links biopolitics not only to neoliberal economics in our own present but to various forms of governmentality stretching back through the nineteenth century). Bioaccumulation names this dynamic of the capitalization of biology for profit within the workings of somatic capitalism. It also works to secure social reproduction, and other biopolitical and governmental aims. Bioaccumulation, in this latter sense, does not have to lead directly to profit but can also function as a means of reproducing the conditions of production (as in social reproduction) or desired outcomes in the biopolitical management of populations in the aggregate. One example of the latter would be the ways in which vaccines or antibiotics enable the health of specific populations (at the risk of creating more resistant strains of viruses, bacteria-based illnesses, and so forth).

In articulating this concept of bioaccumulation, I do not want to theorize it as radically distinct from other forms of capitalist accumulation. While Rose and Kaushik Sunder Rajan theorize "biocapital" as a unique economic formation, employing "capital" in a largely metaphorical sense, bioaccumulation, as I am defining it, is parallel with other forms of accumulation in the world system.[29] It does not create a separate conception of capitalism. There is one capitalist world system, with various regimes of regulation and governmentality intersecting with it. Bioaccumulation is instead one important form of accumulation, one that has grown exponentially in the present. Its workings are central to somatic capitalism, which is not a distinct form of capitalism but rather describes the folding of the body and reproduction into forms of accumulation within contemporary capitalism.

Central to the workings of bioaccumulation as it develops in tandem with modern medicine and technoscience are various forms of accumulation by dispossession as well as commodification. The early history of medicine can be theorized in relationship to primitive accumulation. Early modern medicine worked by the same dynamics that Marx describes as characterizing primitive accumulation: conquest, colonization, theft, and murder. The annals of medicine are rife with the conquest of various domains of biology and nature, the colonization of specific bodies, bodies that often became available via the dynamics of settler colonialism and capitalist enclosure, the usurpation of the earlier, woman-centric profession of midwives and healers, the theft of bodies and biological materials from graves, and the regular killings that took place, not only during the history of colonialism and enclosure but also in the experimental practice of medical techniques that were later abandoned because they proved to be fatal.

The dynamics of accumulation by dispossession are not limited to medicine's infancy and early development. Instead, as Harvey argues, the dynamics that Marx describes as primitive accumulation and locates at the beginning of capitalism are a recurring part of capitalist development. In the nineteenth and twentieth centuries, as medicine reaches maturity, regular forms of accumulation by dispossession accompany medical advances and enable forms of bioaccumulation. These forms of accumulation by dispossession were directed at the bodies of subjects who were either defined as fully outside of the domain of citizenship, via colonialism and slavery, or as politically and economically abject, such as immigrants. For example, Deidre Cooper Owens has charted the use of African American slaves and Irish immigrants as regular test subjects, ones often subjected to surgeries without anesthesia along with other forms of invasive bodily violence, in the development of gynecology.[30] Owens nicely also emphasizes the way in which the same populations also sometimes became medical practitioners of their own, exerting a complex agency that positioned them not only as objects of the medical gaze, but subjects who helped contribute to the discoveries and achievements credited to white, male doctors. But while it is important to attend to the complex positioning of some of these subjects and the forms of agency they employed around it, it is also crucial not to minimize the forms of necropolitical violence that was enacted on populations whose political and economic status limited their agency and made them vulnerable to violent medical experimentation. Indeed, as Harriet A. Washington has demonstrated, the experimentation, without anesthesia, on slave women by James Marion Sims, the ostensible "father of gynecology," represents only one moment in a long and recursive history of medical experimentation on Black subjects in the United States.[31] This history stretches from slave owners and southern doctors "who were active participants in the exploitation of African American bodies" to the infamous Tuskegee syphilis experiment, the nonconsensual use of Henrietta Lacks's genetic material, and contemporary drug testing practices, which often target Black, working-class, and underclass people in the United States, given that such drug trails often represent the only form of medical care available to these populations. This long history also intersects with the unevenness or unavailability of medical care in the for-profit system in the United States for working-class and Black subjects. As Washington notes, this history of experimentation and exclusion work to produce a radically different life expectancy for Black Americans: "The life expectancy of African Americans is as much as six years less than that of whites."[32]

A similar form of accumulation by dispossession, in which the body is appropriated and experimented upon in the name of medical advancement, has taken place with nonconsensual and unnecessary surgeries on intersex patients. The position of such intersex subjects in the United States often was (and continues to be) diametrically opposed to the Black subjects who were and often continue to be experimented upon and thoroughly objectified by the practices of slavery and incarceration, the rhetoric of white supremacy, and the medical gaze. Intersex subjects who were subjected to medical normalization were and are (I am a textbook example) typically white, middle- and upper-class, and overmedicalized. The logic underwriting the medicalized intersex subject is what Clare calls the ideology of the cure rather than experimentation on those who are constructed as less than fully human. Indeed, as Iain Morland argues, it is connected to the production of whiteness as a crucial dimension of the production of normative sexuality.[33] Intersex subjects' exclusion from consent was structured around their status as children and a rhetoric of remediation and cure, rather than undermedicalized exclusion and necropolitical experimentation. Still, the logic of bodily accumulation by dispossession structures the experience of both Black and intersex subjects.

While it is crucial to theorize these forms of accumulation by dispossession as they function within the logic of bioaccumulation, it is also crucial to remember that dispossession is only one of two dynamics by which capitalism generates profits. The other is of course commodification. In theorizing bioaccumulation, we need to pay attention to both dynamics, particularly as they represent different parts of the same process. The accumulation by dispossession of bodies functions in order to test and perfect surgical, pharmacological, and other forms of treatment, which in turn can then be used to generate surplus value and sold as a commodity to (other) biomedical corporations, nonprofit health systems, and consumers. The initial moment of incorporating people into circuits of accumulation by dispossession, where their bodies become testing sites parallels Jason W. Moore's account of the four cheaps. Indeed, we may need to add another cheap: cheap or free bodies (ironically produced by the unfreedom of embodied subjects), which function not only in relationship to bioaccumulation but also the biopolitical and necropolitical dynamics of accumulation more generally. Such forms of accumulation require not only slave labor and those who do, in Gonzalez and Neton's terms, indirectly-market-mediated labor, but also wage workers (the health of whose bodies becomes part of the capitalist's calculus). All of these bodies become debilitated in Jasbir Puar's terms. Thus, like the appropriation of ecosystemic materials (including land, water, and food), various forms of unpaid labor, debt repayments, and forms of cultural knowledge (like the pharmaceutical companies' appropriation of Indigenous medical knowledge), bodies and their component parts and systems become part of what capitalism appropriates in advance of wage work and in order to make wage work profitable. It is also what it appropriates in order to offer commodities to those who can afford them, including the commodity of an optimized body.

While I am theorizing these moments (accumulation and commodification) as separate, it is crucial to understand how they work in tandem to coproduce each other. For example, in slavery, enslaved people, as has often been theorized, are rendered living commodities, but, as such, they do the work of unpaid accumulation for their owners, the products of which are then sold as commodities on the market. Similarly, early gynecology and urology appropriated aspects of sexed bodies (and we should remember the understanding of sex as nonbinary that is central to this book's argument) in order to perfect and profit from various technologies of gender and sex that other patients could consensually request. As C. Riley Snorton has argued, we need to think about the history of gender and gendered medical procedures through the lens of the violent appropriation and experimentation on enslaved women's bodies.[34] The two forms of accumulation (appropriation and commodification) are intimately intertwined, yet we tend to focus on the end of the circuit at the exclusion of the wealth that is accumulated through dispossession. Appropriation is typically centered on subjects who are, in Gonzalez and Neton's words, "abjected" (169). While necropolitics and the violence of what Benjamin describes as barbarism can also define waged work, they function acutely in sites of dispossession, where subjects are rendered disposable, the ecosystem, including various bodies (human and animal), is treated as a free input, and laws of citizenship do not apply (here intersex children's status as dependents becomes paramount, particularly when the surgeries they undergo are nonconsensual and unnecessary).

It is thus crucial to theorize such sites of accumulation by dispossession when we consider the forms of freedom that medicine has also produced around gendered and sexual embodiment and the workings of desire (both the desire to be a certain body and the desire to interact with certain bodies). The freedom to transition and to medically shape your gendered embodiment is one of the remarkable achievements of medical science, producing real freedom in Marx's terms, and has a longer history of appropriation behind it. We need to affirm this freedom, but central to this affirmation is recognizing all the work that went under the name of "medical necessity" and involved not affirmative transformation or the production of health but violent appropriation. It is toward a vision of true freedom (one wrestled from necessity but which doesn't produce nonconsensual violence on another scene) around gender, sexuality, desire, and embodiment that this chapter is written, but before theorizing what this might look like, I want to briefly periodize transformations in biomedicine, situating how different regimes of biomedicine shape our understandings and medicalizations of gender and sex.

Periodizing the Medicalization of Sex and Gender

Before turning to the functioning of medicalization in relationship to the shaping and production of sex and gender in the present, I want to periodize the different ways in which the body, sex, and gender intersect with medicalization and the biomedical production of embodied subjectivities. Schematically, and understanding that all such developments are combined, uneven, incomplete, and sometimes recursive, the emergence of modern Western medicine takes place in Europe and the United States at the end of the eighteenth and beginning of the nineteenth centuries. As Foucault argues, "Modern medicine has fixed its own date of birth in the last years of the eighteenth century."[35] The self-conscious dimensions of this birth are worth noting. As Fredric Jameson has argued about discourses of modernity more generally, they are self-conscious moments that locate a break, one that defines what follows as radically new and mark what just occurred as irredeemably located in the past.[36] While such pronouncements do have the effect of self-consciously willing the modern into being through naming, the actual transformations that modernity denotes are neither so neat, nor do they appear everywhere at once. Instead, forms of nonmodern knowledge and practices continue, although in a more discredited form. Moreover, they merge with even as they are defined as lacking in relationship to, what is defined as modern. We need to both attend to moments of shift or rupture (which is what a periodizing methodology emphasizes), particularly as they become self-conscious, while also attending to the necessarily messier stuff of history, which a too neat periodization effaces.

Before the beginning of nineteenth century, what can be termed the early modern period of Western medicine is engaged in defining itself as a professional practice that worked primarily by forms of experimentation and trial and error. As the list of early modern medical procedures such as bloodletting and the application of leeches suggests, the knowledge of the human body and its functioning was limited by the working theories of medical practice and the limits of technology. Physicians were often viewed with suspicion. They were seen as bloodthirsty experimenters as much as healers. This tension, a version of the dialectic between civilization and barbarism, runs throughout the history of Western medicine. Not only are doctors regularly looked at with suspicion, particularly and understandably by populations who have been exploited for nonconsensual research purposes, but the public discourse around medicine itself regularly manifests ambivalence.

During the early modern period, as before it, much medicine (and certainly the most effective versions of it) was practiced by healers and midwives. Medicine's engagement with sex and gender primarily focused on childbirth. Women were the primary healers and used various lay and folk practices in healing bodies, providing abortions, and assisting with births. As Silvia Federici has demonstrated, the seventeenth-century campaigns against witchcraft were directed primarily at women and the forms of power they held in everyday life, from property to their position as midwives and healers.[37] This produced the uneven destruction of lay medicine. The latter's replacement by professionalized (read male) medicine was one of the central (and violently achieved) transformations of the period. It also became a way of shoring up the professional status of doctors by shifting suspicion onto healers and midwives. This exclusion of lay healers and privileging of professional doctors too can be seen as a version of accumulation by dispossession, which occurs at the early moments in which any given profession is established. And while professions do the crucial social work of standardizing treatment, separating treatment from immediate market considerations, and regulating proper practice, they typically have their initial genesis in moments of appropriation of lay practices and forms of knowledge.

Federici's work in *Caliban and the Witch* is crucial in theorizing this history, but her later work in *Beyond the Periphery of the Skin*, on the violence of the medicalization of gender, makes the mistake, one that has been criticized as transphobic, of not recognizing the positive freedoms that contemporary medicine also enables.[38] Interestingly, this position is visible not just in *Beyond the Periphery of the Skin* but in her earlier work too (as valuable as it is), which, unlike Marx, sees the advent of capitalist modernity only in terms of loss and violence rather than as dialectical movement between the pairs we discussed above (freedom and necessity, civilization and barbarism, biopolitics and necropolitics).

In terms of bodies that challenged normative gender and sexual formations in this period, they were mostly seen as monstrous, although not always in a fully negative way. As Jeffrey Jerome Cohen has theorized, "monsters dwell at the gate of difference" and as such provoke fascination and fantasy along with fear and anxiety.[39] As Foucault notes, the figure of the hermaphrodite (as a premodern conception of intersex people) was a recurring one in early modern (and premodern) representations and helped define the limits of the human.[40] As a figure and a recurring form of embodiment, hermaphroditism functioned in this period to define, as Foucault, David A. Rubin, and Alice D. Dreger have argued, the contours of normative understandings of gender and sex.[41] It represented the constitutive outside to what was constructed as proper human (nonmonstrous) embodiment.

This regime of premodern medicine begins to shift to its modern manifestation in the eighteenth and nineteenth centuries. Rubin describes how this shift was organized in part around the perception of hermaphroditism: "Between the sixteenth and seventeenth centuries, European medical men understood the hermaphroditism within a juridical-natural model as monstrous. However, by the eighteenth-century doctors began to conceptualize hermaphroditism not as a breach of nature but rather as a defective structure. This view allowed European medical practitioners to articulate their role in regard to hermaphroditism as not simply diagnostic but as corrective and normalizing."[42] This turn to ideas of defect and correction helps to usher in modern medicine, where the monstrous gives way to the medical problem in need of repair and normalization.

The shift was of course uneven and occurred in different places at different times. Foucault marks its beginnings in the shift from a conception of vision as the manifestation of rationality to the emphasis on newly a "empirical gaze" illuminated by new technologies of seeing into the body's cavities, illuminating what was "the insistent, impenetrable density of the object."[43] Modern medicine thus turned around a new empiricism, one that tried to locate its concepts in what was rendered newly visible. Such an approach necessitated multiple bodies to work on in order to establish scientific truth. The doctor should be the observing subject and the patient becomes the observed object. Both are to be conceptualized as ideally impassive, even in the middle of intense pain and violence. As Georges Canguilhem argues, the furthering of medical knowledge involved a certain controlled violence in order to make different aspects of the body visible: "To find out what went on inside, several options were available: one could monitor comings and goings, introduce spies into the household or smash the walls partially or totally in order to catch a glimpse of the interior. . . . Experimentation through organ ablation a natural extension of surgical excision."[44] While Canguilhem is describing Baroque medicine in the passage, the drive toward the knowledge of the inner workings of the body became even more forceful, even as it was systematized and made part of a standard practice, in nineteenth century medicine.

We can situate James Marion Sims gynecological experimentation on enslaved women within this modern regime. Doctor, slaveowner, and one time president of the American Medical Association, the "Father of American Gynecology" used enslaved women from his own or surrounding households and plantations to perfect his "silk suture method" of repairing anal-vaginal fistulae and other tears due to childbirth. These surgeries were not consensual and often caused the women extreme pain. As Harriet A. Washington argues, these surgeries, without anesthetic, were marked in their violence: "each surgical scene was a violent struggle between the slaves and physicians and women's body was a bloodied battleground" (2). Moreover, there was no therapeutic justification for the surgeries; he created the fistula and then fixed them: "Each naked, unanesthetized slave woman had to be forcibly restrained by the other physicians through her shrieks of agony as Simms determinately sliced, then sutured, her genitalia" (2). This becomes a process of debilitation in Jasbir Puar's sense. Sims then used the knowledge he gained from these barbarous experiments in order to establish the field of gynecology and open the first hospital for women in New York City, in which his techniques were used to aid white, primarily working-class women. Needless to say, he and his staff operated on white women only when it was necessary and had a therapeutic aim. Sims's surgeries are perhaps the starkest case of accumulation by dispossession of the body in the nineteenth century, but medicine in the century as a whole can be described primarily as a locus of experimentation and accumulation of knowledge. While the bodily appropriation may have been temporary (we are returned to our body after surgery—although a changed one), it led to the acquisition of surgical technique, which in turn is a skill that could be sold as a commodity or used as part of the biopolitical shaping of the citizenry. In order to regularize medicine's ability to heal, such experiments (often conducted on nonhuman animals as well as abjected humans) had to occur with enough regularity to establish scientific knowledge and standard practices.

Within this modern regime, surgical gendering of intersex subjects became more of a regularized practice, one that benefitted from the grim forms of bioaccumulation practiced by Sims as well as from the growth of plastic surgery more generally. The first "sex change" operations occurred in this period, as Joanne Meyerowitz and Jules Gill-Peterson have chronicled.[45] Some of these surgeries were not normativizing but represented moments of medically assisted freedom wrested from necessity. There were the beginnings of a utopian dimension proffered by Western medicine, one structured very unevenly by both class and race, in the possibility of physically changing one's sexed embodiment. This utopian dimension existed in tension with dystopian forms of surgery on racialized, working-class, and/or intersex subjects (the latter being typically privileged in terms of race and class). The motivations for these different surgeries are also important to note. In the case of intersex surgeries, they were supposed to be therapeutic, even as they involved testing and perfecting surgical techniques. The surgeries done on Black women by Sims and other early gynecologists did not even have a therapeutic justification. They were truly forms of experimentation and accumulation by dispossession. Their therapeutic aims were directed at white women.

We can see a parallel drive toward normalization at the turn of the twentieth century in terms of the definitions of nonnormative sexual behavior (what was

defined as "perversions"), sexology, and the taxonomy of various forms of queerness in the work of Havelock Ellis and Richard Von Krafft-Ebing. Indeed, as
Kadji Amin argues, the sexological discourse of the turn of the twentieth century is echoed by the proliferation of micro-identities in the present, even as
those doing the defining has shifted from medical authority to self-definition.[46]
This notion of sexuality attaching to individual identities is, of course, a central
argument advanced by Foucault in the first volume of the *History of Sexuality*,
and he links this directly to the growth of sexology in the same period. As I
argued in the introduction, Foucault's understanding of gay sexuality as the
product of turn-of-the-century sexological discourses needs to be complicated
by the longer history that Christopher Chitty's Marxist account of sexuality
provides.[47] In Chitty's history of the early modern period, a more collective
relationship to homoerotic sexuality developed with the separation of workers
by sex in agricultural, maritime, and artisanal work. This produced the possibility of an autonomous, yet collective, relationship to gay sex, one that was
also specifically laboring-class in origin. Given this earlier history, Foucault's
account of the sexologically derived emergence of gay identity needs to be
understood both as a more middle- and upper-class discourse and an individualizing one. We have both the uneven reification of the sexual subject
and what Kevin Floyd describes as the reification of desire in the early to
middle twentieth century.[48] Sex and sexuality detach from collectivities, of
either the family or the work unit, and become autonomous on the level of
the individual.

If these were the parameters that shaped modern medicine's engagement
with gender, sex, and sexuality, the period after World War II marks an important shift. Adele Clarke, Laura Mamo, Jennifer Ruth Fosket, Jennifer R. Fishman, and Janet K. Shim have defined the period from the mid-1940s through
the mid-1980s as the period of medicalization.[49] This period codified the notion
of modern medicine functioning to sustain healthy populations. It thus took
on an explicitly biopolitical cast. While the biopolitical aspects of medicine
were also evident in the nineteenth century, as Foucault has demonstrated,
the idea of supporting the general population's health and well-being distinguished this version of explicit biopolitics from earlier regimes. While the argument of Clarke and colleagues is focused on the United States, the same
shifts are visible in uneven fashion in other national contexts. Central to medicalization was an understanding of medicine's ability to cure disease, correct
accidents of birth, and stave off threats to well-being. Medicine was understood
to be something that applied to the population of a given nation-state as a
whole, and statistics became increasingly central in measuring its effectiveness.
This emphasis on medicine as collective and as having the responsibility for a

population considered as an aggregate, even as it also focused on the treatment of specific individuals, echoed the political-economic logic of Fordism in this period. A standardized conception of health became central to the era. Rather than the intensively individualized notion of health that we get in the later period of biomedicalization (which I will discuss), health, just like production, was serialized and massified. This was the period in which vaccines helped irradicate diseases on a grand scale. It was also the era of standardized treatments of various diseases and conditions, from cancer to heart disease. Central to this era, as well, was the ideal of curing ailments, rather than maximizing health (which is a later development of biomedicalization).

Given the logic of standardization here and the idea of the nuclear family, which was economically reproduced via the idea of the family wage, this was an era of intense normalization. Intersex surgeries were given new justification, as we saw in chapter 1, by John Money's plastic yet binarized conception of gender. These surgeries became part of standard practice and were given the rationale of being a psychological necessity for intersex infants, who were supposed to be operated on before their gender identity took shape. As David A. Rubin argues, in the era of medicalization, intersex surgeries became the norm rather than the exceptions as part of a larger regime of treatment: "Twentieth-century biomedical experts developed a range of surgical and hormonal techniques to 'normalize' infants born with intersex conditions. In this sense, the stigma and trauma persons with intersex embodiments face, including unwanted genital surgeries, hormone treatments, repeated medical inspections, and family shame and secrecy, are fundamentally related to gender and sexuality as regulatory structures."[50]

These normalizing surgeries, which often involved vaginoplasties and phalloplasties, were undertaken to produce new normalized and ostensibly happier (because properly sexed and gendered) subjects, and thus produced sex as a biomedical commodity. Not only was the production of a proper sexual organ a product, but the intellectual property around the medical techniques also functioned as a commodity. To turn to my own experience for a moment, I often had various surgeons try new techniques out on my recalcitrant body. Yet, since these surgeries on a physical level often produced more surgeries (because of complications produced by scar tissue) they were also a locus of accumulation by dispossession (on the levels of material practice and intellectual property).

In theorizing the commodification of these new surgical techniques and the organs that they promised to normalize and/or create, it is important to remember that the U.S. medical system is privatized and unevenly supported by insurance. These undertakings thus function within a larger capitalist market. Even in places like Germany and England, where universal health care was a core part of the medicalization of everyday lives and represented parts of its utopian promise, surgeries still had differential costs, and thus had a relationship to commodification as well as the biopolitical shaping of populations. Finally, it is also crucial to recognize that medicine functions globally as part of the capitalist world system and so is defined by radical unevenness in terms of the overmedicalization of certain populations (unnecessary surgeries on intersex infants being one marked example) and the lack of basic access to medical care.

Intersex surgeries, along with early sex change surgeries and hormone protocols, functioned as a locus of accumulation and experimentation that has enabled better surgical options for transitioning in the present. This is part of the utopian promise of urology and gynecology in our own era, but it is important to remember that the possibilities it now proffers were built on nonconsensual surgeries both on Black slave women and on otherwise relatively privileged intersex children. Thus, we need to attend to the contradictory formation of biomedicine in its long history, one that is shaped by dialectics and tensions between utopia and dystopia, civilization and barbarism, biopolitics and necropolitics, necessity and genuine freedom.

The "civilizational" promises (in Benjamin's terms) of the medicalization era were captured most forcefully by the attempts by many nations to make health care universally available. This is indeed a genuine utopian achievement, one that has been undermined in our own era of neoliberalism and biomedicalization. Yet, it is important to remember, as well, that normative conceptions of what did and did not constitute necessary medical treatment, which are in turn tied to, as Rubin argues, normative conceptions of gender, sex, race, and class, still play a sorting role that can produce dystopian and contradictory effects. For example, while nonconsensual, "corrective" surgeries for intersex children were regularly supported and covered by insurance, consensual surgeries that support or enact transition were typically not covered or supported. As Jules Gill-Peterson and Joanne Meyerowitz demonstrate, finding a surgeon who would perform a "sex change" operation was often quite difficult. It also involved one being independently wealthy, since it was not covered by insurance. Thus, there was a necropolitics at work (often resulting in subjective or literal death) for all of those who could not gain access to such medical procedures.

If the era from 1945 to 1985 or so represented the moment of medicalization, the period that follows (1985–present) is one of what Clarke and colleagues term biomedicalization. It is also the era of what Nikolas Rose describes as "molecular biopolitics" and what Sarah Franklin and Margaret Lock, like Rose and Rajan, describe as the period of biocapital.[51] These different developments are overlapping. Each emphasizes the individual and the cellular even as they are macrosocial developments. Each also imagines biology as deeply enmeshed with financial and social speculation, in which new forms of bioaccumulation emerge in the promise of various forms of embodied and biological futurity.

Clarke and colleagues define biomedicalization as a reconceptualization of biomedicine in neoliberal terms. As Foucault has argued and Wendy Brown has theorized at length, neoliberal biopolitics is organized around the dismantling of larger systems of social welfare and collective health.[52] These are replaced with individualizing discourses, interventions, and forms of socioeconomic sorting, in which human capital becomes the basis of measuring who deserves social and medical investment and who does not. Those with the most human capital, which is measured, as Foucault argues, in terms of "innate elements and other, acquired elements,"[53] are worthy of investment and support. Those who are not are divested of any social support. On the level of the political economy, neoliberalism applies the logic of financialization to the entirety of the political-economic system. People, because of their position in the market (which neoliberalism narrates in terms of life choices, entrepreneurial investments in the self, and innate capacities), are seen as good or bad investments, and social support should be given to those who represent promising return on investment.

It rewards those already privileged by class and punishes (through the removal of social support) those who are on the losing end of the political economy, that is, those who have not properly managed their human capital or whose capital is innately or structurally minimal. The large forms of biopolitical management, such as welfare systems, investments in collective health, and state investments in education that were central to the earlier period of Fordism and medicalization, are replaced with private investment and maximalization of the capacities of those who are imagined to be deserving individuals. In medical terms, this translates to a shift from maintaining the health of the collective to a logic of maximalizing health and wellness on the individual level. While the individualizing dimension of biomedicalization opens up some spaces for individual agency, often in the form of informed consumers of health who are increasingly seen as comanaging their own treatment, and dovetails with the preventative health movement, it also turns health into a moral rhetoric, in which one's health is a measure of one's moral worthiness for treatment. These practices combine to produce a radically uneven landscape of medical access and care, with obscene expenditures for those who can afford and "deserve" elaborate medical procedures and an absence of basic care and support for those who cannot afford it and are deemed unworthy.

More generally, neoliberalism changes the map of accumulation by dispossession and exploitation. Human capital becomes the basis for proving worthy of exploitation and thus a wage. In this way, human capital is seen as something that is extracted by a given employer, blurring the line between exploitation and accumulation. It also renders those undeserving of investment as surplus populations, those who find ways of surviving in what Michael Denning describes as wageless life. Their wageless position situates them as ideal for various forms of biomedical experimentation, testing, extraction, and other forms of accumulation by dispossession.

In order to present a full account of these forms of accumulation by dispossession, we need to address what Rose defines as molecular biopolitics and what Franklin and Lock describe as biocapital. If biomedicalization represents a shift to the individual as the main social unit of bioeconomic and capital investment, the other dynamics that emerge from these new technologies and market formations focus on the level of the cell and the molecule. Yet, as I detail these transformations, it is crucial to remember they are often framed in terms of the individual human or organism. Central to the emergence of these dynamics is the growth of genetic knowledge and various forms of nanotechnology that enable not only the observation but manipulation and creation of genetic and other forms of nanoscale biological materials. As Rose puts it, "the laboratory has become a kind of factory for the creation of new forms of molecular life." For Rose, this produces what he terms an "ethopolitics" which "concerns itself with the self-techniques by which human beings should judge and act upon themselves to make themselves better than they are."[54] The neoliberal dimension of this logic is clear. Franklin and Lock's understanding of biocapital emphasizes how molecular biopolitics intersects with the workings of contemporary capitalism, underscoring the connections of biological futures and biotechnologies to the futurity of financial markets. While I do not see biocapital as producing an entirely new mode of capitalism, it does represent a crucial mutation in the logic of both accumulation and commodification in which life becomes capitalized, what Franklin and Lock describe as "the capitalization of germ plasm, or life itself." They go on to describe the various biological products (which I am sure have expanded since the publication of their chapter in 2003): "In our midst, transgenic mice, cloned sheep, purebred dogs, and parthenogenic shrimp metamorphosed into new pathways of capital accumulation. Deep-sea enzymes, suspended human embryos, extraterrestrial cell lines, human genes, and good-as-dead bodies emerged as significant new actors in social and commercial life."[55] Central to their conception of biocapital is the ways in which these newly capitalized materials blur and combine reproductive and productive technologies, accumulation by dispossession and commodification.

Extractivism becomes generative of new products which produce a different relationship to embodiment: "Even more precisely, it could be said that this mode of generating biocapital is driven by a form of extraction that involves isolating and mobilizing the primary reproductive agency of specific body parts, particularly cells, in a manner not dissimilar to that by which, as Marx described it, soil plays the "principal" role in agriculture. In other words, according to [Charis] Thompson, 'the biotech mode of reproduction does not alienate one's labor from the person so much as alienate one's body from one's person."[56]

It is striking that Franklin and Lock theorize biocapital accumulation in a manner parallel to Jason W. Moore's discussion of agricultural production and the four cheaps. Here it is cheap life or cheap bodies that become the locus for extraction and accumulation. The extracted material can, in turn, be transformed into biocommodities and tied to both embodied and financial futures, given that biocapital relies ever more fully on private investment and equity. Moreover, the measurement of the value of such biocommodities is the futurity that they promise for those who are privileged in terms of global divisions around class, nationality, and race.

So what does this all mean for understandings of sex, gender, and sexuality in the present? First, as I argued in the introduction, it changes our understanding of embodiment, subjectivity, and desire. Neoliberalism places an emphasis on the competitive individual rather than group solidarity. Identity categories, in this context, rather than being the basis for collective forms of identification and solidarity, increasingly become micrological and competitive. Similarly, they become abstracted from our embodiment and function along the lines of what I elsewhere have termed avatar fetishism.[57] I define avatar fetishism as the fetishizing of an abstracted and manicured conception of the self, one that corresponds to the various online and televisual conceptions of self that we construct. I oppose this conception to what I define as "embodiment envy" in which the globally privileged (who are defined by avatar fetishism) have an envy of those on the precarious end of the global divides around class, race, gender and sexuality, whose work (industrial, agricultural, service, affective) is defined as fundamentally embodied and who are perceived as more sensual and sexual. We already addressed some of this racialized history in the discussion of the flesh in chapter 2. Here I want to suggest that labor and class position workers differently in relationship to embodiment. In all cases, however, the advent of biocapitalism and molecular biopolitics produces a situation in which the body is merely a container for the real scene of economic and social transformation. Thus, rather than the social being defined by connections between people, it is defined my molecular dynamics within people. Becoming molecular also functions to separate people from each other. We are competitive assemblages of various biomaterials and biofutures. Sex, as material, becomes effaced (except where it is legislated in reactionary ways in anti-trans legislation, as Paisley Currah demonstrates), replaced by the cultural and less materialized concept of gender.[58] Self-construction and maintenance become the core of the self. Similarly, as Jordy Rosenberg has argued, sex as desire becomes similarly molecularized.[59] Desire between people becomes secondary to the desires that function within people.

Rethinking Biomedicine outside of a Capitalist Framework

As long as our thinking about biomedicine remains within a capitalist framework, the forms of contradiction and violence that I have detailed throughout this chapter will remain in place. Barbarism will always shadow civilizational accomplishments. Freedoms will always be used to justify necessary violence on another scene. And biopolitics will always produce necropolitics as its double. Certainly there are reforms that can happen within capitalism, but as a world economy it is fundamentally built on profound inequalities, the sorting of populations into a small contingent of winners and a much greater number of losers, and a logic of endless growth in a world ecology that is already strained to the breaking point. While seemingly tied to new products and possibilities that can promote human flourishing, capitalist biomedicine, like capitalism in general, sustains itself by brutal competition and by exploiting and extracting value from waged laborers and from the work and the possessions of the nonwaged, whether these be embodied, intellectual, or territorial. Built around endless growth, capitalism thus fundamentally exhausts the systems that it uses to produce surplus value and the commodities that promise human flourishing.

Given its imperative of endless growth, capitalism is also fundamentally colonizing. We see this in all the forms of accumulation by dispossession that organize its logic, from the appropriation of land, the destruction of ecosystems, the exploitation or "removal" of Indigenous life ways, the appropriation and commodification of the body (including the brain), and more. There can be no decolonization worth the word without a fundamental transformation in our political economy. Yet, as the authors of The Care Manifesto argue, the anticapitalist transformation of the global economy and the world ecology does not have to happen all at once (it is hard to imagine that it could).[60] We need to begin the transformations on local and regional levels even as we work in solidarity with other sites of transformation to finally change the fundamental organization of the world system as a whole. In the spirit of such a transformation and as a model of what can perhaps be achieved on the local, state, or regional levels, I end this chapter with a list of sites of possible transformation in biomedicine, particularly as it shapes sexed and gendered embodiment. These transformations can contribute to building a globally integrated medical system that that is not fundamentally predicated on exclusion and violence in one locale in the name of maximalizing life in another.

1. Medicine everywhere must be socialized. Medical care should be a fundamental right and not a privilege. Moreover, disparities in care should be seen as a problem. Privatized medical systems, as demonstrated most forcefully in the contemporary United States, produce too many people who lack basic access to care. They also produce fundamental irrationalities in terms of cost (the United States spends more per capita and has much worse health care than nations where it is effectively socialized) and dynamics of overmedicalization and undermedicalization. Advances in bio-medicine and its application cannot be left to the whim of market competition. Instead, we need to produce a set of policies that are organized around giving all people fundamental access to medical care and support. In terms of producing positive rights around embodiment, such policies would support transitioning, reproductive rights, sex education, and sexual health.

2. Consent must be affirmed or sought (when possible) not only in terms of patients and doctors but at all levels of biomedical development. While consent has limits as a paradigm under capitalism, in a socialized context, it provides a crucial locus of input by those who are otherwise objectified in medical discourse. Within such a framework, unnecessary intersex surgeries would not be done without patient consent. If we need to wait until a patient is old enough to consent in a reasonable manner, we should do so. On the other hand, medical transitioning (through pharmaceuticals or surgery) should be allowed when the person in question consensually requests it. To enable consent in these differing contexts, we may have to construct different ages of consent for different procedures or practices. While we may want to keep eighteen as the age when one can sexually consent as an adult, we may want an earlier conception of consent for both transitioning and "corrective"

procedures on those who are intersex (parallel to the ways in which we understand sexual consent between minors). In these cases, something closer to puberty makes more sense. Emphasizing the consent of the person who is undergoing the procedure will forestall the present contradiction in the United States in which transitioning surgeries to minors are imagined by transphobic laws and discourses as "child abuse" while in many places absolutely nonconsensual surgeries on intersex infants are routine. If consent were insisted on at all stages of medical research and practices, this would also avoid the violence of experimenting on certain abjected populations in the name of assisting or producing medical care for others. Moreover, given a larger socialized context, medical research would no longer be able to use the promise of money in enticing the desperate to participate in research that provides nothing for them therapeutically. Histories of biomedicine would also be dialectical (as I have attempted to do in this chapter), narrating the experiences of those who were used as experimental test subjects in the name of medical advancement. This also would apply to the use of nonhuman animals in testing, particularly their use by corporations for various products. Their use in medical testing involves a more complex discussion, but we would at least be able frame the question in ethical rather than cost-effective terms. Finally, at least until the achievement of genuine socialism, black or shadow markets for medical supplies (such as hormones for transitioning) should be accepted as necessary. Until there is economic equality, such markets produce access for those who cannot afford legal access to care. Moreover, when states decide to stigmatize certain populations in the name of collective health, the black market becomes a crucial mode of access.

3. Advances in biomedicine need to be measured not only in terms of their differential socioeconomic effects but also in terms of their ecological ones. The era in which we could ignore the fundamental reality of the climate emergency has passed. Modernity has allowed humans to wrestle great freedom from the necessities of life on this planet. Yet, it may be time, as I suggested, to partially flip this dialectic. We may need to figure out what necessities we may need to embrace in enabling the freedoms and survival of future generations. This may mean some hard choices will have to be made around what materials we use and how we use them in biomedicine. A truly sustainable biomedicine would be a remarkable

achievement and one we should strive for. Part of this would be to produce a pedagogy around it (as well as other technologies) that traces the biomedical advance at all stages of production—tracing the commodity chain that shapes it, as well as the workers and test subjects that contributed to its genesis, but also its ecosystemic genesis and the effects of such a genesis. Just as commodity chain mapping is a central practice of Marxist pedagogy, we need a similar mapping around ecological affordances and effects involved in the generation of biomedicine.

4. Finally, we need biomedicine that can enable embodied and consensual sexual flourishing for all, including all the kinks, desires, identifications, and practices that make up a rich and diverse sexual society. In the next chapter, which theorizes what I term the sexual commons and the embodied commons, I articulate this vision of sexual flourishing more fully.

4

The Sexual and Bodily Commons

More than on couches, it is in literature, in art, and in revolution that sex speaks—and speech makes itself sexual. Simultaneously, a major transformation occurs, that of an entire social and technical praxis which desires to recreate the world, desire's own speaking out and language's desire not to say but to make love.

JEAN-LUC NANCY

Nothing seems more amenable to the discourse of privacy than sex.[1] Certainly queer theory and feminist theory recognize that forms of ostensibly private experience are shaped by public discourses, institutions, practices, and economic formations. Central to feminist theorizing in the 1970s was the recognition that the private is public, that privacy itself was an ideological discourse used to deny women rights around the forms of manifest inequality, exploitation, and violence that they experienced in the so-called domestic sphere, from the appropriation of value and care in social reproduction to the exclusions from aspects of the public sphere and on to sexual violence and domestic abuse. Similarly, queer theory at its most radical also emphasized the public dimensions of sex, most famously in Lauren Berlant and Michael Warner's celebrated essay, "Sex in Public."[2] Yet even in these important theoretical interventions, the assumption remains that sex and the body are irreducibly tied to individual subjects (even as consensual fucking necessarily involves at least a minimum of intersubjective communication and interaction). Even the work of Jacques Lacan, which has done so much to reframe psychoanalysis in a fundamentally social direction, is organized in part around the dictum that "there is no such thing as . . . sexual relationship."[3] While the meaning of this dictum is complicated, and it can be read, as I do, as framing both the sexual and the social as internally split, thus not reducing the social to the level of the atomized individual, Lacan too seems to pose the idea of a collective relationship to embodiment and sexuality as ontologically fractured. Even Marxist theory, perhaps the most socially oriented body of theory there is, tends, with a few visionary exceptions, to bracket questions of sex and embodiment. Moreover, when Marxism and actually existing communism do address questions of reorganizing or reimagining sexuality, the family, and the body in fundamentally collectivist terms, it is often seen as a monstrous overreach, even by otherwise committed leftist scholars.

Why this emphasis on the irreducibly individual and often private experience of sex and embodiment? There are a number of interrelated reasons, some more ideological than others. On one level, the idea of privacy and the (private) ownership of one's own body is a central tenet of Enlightenment thought, particularly as articulated by John Locke, and has become a fundamental feature of the liberal state for subjects who are extended full citizenship, even as it works to limit the freedoms of many other subjects. Indeed, not only do contemporary conceptions of sex and embodiment depend on ideas of the private self, but also ideas of rights, consent, self-fashioning, and economic entrepreneurship. Neoliberalism, as theorists from Michel Foucault to David Harvey and Wendy Brown have demonstrated, depends fundamentally upon an ideology of the individual as self-entrepreneur, in which the mass-scale economic workings of the global economy are reduced to the concept of individuals as the primary agents of their own success or failure.[4] It is also crucial to remember that these forms of individual self-possession and self-entrepreneurship are fundamentally not available to all, as the long history of those who are excluded from Enlightenment conceptions of selfhood demonstrates. So, on one level, we are dealing with a core ideology of the social, one that has deep philosophical roots and manifests in the late neoliberal present in particularly pernicious ways.

As I suggested before, the production of sex and sexuality as private is also a legacy of the uneven and never fully successful production of public and private spheres beginning in the eighteenth century and becomes more generalized with the growth of wage labor and the reduction of the definition of work to those who receive a wage. While there have been important challenges to the ideology of separate spheres—and it was an ideology, one with powerful material effects, rather than a fully realized reality—Nancy Fraser has demonstrated the ways in which the intrusion of waged work with the introduction of industrial capitalism, fundamentally changed conceptions of gender and labor, with women often relegated to the private sphere in which the labor of reproduction was newly abjected and the definition of the male laborer as wage worker became the new standard by which the concept of work was understood.[5] The uneven splitting off of reproductive work (which was also shaped and complicated by divisions of class, race, and citizenship) from wage work has the effect of rendering official conceptions of sex and embodiment as continuous with the familial, now bracketed off into a private or domestic sphere. Such an ideology was complicated by the very real embodied dimensions of industrial labor, which often employed working-class women and children, and the ways in which unofficial forms of sexuality from the homoerotic to sex work functioned in public.

With the neoliberal reforms of the past forty years, the ideology of the private has lost some of its gendered quality. Instead, it has become the central pillar of social good and the ostensibly frictionless workings of the market. In the nineteenth and early twentieth centuries, the ideology of separate spheres was used to segment the labor force and create different locations for waged and unwaged, official and unofficial labor. In the neoliberal present the private has basically merged with what used to be the public, using the concept of human capital and the ideology of corporate efficiency to produce a thoroughly atomized and individualized conception of what used to be the public good. Citizenship is no longer measured in terms of social provisions and collective flourishing (however uneven) but in terms of private gain, the liquidity of credit, consumer access, and choice. The family and the consumer have replaced the citizen and the worker as the prime locus of social identification. Of course, this shift has not been without its ambiguities. The strict gender hierarchies produced by the Fordist conception of the family wage have given way to the two-career or single-parent household. While this has meant greater access to direct wages for (what is left of) middle-class and upper-class women, it has also contributed to the downward mobility of many women and the feminization of poverty. Moreover, as Cinzia Arruzza, Nancy Fraser, and Tithi Bhattacharya argue, the reduction in real wages that has underwritten the dissolution of the family wage has meant the shifting of much of the burden of childcare and social reproduction onto poor women and women of color, whether this work is waged or otherwise.[6] Similarly, the uneven dissolution of the Fordist and pre-Fordist ideology of the public sphere as thoroughly masculine has combined with the powerful struggles for rights and public recognition of all of those excluded from the Fordist compact to produce an economic and public sphere in which women, people of color, and queer folks gained rights, recognition, and certain forms of economic access, even as such access was being structurally attenuated for all via a growing class divide. Identity, first as a collective conception that held much political promise and second as its neoliberal revision along individualized and atomized lines, became a central political and social concept. Sex and embodiment have similarly become experienced as increasingly atomized, personalized, and algorithmicized in late neoliberalism, as I detailed in the introduction. Within such a framework, it is not surprising that both embodiment and sexuality are experienced primarily as individual and private identities.

Of course, there is also the seemingly irreducibly individual experience of embodiment and sex on an existential or phenomenological level. Our bodies may share many common features, materialities, and forms of biosocial organization, but this commonality is experienced as individual to each consciousness. Subjectivity can be collective and not merely individual, but we tend to experience aspects of embodiment and our desires as, like death, irreducibly singular. It is all fine to think about collectivity, but when one is sick or when one has desires that are not affirmed by the social, we tend to experience such moments in terms of individual suffering or anomie. While I think it is crucial that we reorient our conception of sex and embodiment around more collective concepts and structures, it is important to not efface these moments of isolation that can also be central to human subjectivity. Indeed, one measure that a collectivist project has become coercive rather than affirmative is that the dialectic between the individual and the collective becomes entirely effaced, as Theodor W. Adorno argued.[7] He saw the dangers of pure collectivism in the workings of Stalinism and (in a very different way) in Naziism. In the United States in the present, and increasingly in much of the neoliberal globe, the opposite danger has become manifest: the absolute negation of the rights, needs, and supports for collectivity in the name of the rights and "freedoms" of the individual, as Elisabeth R. Anker cogently argues.[8]

Becoming Collective

So what if we begin to conceptualize sex and embodiment in more collective ways? What commonalities can we start to conceptualize that structure a fundamentally human orientation to both embodiment and sexuality, even as theorizing such commonalities may finally push us in the direction of posthumanism? Similarly, what if we begin to conceptualize the body, the workings of desire, and human subjectivity as nonautonomous, as always functioning within, dependent upon, and necessarily shaped by a larger ecosystem, cultural system of meanings, and political-economic context. In other words, what if we theorize the human being as fundamentally existing in what Jason Read (after Gilbert Simondon) has termed "transindividuality" and as being what Stacy Alaimo defines as "trans-corporeal"?[9] Such a conception of the human is not merely present in the most visionary of contemporary theory, it was also central to Marx's early concept of "species being."[10] For Marx this concept is produced by the human relationship to and transformation of the environment (what Marx terms "inorganic nature"): "in his *working of* inorganic nature, man proves himself a conscious species-being, i.e., as a being that treats the species as his own essential being, or that treats itself as a species-being" (76, italics in original).

Humans thus realize their collective commonality in their relationship with the material world and ecosystems. This relationship is fundamentally an active one, we realize our sensuous relationship to the material world by transforming it through labor. In chapter 2 we explored how this conception of species being persists in forms of racialized consciousness and embodiment around what is termed the flesh, precisely because of the different ways in which slavery and unwaged rather than waged labor functioned in relationship to the body as a commodity without rights, one that is part of the process of accumulation by dispossession, in contrast to the alienation and reification produced by the exploitation of wage laborers with rights.

Labor, when not alienated and reified in capitalist exploitation, is fundamentally enriching and collectivizing. It produces a sensuous relationship with both the material world under transformation and with others. Of course, the concept needs to be reworked in the present, emphasizing that the human is not the only species or entity acting within what Jason W. Moore has termed the "world-ecology."[11] Marx attempts to distinguish human activity from animal activity by emphasizing the conscious and aesthetic dimension of the former, but, as various posthumanists and animal theorists emphasize, we need to attend to the agency of various nonhuman actants as well.[12] All entities in the ecosystem (humans, animals, plants, soil, climate, minerals, cultural production, the built environment, infrastructure, and so on) have to be theorized as part of a mutually sensuous and transindividual activity. This productive sensuousness is formed when human labor shapes and is shaped by other material actants. While it is important not to efface the often violent ways in which, particularly under capitalism, humans transform the ecosystems in nonsustainable ways as well as the primary responsibility humans hold for climate change, such an expanded conception of species being would emphasize the co-constitution of the ecosystem and the forms of sensuousness that takes place between trans-corporeal and transindividual beings. I term this expanded conception of species being, as a mode of transspecies being, one that R. A. Judy locates historically as intertwined in a collective conception of the flesh.[13]

This concept of transspecies being underpins my discussion of the embodied and sexual commons that follows in this chapter. Central to this theorization will be the insights proffered by Marxist conceptions of the commons and collectivity, such as those posited by Read and Moore. It will also rearticulate collective desire as necessarily central to the most radical work done by queer theory, gender theory, psychoanalytic theory, critical race theory, and indeed Marxism. Before articulating each of these concepts, however, I think it is important to briefly provide a historical account of why thinking the collective has become such a challenge in the present. It is to such a history that I turn next.

The Slow Erosion of Collective Vision

I have told a version of this history elsewhere in this book, primarily in terms of the economic and social transformations produced by the decline of Fordism and the growth of neoliberalism and biocapitalism. Here I want to tell the story from within the logic of theory, artistic production, and academic discourse. The mapping and periodization I am going to provide will be inadequate and can be criticized by the very theories I am presenting here as privileging a geographically and temporally situated history as if it were general. Such are always the dangers of periodization and spatialization, yet to do neither is to fall into the trap of radical particularization, in which no ability to scale up from our private or local experiences is possible. As I have detailed, such radical incommensurability of individual or undifferentiated experience is already one of the central ideologies of our time. I offer this periodization as one very simplified and generalized attempt to produce a schematic account of theoretical reflection and artistic production since 1900 or so. It obviously can be critiqued and should be. It is merely a heuristic.

If one of the characteristics of theory in the era that we call modernist was an emphasis on universality, it was this very tendency that was challenged in the era that we inadequately termed postmodernism. Our own moment of climate emergency, growing fascism, and late neoliberalism are characterized less by one theoretical tendency, but instead a series of them that each exist in discrete isolation, with little communication in between. As David Harvey, among others, has argued, central to much modernist artwork was a central tension between the universal and the particular, the eternal and the ephemeral.[14] Modernist art often tried to link these oppositions through a dialectical leap from one register to the other. In this way it contrasted with the moment of nineteenth-century realism, which often provided a midlevel mapping of the relationship between characters and their social milieu, individuals and the growing urban or national space. For modernism, it is already as if these two poles cannot be imagined fully without a sudden shift in register from one to the other. What we sometimes call modernist theory was similar in orientation. It tended to articulate a universalist vision and then situate the individual subject within such a vision. Freudian psychoanalysis thus posits its conception of the unconscious as universal, a fundamental trait shared by all human beings, even as its form takes on a distinct formation within each subject. We thus have this shuttling from the individual subjective to the universal and back that characterized a certain amount of "modernist" theory. While some modernist theories and philosophies tended to emphasize the subjective side of the pole, others tended to emphasize the universal. Phenomenology and existentialism, like psychoanalysis, tended to emphasize the subjective pole of the opposition while positing universal structures. Marxist theory and structuralism, on the other hand, tended to emphasize the universal. The subject (especially the collective subject for Marxism) was situated within this universal, but the emphasis was on larger forms of structure, contradiction, and, in Marxism, the universal movements of history.

Discourses around sexuality, sex, and gender were similarly split between an individual understanding of the subject as object of study (the psychoanalytic case history being one exemplary model) and a drive toward universalizing taxonomies (the sexological taxonomies of Krafft-Ebing being, perhaps, the most famous). Within such a framework, sex and gender were understood as having normative and pathological poles. While psychoanalysis at its best suggested the presence of pathology within the ostensibly normative, sexology created a complex and exhaustive taxonomy of pathologies. Sexology proliferated sexual pathologies, in some ways paralleling the proliferation of sexual identities in the present, as Kadji Amin notes, yet the aim, as in structuralism, was to provide and account of all possible sexual pathologies and their variations.[15] I have provided an account of the complex dance performed by ideas of sex and gender in this period in chapter 1, and I will not rehearse it here. Suffice it to say that they were both very much in play as concepts in this modernist moment, even as their meanings slipped around, sometimes in surprisingly chiastic ways.

If the midcentury moment represented a complicated shift between two regimes (what inadequately got called the modern and the postmodern), then by the 1970s or so and through the last three decades of the century, a very different theoretical and artistic logic was dominant, at least in the most celebrated theory and art in the period. Central to postmodern art was a challenge to the universal and metaphysical claims of modernist art. Replacing it was art that was reflexive, political, and antimetaphysical (which is different from nonmetaphysical—it called attention to the inadequacy or contradictoriness of any metaphysical position). The art interrogated its enabling possibilities and often reflexively critiqued the very institutions, practices, and discourses that enabled its production. If Fredric Jameson argued that postmodern art was primarily about pastiche, I think such an account only applies to the most depoliticized version of the postmodern, such as the use of historical quotation and pastiche in much ordinary postmodern architecture.[16] More often, as Linda Hutcheon argued, there was a political charge to the use of postmodern irony.[17] The artwork interrogated its own materials, metaphysical presumptions, and the conditions of its own production. Brian McHale famously argued that if modernist fiction was about epistemology, exploring perception and the apprehension of a material world, postmodern fiction was ontological, imagining and constructing multiple discrete and incommensurate worlds.[18] I always found McHale's account unpersuasive, perhaps because I always saw an ontological and epistemological dimension to both modernist and postmodernist fiction; it is just that modernism privileged a singular, consistent world, while postmodern proliferated multiple inconsistent ones. While this discussion of postmodern art and literature may seem only distantly related to the discussion of sex and embodiment, this conception of multiple incommensurate worlds presages how gender and sexual identity is increasingly be experienced in our algorithmic present.

In terms of theory, a similar shift occurred. This shift was often characterized as the movement from foundationalism to antifoundationalism or, in philosophy, from modernist philosophy (which encompassed everything from Kant to the phenomenologists) to postmodern philosophy. As Fredric Jameson argues, theory itself as a concept, really comes into being with this emergence of antifoundationalism (although, as I have argued elsewhere, it is not reducible to this tendency).[19] Central to much postmodern theory was a sustained and political interrogation of universalist, metaphysical, and normative concepts assumed by modernist thought. Thus, the ordered formalism of structuralism was challenged by the poststructuralist emphasis on the way in which systems, philosophical, political, linguistic, or social, are fundamentally incomplete and contradictory. As deconstruction especially demonstrated, they necessarily contain the logic of their own undoing. Moreover, their claims to universal, systematic, or disinterested knowledge can and should always be challenged as particularist, inconsistent, and politically motivated. Indeed, many of the most powerful versions of postmodern theory demonstrate that universal and normativizing claims are profoundly political. They serve the interests of power. Thus feminist, postcolonial, and queer theories all work to challenge universalizing logics that privilege specific formations power (the imperializing, sexist, and homophobic) and particular subjects (the colonizing, white, straight, and male). Central to the theoretical revisions undertaken by postmodern theory is the rejection of grand narratives articulated by Jean-François Lyotard and the privileging of more localized, contingent, and politicized narratives.[20] Similarly, such a position also asserts that no singular truth can be applied to all situations. Instead, truths are the product of language games and particular meaning systems and are incommensurate with each other.

In terms of gender, sex, and embodiment, postmodern theoretical accounts tended to emphasize an oppositional and contestatory set of meanings. If the truths privileged by a given society tended to minoritize, pathologize, or exclude various forms of otherness, then postmodern theoretical approaches such as third-wave feminist theory, queer theory, postcolonialism, and disability theory took such otherness as the starting point for not only a critique of dominant practices but also a recognition of alternative cultural practices, lifeways, and states of being. Similarly, even if such theories had difficulty articulating a new set of (more just and inclusive) norms and visions, they were thoroughly political—situating themselves as fundamental challenges to hegemonic forms of exclusion, oppression, and pathologization. Central to 1990s gender, queer, and critical race theory as well, as I have argued elsewhere in this book, was the notion of cultural or linguistic construction. Within such a framework, not only are such categories constructed, having no foundational essence or biological core, but so is subjectivity itself. As such subjectivity is thoroughly contingent, the product of contradictory cultural discourses. Even the Marxism of the period tended to emphasize the thoroughgoing constructedness of the subject (Althusser) and the cultural dimensions of economic transformation (Jameson), while also underscoring the different material determinations of both. Lacanian psychoanalysis also emerged (unevenly in translation) in the United States in this period, but echoing the Marxism of the era, it presented the linguistic construction of the subject and the unconscious in relationship to imaginary identifications and nonsymbolic determinations of the real. It is not accidental that this book is organized primarily around these versions of Marxism and psychoanalysis. Central to both approaches is an attention to both the constructedness of subjectivity and that which shapes, overdetermines (to use Althusser's language), eludes, and exists in contradiction with the symbolic. Unlike older structuralisms, it also imagines the social field as shaped by contradiction and antagonism. Such an approach allows me to maintain both a materialist and a soft-constructivist approach to the production of sex, gender, and sexuality.

Assuming that the postmodern era existed (and there are those who argue that it was never more than a fashionable academic concept) it seems to have run out of steam around the beginning of the new millennium. While there are some who still use the phrase "postmodern" to describe the present, most scholars agree that it no longer seems to be an adequate account of the world in which we live. While neoliberalism seems to have replaced postmodernism as the central descriptor of the present (in this book too), it lacks the explanatory mobility (what others might call the imprecision) that the earlier term possessed. Like modernism before it, postmodernism has the virtue (or vice) of describing not only an intellectual approach, but a leading set of artistic practices, and a dominant social formation.

So how do we characterize theoretical production and its relationship to the dominant texture of everyday life in the present? It does feel as if we live in a decidedly different moment than the moment of high constructionism, globalization, and cultural hybridity. If everything in postmodernism felt lighter than air, then most things in the present have fallen back to earth. We live in a moment of walls, paranoia, and fantasies of ethnic, national, and sexual purity. In contrast to postmodernism's promise of transcending the material and the natural, we also live in a moment when the pressures of the material and the ecosystemic are experienced as ever more forceful. Whether it is the fundamental challenge and threat represented by the climate emergency or the reminder of our biological vulnerability produced by the COVID pandemic, the postmodern fantasy of nature being abolished or transformed into culture reveals itself to be profoundly misguided. Similarly, on an economic level, despite various bubbles and their collapses (the 2008 housing market and financial collapse being the most significant), the promises of endless if profoundly unequal growth that characterized the rhetoric of globalization have given way to a recognition that capitalism may actually be characterized by a long downturn in profitability since the 1970s and that growth that the world system has relied upon to exit such downturns in the past is inimical to the ecological survival of humanity and the other lifeforms that occupy the globe.[21]

Within the cultural sphere, there have been different responses to this moment. In the visual and plastic arts, self-referential irony and political critique has given way to multimedia, installation, and environmental art. In literature, here conceptualized broadly to include popular genres, many of which have achieved canonical status, we find a complicated antinomy (more of a Jamesonian than a Kantian one) between texts that focus primarily on the individual, such as the explosion in the publication and popularity of the memoir, autofiction, and autotheory and those that take on a planetary and even extraplanetary focus often through tales of the near or distant future. In the case of the latter I am thinking of the way in which contemporary science fiction and climate fiction, often with a directly utopian or, more often, dystopian cast has become a central focus of academic scholarship in the present. This dystopian emphasis is also everywhere present in films and television, from *Don't Look Up* and *Squid Game* to *The Hunger Games* and *Annihilation* (even as the possibility of rebirth is always present).

As similar antinomy structures contemporary theory. Parallel to the explosion of memoir in the present is the emergence of autotheory as a dominant genre. Theory, which used to attempt to explain macrological and structuring dimensions of everyday life and used to be organized around a fundamental encounter with otherness has now, in one of its guises, shrunk to theorize the self, which has in turn been writ large. If I began this book by emphasizing the way in which gender, sex, and sexuality have increasingly been organized around a noncontradictory and micrological conception of identity, one that is informed by the algorithmic structures of communication and representation in the present, then the genre of autotheory becomes micro-identity's privileged theoretical articulation. On the other hand, parallel with dystopian science fiction we have the emergence of speculative realism, which challenges the antirealist position that has been central to philosophy since Kant (that is, that we cannot fundamentally know anything about reality in itself but only as it exists for us), articulating instead a new realism, but a wild one.[22] It argues that we need to return to theorizing what exists—hence the return of ontology as a central theoretical category in the present—but such a turn to realism still remains speculative, given the limitations of human perception. While this turn toward realism is admirable in a present defined by climate change, profound inequality, and limited resources, much of speculative realism takes on a kind of otherworldly cast. Rather than theorize the real possibilities, contradictions, and limits that structure human and nonhuman existences, too often it theorizes existence in relationship to the universe as such (as in Meillassoux and Brassier) or becomes a nihilist account of the horrors of the extant (Thacker).[23] Even object-oriented ontology, which is perhaps the most this-worldly of speculative realisms, tends toward theorizing objects in and for themselves rather than in how they shape and interact with humans, animals, and plants. The exception here is the work of Levi Bryant, which consistently theorizes the material in relationship to the human and to ecosystems as well as to other objects.[24]

Another promising development of theory in the present is new materialism. Emerging out of feminist science studies, much new materialism emphasizes the materiality of both bodies and ecosystems. In contrast to the grand theorizing of speculative realism, its theoretical claims are narrower and more precise. Central to much new materialism, from Karen Barad to Mel Chen, is an account of the embodied subject or self, including the racialized self, as it encounters a material world.[25] Chen emphasizes the ways in which ontologies and ideologies of race complicate Western understandings of matter and the differentiation between subject and object. The focus, like the turn to ecological and assemblage art in the plastic arts (or field recordings in the sonic arts), is relationship of the embodied subject to the ecosystems and to the politics of materiality. Central to much of this work is also a Deleuzian emphasis on flow and becoming, focusing on the interchange between bodies and ecosystems or nonhuman entities. New materialism provides a powerful framework for theorizing the materiality of the body in ways that insist on its relationship to the material world and its embeddedness in ecosystems. As such it presents a crucial riposte to the contemporary emphasis on the autonomous individual and the logic of micro-identities.

What seems to be missing from all these frameworks, however, is a conception of scale that can link the subjective and broadly social, human and non-human flourishing to the world ecology and economy. Predictably, it is contemporary Marxist theory that has addressed these questions of scale most effectively while taking on a more materialist cast, whether it is the focus on the structuration of existence by the workings of the value form, the shaping of life possibilities via Marxist versions of biopolitical theory, or a new emphasis on the intersections of the economic and the ecological in eco-Marxism.[26] Central to some of these newer approaches to Marxism is the concept of the commons as well as the immediate production of communist relationships or communization, as the Endnotes collective has theorized. It is to the idea of the commons, as one such attempt to theorize the human relationship to the political economy and the world ecology to which I will turn next. Unlike much recent theorizing of the concept, I emphasize the need to intertwine the common and the public, theorizing the necessary entanglement of the commons, the state, and the global economy. As *The Care Manifesto* argues, we need to scale up our solutions in order to address the global framework at which humans can transform the immiserated, destructive present and produce a more just and resilient future.[27] In what follows I look to building relationships between various instantiations of the commons, the state, the world system, and world ecology in order to overcome the antinomies of contemporary theory and imagine a way we can link different struggles into larger forms of pollical economic, ecological, and social transformation. Of course, the focus here is on sex and embodiment, but I hope it might provide a model for other necessary transformations. Key, as *The Care Manifesto* articulates it, is a recognition of interdependence, or what Jason Read terms, in a more philosophical and political-economic register, transindividuality.

The Commons and Transindividuality

The commons is a key category for theorizing "transindividuality." Read argues that transindividuality represents a fundamental conceptual shift from most contemporary social and economic thought which privileges the individual at the expense of the collective. As I have already said, contemporary neoliberalism and even many of the discourses that are supposed to challenge it seem unable to think forms of collectivity without either further unraveling them to the point of atomization, as in the growth of micro-identities, or overshooting them to the point that human action and social formation become relatively meaningless, as in much speculative realism. Read argues that our inability to think the individual and the collective together is not just an effect of neoliberalism but a theoretical inheritance of the Cold War in which American individualism was celebrated over and against Soviet collectivism, the latter being read as fundamentally totalitarian—and it is striking in this ideological framing that it is not the Soviet state that is the locus of the totalitarian but any attempt at collectivity as such. While the discourse American individualism, as Richard Slotkin has demonstrated,[28] fundamentally predates the Cold War, Read is certainly right that the latter, as it combines with ideas of human capital in neoliberalism, creates a social imaginary that thoroughly privileges the individual at the expense of the collective. And yet his vision does not exclude the individual

> Eclipsed by such a social imaginary is not only collectivity, but more importantly the point of intersection between collectivity, or social relations, and the individual. The two have become a strict binary: either we think in terms of the individual, making it both an analytic and evaluative center of our thought, or we affirm an all-encompassing collective, which washes the individual away in a night in which all jumpsuits are grey.[29]

Crucial to Read's argument is the understanding of transindividuality as constructing a mutual relationship between individuality and collectivity. Rather than being in opposition or, as he puts it, "a strict binary," the two constitute each other and depend upon each other for their emergence. For example, Marx's account of the figure of the bourgeois individual only takes shape with the large-scale and collective emergence of capitalist social relationships. Individuals are less an opposition to the collective than a product of the way in which we conceptualize and politicize the collective. The opposite is also true: our conception of collectivity depends, in part, upon how we conceptualize and politicize the position of the individual. Neither term is static, nor are they, to use Read's words, in a zero-sum game. Instead, both are historical categories that change over time and in relationship to each other. Similarly, they are categories of world making; they are construction materials for the social. In what follows, I want to think of the individual and the collective as dialectical categories, ones necessary to each other and always in motion. What one of these categories means is always an effect of the other. Moreover, their definitions are in motion rather than static.

In arguing for a sexual and embodied commons, then, I am not arguing for a sexual and embodied free-for-all. This is not a vision of a 1970s-style sex cult (you can tune into *People Magazine Investigates Cults* if you are looking for your fix, and I may just join you). Nor am I arguing for a negation of individual rights, desires, or practices. While it may be somebody's kink, the world of gray Hegelian jumpsuits imagined by Read does not sound sexy enough to build a sustaining vision of collective sexuality around. Moreover, whatever its theoretical limitations, individual consent in sexual and embodied matters is too crucial a concept for preventing forms of sexual and embodied coercion to jettison it in relationship to some collective vision of sexual world building. Still, even though we want to affirm individual relationships to consent, desire, fantasy, and practice, this does not mean that such ineluctably individual dimensions of sex and embodiment form the horizon of what can be imagined and built in terms of producing collective embodied and sexual flourishing. Before articulating this vision of a sexual and embodied commons, it is crucial to provide a more general account of the concept of the commons. It is to such an account that I turn next.

Defining the Commons

Simply put, the commons describes what is common to people outside of and in opposition to both capitalist conceptions of private property and state notions of the public. It is what is shared, produced, and exchanged in common by people. Michael Hardt and Antonio Negri define it as a "democracy" that "is imaginable and possible only because we all share and participate in the common," which they define as both the "wealth of the material world" and "forms of social production such as knowledges, languages, codes, information, affects and so forth."[30] Thus, they emphasize both the wealth already present in the material world, with which we have an ecosystemic relationship, and the wealth and forms of connection that human communities build through collective production, including more obdurately material infrastructures and the more immaterial (or, precisely, alter-material) infrastructures attaching to language, information, and affects. In theorizing a sexual and embodied commons it will be important to keep both of these meanings in mind.

Building off of Hardt and Negri while also revising their vision, Christian P. Haines and Peter Hitchcock provide the following poetic definition of the commons, which I find compelling in its attention to concept's multiplicity:

the commons is: a genre of practice, hence *to common*: to transform
matter into something shared in common, to deprivatize social relations and material resources; a history: precapitalist customs of resource sharing, as well as the emerging forces of production associated
with digital capitalism; a mode of governance or institutionality, ulti-
mately an non-state-based, non-property-based means of coordinating
activity and participating in collective life; a generic capacity for sociality and solidarity, perhaps located in a specific social class but shared
universally as a presupposition of sociality as such; and a political
event: a complex mode of transition to a postcapitalist society.[31]

This definition is rich in its complexity, and I cannot do full justice to it
here. However, I do want to call attention to a few of its crucial formulations.
While they talk about the commons as singular here, and we need to think of
all the different forms of the commons as intersecting and forming one common, they also emphasize that there are many different manifestations of the
commons within this overarching category. The special issue of *Minnesota
Review* that Haines and Hitchcock introduce here is a perfect example of the
multiplicity of commons, addressing topics such as the queer commons, the
energy commons, the common university, the Indigenous commons, and more.
Haines and Hitchcock also emphasize that the commons is fundamentally
about production. It is a common practice, a form of producing collective
flourishing by transforming matter for the sustenance of life and communities.
As such, it is fundamentally about deprivatizing the lifeworld, making the
infrastructure and practices that sustain it collective. As they also note, the
practice of the commons, while having a potentially universal horizon, is often
associated with specific class or class fractions that have different relationships
to production as well as to race and gender. Thus, it is often a practice of the
working class or underclass and exists in excess of their waged work or the
conventional practices by which the work of social reproduction is done. One
thinks of collective forms of childcare or community parenting within working-
class and/or communities of color, to take just two examples. One also thinks
about other forms of mutual aid as Dean Spade theorizes them, including
"vibrant social networks in which we not only do work in a group, but also have
friendships, make art, have sex, mentor parents and kids, feed ourselves and
each other, build radical land and housing experiments, and inspire each other
about how we can cultivate liberation in all aspects of our lives."[32]

As Haines and Hitchcock also argue, the commons also long predates capitalism (although it often takes on different characteristics within capitalism),
being a fundamental way in which social life has been organized throughout

much of human history. It also, hopefully, will long outlast capitalism, especially if we hope to persist and flourish on this planet for more than the next century. Finally, the commons may be anti-state in its pure form, but it is not anti-institution. Institutions and the building of social structures and relations are crucial dimensions of the commons.

Such forms of common life can be privatized and capitalized, as is evident in the workings of accumulation by dispossession whether it be, as Elizabeth Maddock Dillon has cogently argued, the privatizations produced by racialized plantation capitalism in the early modern world, the primitive accumulation produced by enclosures and the building of factories in eighteenth-century England detailed by Marx, or the forms of privatization and appropriation of public goods (such as education or health care), collective practices (such as the appropriation of Indigenous medicinal knowledges by pharmaceutical companies), and the privatization of life chances through the creation of individual and collective debt by contemporary forms of financialization that, as Maurizio Lazzarato has argued, work to colonize the future as well.[33] The commons forms in opposition to these dynamics and persists beneath and beside them (take, for example, what Dillon describes as the "provision grounds" produced by slave populations in which they grew their own food for "sustenance and local exchange"), or the way that forms of public sex and cruising, as Samuel R. Delany and José Esteban Muñoz have differently argued, can function in noncommodified spaces such as public parks, libraries, and restrooms or in excess of the commercial uses of given spaces, such as bathhouses and clubs.[34]

Such persistence within explicitly capitalist spaces, whether the plantation or the contemporary city, suggests the political limits of certain conceptions of the commons. It does not challenge capitalism so much as persist as a distinct set of cultural practices within it. Yet it also suggests that the commons is never thoroughly eradicated and can be scaled up and rearticulated in ways that can fundamentally transform the social. Even in profoundly necropolitical spaces such as the plantation or the divested urban warzones such as many of the parts of Chicago that produced footwork and drill scenes (which, while sometimes capitalized, often function as spaces of the commons in terms of shared YouTube videos and the like), the commons persists. This very persistence demonstrates ways of organizing social life in opposition to the violent forms of accumulation, immiseration, and inequality that are fundamental to the capitalist world system.

The relationship of the commons to the state is more complicated. The critique of state actions and of state violence toward various populations (both internal and external) and what they hold in common is a crucial dimension of theories of the commons. Yet dismantling various states and their remaining (although deeply compromised) institutions before dismantling and transforming the global capitalist economy, rather than being radical, enacts one of the core goals of neoliberalism. Indeed, too much contemporary and ostensibly left theory, particularly in the United States, reproduces the logic of neoliberalism with its hostility to social institutions. Thus, while Foucauldian critique is valuable and necessary (particularly in its focus on biopolitics), without a vision of a better and more just future society, it can slip imperceptibly into an affirmation of the local and libertarian. Theory becomes a version of what Anna Kornbluh calls "anarcho-vitalism," or a celebration of the formless, immanent, and local with no attention to the need for complex formal and institutional structures, some necessary verticality, and the ability to work at the necessary scale to have fundamental social, economic, and ecological impact.[35]

Certainly, it is crucial to critique state institutions and such critiques should be in the service of making them more just, democratic, and supportive of positive liberties, but to see them as the central locus of exploitation and violence globally is to miss the ways in which many of them can be used to promote positive liberties and set limits on the ravages produced by global capitalism. To the degree that they do not function this way anymore, it says more about the destruction and repurposing of social institutions under the aegis of supporting capitalist accumulation than it does about the structural impact of institutions as such. There is no way of making capitalism just. It is fundamentally organized around inequality, the destruction of necessary ecosystems, and the immiseration of the many to the profit of the few. To put it bluntly, the fundamental locus of violence in the present is the capitalist world economy. While much violence has been done in the name of state institutions, particularly as they have aided and abetted imperialism, capitalist accumulation, warfare, and the policing, incarceration, surveillance, and enslavement of various marginalized populations, theoretically the role of the institution is more neutral. Institutions are not inimical to collective flourishing. Indeed, when they genuinely and justly promote public good, as in providing fully accessible (that is, free to the user and invested in undoing various forms of social inequality) public education, public health, environmental sustainability, and general socioeconomic flourishing, they become the fundamental building blocks of a society.

Of course, the question of institutions is different than that of the state, and if we build strong enough and just transnational institutions the state may begin to be an unnecessary and parochial entity. The best theories of the commons, such as Hardt and Negri's account of the common and Imre Szeman's argument for an "energy commons," recognize that robust institutions are a feature of any genuinely realizable collective enterprise that persists beyond the immediate moment of activism.[36] At the point that we have developed robust and lasting transnational institutions, we may want to hasten the state's demise. But until we can build such institutions and transform the fundamental features of the global economy, state formations, particularly in their role in sustaining life (fundamentally in their biopolitical role and not in their necro-political one, although disentangling these two is of course complicated and perhaps never finally possible), may be necessary to maintain. Central to the most powerful visions of the commons are socialist and radically democratic institutions, including what Cesare Casarino calls the common university, what Szeman calls the energy commons, and we can add a series of other in-stitutions: the health commons, the commons for economic flourishing, the ecological commons, and as I will argue, the sexual commons and the embod-ied commons.[37]

Before theorizing the sexual and embodied commons, it is crucial to first turn to theorizing what Stefano Harney and Fred Moten call the undercom-mons. If the global economy forms in a dialectical tension from above with the commons as it creates and repurposes social life, the undercommons forms in dialectical tension with the commons from below (to use Harney and Moten's spatial metaphor).[38] Being underneath, here, is not merely a negative concep-tion, as in being exploited, oppressed, or disenfranchised. It also suggests a series of positive qualities, including a closeness to infrastructure, to the ground, the earth, the street, and to the most intense effects of power. For Harney and Moten, the undercommons is their figure of those who have been dispossessed, made fugitive, made alien not only by settler colonialism and the state as it has practiced anti-Blackness and anti-Indigenous racism, but also by many con-ceptions of the commons itself. Susan Hegeman argues that the idea of the commons is central to contemporary Indigenous political struggles: "But whatever its limitations as a concept, the idea of the commons persists in po-litical discourse, and it is particularly prominent in the political arsenal of ideas animating current international indigenous politics. Indigenous leaders and their allies have invoked the language of the commons to assert their stakes in struggles over traditional forms of knowledge and over key resources, including land, water, and even the climate."[39]

Indeed, as we discussed earlier, any nonprovincial account of the commons must recognize that it has been a fundamental dimension of human organiza-tion long before the histories of both capitalism and Euro-American imperialism, whether it is the collective resource use and stewardship in Indigenous societies and peasant communities or the ever-present work of social reproduction. Yet, in too many conceptions of the commons coming out of Euro-American theory the prehistory and ongoing history of the dispossession of the commons by the intertwined histories of capitalism, slavery, and settler colonialism, dispossession that typically takes place not only along class lines but raced and gendered ones as well, is ignored or forgotten. The question of "whose commons?" becomes crucial.

It is in response to this question that the concept of the undercommons becomes central. The production of the commons as a genuinely democratic and communist enterprise is never without conflict and struggle. Instead, it represents the beginning of a new chapter of history rather than the end. The undercommons, then, represents a crucial locus of struggle around the definition of the commons. It is the idea of the commons as articulated by those who have been dispossessed, disenfranchised, and rendered fugitive. It thus dialectically challenges the institutions of the commons to recognize this history of dispossession and be transformed accordingly. The commons and the undercommons in such a vision (like the various manifestations of the commons and institutions of governance attaching to them) function in a necessary dialectical tension with each other.

The Sexual Commons

What if we conceived of sex as fundamentally transindividual? What if we assumed, as I argued in the earlier chapters of this book, that it is fundamentally social? It always involved a relationship to otherness, one that not only is present in the existence of actual others either individually or collectively but also in relationship to the other within, the unconscious and its fundamentally extimate relationship to our egoic sense of self. As Read theorizes it, the individual and the social are always realized in relationship to each other. So, if we have sexual subjectivities or sexual desires, these emerge and take on significance only by being routed through the social, whether this social dimension is recognized by the larger society or not. Ideas of individual property, which individualist notions of identity (that is, micro-identities) affirm, become a fundamental way of effacing the social and collective constitution of sexuality, just as bourgeois conceptions of private property both depend on and obscure the fundamentally social production of everyday life.

So what if we take this collective dimension of sexuality as our starting point for thinking about a better and more just way of organizing and conceptualizing sexual life? Since we are able to imagine a political, economic, and energy commons, it is not clear why we cannot imagine a sexual commons. While, as I argued earlier, state structures may be necessary to produce a scaled-up

politics of economic, ecological, and social justice, at least until we have institutions vibrant and powerful enough to resist capitalist incursions and contribute
to the transformation of the world economy, the state seems a particularly
problematic entity through which to regulate sexuality. As with the long history
of state dispossession of and genocidal violence toward Indigenous communities, the history of various state undertakings in regard to sexuality is a grim
one. States often work to impose a particularly narrow, constrictive, and violent
conception of sexual normativity (take the long history of the criminalization
of homosexuality in the United States as merely one example). Various state
biopolitical programs have often functioned to dismantle reproductive rights
(limiting childbirth, demanding it, nonconsensually sterilizing specific populations, and so on), and recast sexuality in a firmly heteronormative reproductive
framework. States have often embraced sex panics and used them to their own
ends. Finally, until the framework and application of liberal law itself is transformed, too much state practice is organized around both a carceral logic
(particularly in the United States) and an individualist one, which is not to say
that states do not have a role in protecting positive liberties, like the legality of
consensual sexual practices, however nonnormative, and the rights and practices that underpin what Loretta J. Ross and Rickie Solinger term "reproductive
justice."[40] But the state is finally not what will enable or produce a genuine
transformation in sexual cultures. The state will need to be transformed by a
flourishing sexual commons, one that may be localized in different places but
one that may also be transnational in scope, and the institutions it produces.

I want to propose an idea of the sexual commons and rather than casting
this conception in the framework of rights, which quickly shifts the entire
discussion to notions of individual liberty and its carceral removal, I want to
cast it in terms of responsibilities and pleasures. Such a discussion of responsibilities is inherently normative. While the critique of normativity has been
a crucial dimension of queer theory and I want to maintain its focus on the
ways in which discourses of normativity can justify various forms of sexual
exclusion and violence, I agree with José Esteban Muñoz's powerful account
of the limits of the "anti-social" and "anti-utopian" strain of queer theory and
his positing of queerness as fundamentally about imagining a better sexual
future.[41] Queerness needs a normative vision of the future even as it maintains
its investment in critiquing heteronormative discourses. In imagining such a
queer version of the future, my own approach echoes that of Samuel R. Delany,
who argues in Times Square Red, Times Square Blue that his "argument's po-
lemical thrust is toward conceiving, organizing, and setting into place new
establishments—and even entirely new types of institutions—that would offer
the services and fulfill the social functions provided by the porn houses that

encouraged sex among the audience."[42] We absolutely need to imagine such institutions of collective sexual flourishing. We also need to imagine a collective sexual ethos. This is what I articulate below. While my emphasis on pleasures, in what follows, takes its inspiration of Foucault, particularly in the first and second volumes of *The History of Sexuality*, the vision here, unlike the seemingly micrological focus of *The Uses of Pleasure*, is toward a large-scale social enterprise.[43]

The sexual commons recognizes that sex (even the seemingly most individualized, asexual, or antisocial of sexual practices) is fundamentally social. It is part of the social glue that binds humans together and connects them to the larger world in which they exist. Of course, sex often has a great deal of negativity bound up with it too, whether this negativity is a product of unconscious trauma (which Laplanche places at the center of the formation of sexuality as such via enigmatic signifiers and trauma theory often sees as shaping sexual development) and unacceptable wishes, whether it is the product of fantasies (which are culturally mediated although not reducible to cultural determination), or whether it is an effect of the extimacy of the drives (or drive in Lacan's conception, in which the erotic drive and the death drive are one in the same).[44] Precisely because sex involves both positive pleasures, ecstasies, and intimacies and negative (and here I use the term in a descriptive sense, not in terms of moral judgment) fantasies or drives around sadism, masochism, and egoic destruction, sex needs to be thought about in terms of responsibilities as well as pleasures.

The sexual commons involves the following responsibilities and pleasures:

1. The pleasures and responsibilities that come with the creation of material institutions supporting not only public sex but the exploration of different sexual pleasures and different forms of sexual expression. On the most material of levels, a sexual commons would involve publicly supported institutions for the practice of consensual sex in all its forms. These would be spaces of collective sexual pleasure and responsibility. Such institutions have been central to the long history of queer community formation, including bathhouses, buffet flats, leather bars, dungeons, cruising spaces, adult theaters, adult stores, public parks, and more. While some of these institutions have also been part of straight culture, public sex itself, like other nonnormative practices, is often perceived as by definition queer. Moreover, historically, the queer community has taken the lead in producing such spaces. We should follow this lead. While by necessity, these spaces have typically been commercial

and for profit (although many of them are run as a labor of love and community building), we can look to them to build a set of institutions that are common and anticapitalist. Moreover, the practice of cruising in public spaces, as has been differently described by José Muñoz and David Wojnarowicz among others, is fundamentally noncapitalist, transforming public spaces into a sexual commons.[45] We can look to the practice of cruising as a guide for building new noncommercial public sex culture that can be part of a democratic socialist society. While these institutions would be publicly funded, they would be run by the communities themselves rather than by the state (hence they would still be a commons). Certainly, the different practices and communities supported by the sexual commons would need to be reflexive about who is included and who is excluded in its different instantiations, but this would be decided collectively and democratically, rather than by the market (take the disappearance of lesbian clubs in the present as one example of what happens when we let the market be the mediator of sexual institutions). Such democratic, common spaces would be the basis for a material sexual commons, one that can be an integral part of a larger democratic socialist or communist society.

2. The responsibility to recognize the social dimensions of sexuality and the pleasure that this recognition may generate. I have already made this argument in the introduction and chapter 2, but I will recap it briefly here. Sexuality, however, individualized, eschewed, unconscious, or unfelt, has its initial genesis in our relationship to otherness. Sex forms as an internal other as well as an externalized dimension of the subject. And while we can organize our relationship to sexual or erotic pleasure (or its absence) however we want, it is crucial that we recognize that it is a social entity that we are individually articulating, one that we have a responsibility to beyond ourselves.

3. The responsibility of and pleasure in enabling sexuality to flourish (whatever form this flourishing takes) for both groups and individuals. Sexuality is something that we should affirm and take pleasure in as a source of social connection and as an expression of collectivity. In making this argument, I am not thinking merely about active physical sex but the erotic dimensions of world building and making, whether such building and making involves intellectual work, physical work, affective work, or some complex mix of all of these. In arguing for the dimensions of pleasure involved in work, I

do not want to efface the physical exhaustion and bodily violence that can be produced by work, particularly under conditions of exploitation, coercion, or oppression. I do want to affirm, however, that work at its most pleasurable and satisfying can be about realizing social desire. Such desire has its roots in sexuality and often maintains an erotic and pleasurable dimension. One product of the degradation of work and the expansion of our identification as consumers under neoliberalism is the fundamental separation of work and pleasure. Yet the two can and should inform each other.

4. The responsibility to recognize and the invitation to enjoy the individuated and unconscious dimensions of sexuality in each subject. So many of our notions of sexuality stem from the idea that we direct and control it in a rational way. Certainly, we have a responsibility to subjectify our relationship to sexuality, which means recognizing ourselves within it, taking responsibility for it, and bringing what we can of it into the symbolic. Yet, we fundamentally exist in an extimate and decentered relationship to it; it typically has its own motive force. While we can take responsibility around acting or not around our relationship to sex, sex (as physical desire) itself is fundamentally recalcitrant to conscious shaping. It resists being cleaned up, gentrified, or domesticated (unless this is part of its kink). As someone who enjoys domestic pleasures and cleanliness, these are not negative categories for me. I am just indicating that sex, as physical desire, tends to resist too much social shaping. This is why it is fundamentally absurd when people try to argue that sexual orientations can be changed through willpower, whether these demands to change it are from the right (the idea that homosexuality can be "cured") or the ostensible left (the idea that one should desire all embodiments and identities equally, as in pansexuality—if one is pansexual that's excellent, but it does not function as an elective choice). On a symbolic level we can and should strive for fundamental equality, but sexual desire is both willful and particular. As I argued earlier, it comes initially from outside of us and remains an intimate stranger.

5. The responsibility to attend to the workings of power in relationship to sexuality and attendant pleasures it may produce. It is crucial for us to realize that power functions in sexual relationships just as it does in the rest of society. In making this argument, I am not arguing for a concept that ostensibly good or proper sexual relationships involve people with equal social power. Too many

affirmative sexual relationships and encounters with difference would be excluded from such a framework. Moreover, differences in power, in social situation or location, and cultural background can be, and often are powerful aphrodisiacs in both directions. What I am arguing for is that we need an individual and collective sense of responsibility around how power plays out in relationships and whether such forms of power are pleasurable and largely affirming or whether they merely reproduce and exploit the violence of inequality. Of course, given the much more equitable and just society that this chapter (and book) attempts to imagine, some questions of power will hopefully be obviated. Yet it is hard to imagine a society in which power and hierarchy are absent. Moreover, I am not sure we want to. The left needs to embrace power while being responsible with it. It too is a fundamental building block of the social. Thus, rather than ruling sex out in workspaces we need to work to insure its consensual dimensions. Legal adjudication of such relationships should be less focused on hindering liability and more focused on supporting those who are on the less powerful end of such relationships. It should also be invested in affirming relationships that are clearly consensual, whatever the differential in power, as long as both parties agree not to be part of a direct relationship of supervision, authority, or oversight. One symptom of the attempt to purge sex from workplaces and other public spaces is the depressing turn to (or return of) fantasies of incest in contemporary porn. The sexuality that is repressed from the public sphere returns in the familial space of the private.

6. The responsibility to recognize that sex involves labor as well as pleasure. While many of us would love to be able to thoroughly separate the pleasurable dimensions of sex from the more laborious aspects of it, the two are inextricably bound together. Even masturbation involves a certain baseline of labor to achieve its pleasures. Moreover, sex contributes to several different forms of social reproduction. Sex can of course be involved in the literal process of human (and nonhuman) reproduction, and it is crucial to recognize the labors attaching both to conception and to the work of pregnancy and giving birth. There is a reason that the latter process is called "labor." Yet the designation should not just rest there. Pregnancy and childbirth are powerful and exacting forms of labor. It is not just with the birth of children that the work of social reproduction begins. Pregnancy and childbirth are often narrated in

heteronormative terms. Such narratives fundamentally obscure how queer a process pregnancy and childbirth can be. First it is not just women who can carry children and give birth. Second, as Sophie Lewis argues, various frameworks of surrogacy, single parenting, and collective parenting work to complicate the conventional understanding of the relationship between childrearing and motherhood.[46] While it is crucial to emphasize the work is done by the pregnant person (surrogate or not), it is also crucial to recognize the other forms of work that go into the process, from the work of other caregivers to doula, midwife, and medical work. Of course, the work attaching to the physical reproduction of the species is not the only form of labor associated with sex. Far from it. The act of sex involves physical exertion and affective labor. Indeed, when money is exchanged for such labor, we call it sex work. While it is crucial to theorize the distinctiveness, distinctive risks, and forms of exploitation, as well as affirmative possibility, attaching to sex work and produce laws and practices that legalize and protect it, it is also important to recognize that all sex involves a version of sex work. Such a recognition may help to destigmatize sex work and help produce better working conditions around it. Even as we imagine a socialist or communist commons in which labor is decommodified and the social dimensions of labor are affirmed, official sex work may persist, even as what it is exchanged for it may change and the conditions under which it operates hopefully improve. But in asserting that all sex involves sex work, I want to emphasize the way in which even sex that doesn't involve the exchange of money or involves a great deal of pleasure also involves work, often including the work of connecting to and caring for those with whom you fuck. This is true as much in a different way with anonymous or casual sex, where particular attention needs to be paid to consent and the reality of being with someone whose fantasies, desires, and limits are less intimately known. Recognizing that all sex involves sex work also help mark when one feels like the work component is too much and the pleasure component is too little, without pathologizing ambivalent but consensual sex (and I think almost everyone who has an active sex life has had this experience). While we should feel empowered to reject sex (here again is where theories of asexuality have made an important contribution), the mix of pleasure and work reveals the way in which sex, in its banality and repetition, can become less than fully desirable. It underscores the ways in which many of us do certain activities because it pleases our partner and functions as a form of consensual care. It also gives us a labor-based language to articulate as much and to demand different conditions of pleasure and work. Finally and, hopefully, most important, it also invokes the utopian promise of dissolving the line between labor and pleasure, in which work itself is a core element of pleasure. Central to many midcentury Marxist visions, particularly those of Adorno and Marcuse, was the undoing of the reification of work and leisure into separate spheres and the degradation of the former into meaningless drudgery and the latter into commodified pleasures.[47] For Marcuse, then, pleasure and work become one—fusing to produce the pleasure of aesthetic production. I will add that there is a deep pleasure that is also an affirmative form of labor, involved in sex of all sorts and with all kinds of partners. Indeed, the sexual and the aesthetic merge here. This is one of the core things that a sexual commons would affirm. Of course, as Adorno regularly warned, the undoing of an opposition can function in dystopian as much as utopian ways.[48] So, under neoliberalism and the gig economy, work and nonwork become increasingly blurry and even play, like endlessly replaying the battle in a From Software game (like *Soulsborne* or *Elden Ring*), can come to feel more grueling than one's paid labor. Still, it is crucial to affirm the pleasurable dimensions of sex as well as the labor that can be involved. For example, a friend who is a masochist in bed said that playing *Soulsborne* and other From Software games felt like a form of pleasurable masochism. If that's your kink, all power to you! Sex is interestingly a part of our lives in which work and pleasure have not been set in full opposition. As such, at its best, it can function as an index of what a nonreified world might feel like, where work produces pleasure and pleasure is derived from work.

7. The responsibility to recognize and work with cultural and subjective differences around sexuality and sexual practices as well as the pleasure of learning and engaging in different sexual practices. Here is where the importance of not losing focus on difference in producing a commons becomes particularly important, whether such differences are cultural or individual. Similarly, here is where Read's notion of transindividuality becomes important. We cannot efface individual and cultural differences around sexuality without potentially doing violence. Certainly cultural notions and investments can change, hybridize, and transform, but such transformations

should happen not through unilateral coercion or imposition. It is crucial to maintain a healthy valuation, respect for, as well as critical evaluation of different cultural practices around sex. This can extend from different sexual practices in different world cultures to different subcultural practices within a given culture. As with ethnographic knowledge when practiced at its best, it is crucial to understand a set of processes from within before evaluating them from without. It is also crucial to reflect on one's own positionality in analyzing or critiquing a given set of cultural practices. I am not advocating cultural relativism. It is important to be able to criticize, speak and fuck across cultural divides and it is important to devise ethical and political principles that can be agreed upon and shared across cultures. There is as much truth gained from looking from without as looking from within at a given cultural or historical formation. Indeed, both perspectives are necessary. What I am advocating is that we be reflexive and careful when looking from both vantages. Rather than the opposition between criminalization of certain practices (like genital mutilation or extreme forms of BDSM, which can produce lasting harm) and a cultural relativist or libertarian affirmation of them, we need to develop a critical, thoughtful, cross-cultural dialogue around these issues, paying particular attention to the most impacted or marginalized within a given cultural or subcultural context. This responsibility then directly connects with the next point.

8. The responsibility of recognizing that violent and nonconsensual sex can produce trauma and the responsibility of care and healing that must take place around such traumatic experiences. It is crucial that we recognize the ubiquity of sexual violence. This has been one of the important dimensions of the #MeToo movement not only in the United States but around the globe and the crucial work done by feminist theory and organizing over the last fifty years. Yet it also is crucial that we do not make sexual violence the master trope by which we understand sex itself. While sexual violence is far too common, sex as pleasure is at least just as common, I would suggest. #MeToo, at its best, was trying to reclaim sexual pleasure by calling out the routinization of sexual violence. While aspects of the movement have been criticized in terms of whose voices got heard and credited (Black activist Tarana Burke started the movement, but Alyssa Milano and other high-profile celebrity activists got all the credit) and in terms of conflating radically

different forms of nonconsensual acts from nonconsensual cheek kissing to the most brutal of sexual assaults (as Oliver Davis and Tim Dean have noted), the movement has crucially contributed to the recognition that sexual violence is a routinized part of many societies and cultures and that this disproportionately affects women, including transwomen, and those feminized by the culture.[49] Because of its pervasive nature, the conventional response by liberal law of incarceration and individual responsibility, always unequally applied in terms of class and race, feels like it merely contributes to a culture of violence (or, at best, a bad status quo) rather than providing a solution to it. This carceral approach particularly becomes fraught given that rape in prison is also a major problem (I do not want to equate all sex in prison with rape, a discourse that reproduces homophobia, but it is also a pervasive problem, one we should be concerned about if we are opposed to sexual violence). So, in solidarity both with movements against cultures of sexual assault like #MeToo and in solidarity with the movements for the decarceralization of American society, such as the prison and police abolition movements and the advocacy of community policing, the sexual commons would need to rethink how we respond productively to sexual violence and its regularity. First, I think making this a collective responsibility rather than an individual one is crucial, both in terms of helping the person who has been assaulted heal and find a way of living a rewarding and pleasurable life again (to the degree that it is possible, given that responses to trauma vary greatly) and transforming the cultures of sexual violence that have made it such a routinized occurrence. We need to create collective cultures of healing and transformation. The focus, of course, should be on the safety and recovery of the person assaulted and those who also may be vulnerable to assault by the same person or people. In terms of the perpetrator, steps should be taken to make sure that the violence is not repeated. But in terms of challenging the routinization of sexual violence, it is fundamentally a matter of producing the larger cultural transformations that the sexual commons promises. Some of this work is educational and pedagogical (and the dearth of sex education in the United States in the present is one of the main culprits in the regularity of sexual assault in this country). Some of this is about transforming sexist and masculinist cultures. All of it is about making sexual violence the responsibility of all.

9. The responsibility and pleasure of talking about sex. Sex is not only
   about bodies fucking, but also about discourse. Lacan famously begins Seminar 11 with the following declaration (which I used as the
   epigraph for chapter 1): "In other words—for the moment, I am not
   fucking, I am talking to you. Well! I can have exactly the same satisfaction as if I were fucking. That's what it means. Indeed, it raises
   the question of whether I am not fucking at this moment."[50] Lacan
   is precisely right here. Sex not only informs our explicitly carnal actions, but it also motivates and shapes our discourse. As desire, it is
   also the glue that binds social relationships. So rather than try to
   contain sex or remove it from public discourse, which various kinds
   of institutional and workplace edicts attempt to do, we need to recognize that sex is fundamentally already part of public discourse.
   Indeed, it is one of the latter's foundations. In arguing this, I am
   not arguing that all discourses are permissible in institutions and
   workplaces. Of course, explicit sexual discourses in such spaces can
   be used as forms of harassment and symbolic violence and there
   should be recourse to stop such actions. What I am arguing is that
   the goal of eliminating sex as discourse (and as a consensual activity for that matter) from the workplace or various institutions is fundamentally misguided. Indeed, the activity is doomed to fail. For,
   given the capacious conception of sex that has been central to this
   project and that is central to psychoanalysis at its most radical, sex
   underpins the workings of sociality itself. If anything, we need
   more discourse about sex, in the classroom, in the general society,
   in the bedroom, and in the sex club. Such a commitment to sexual
   discourse in all of its forms would be part of the sexual commons.
   As I mentioned, one of the real crimes of the past fifty years in the
   United States is the destruction of sex education in grade schools.
   Moreover, given Florida's ban on the use of the word "gay" and its
   war on transgender people more generally, teaching risky material
   can get you into administrative trouble these days. The climate for
   teaching about sex, particularly queer, kink, and other nonnormative sex practices is becoming ever more hostile. And yet the need
   to talk about sex is never more pressing. Samuel R. Delany may be
   correct in arguing that the first waves of widely available, filmic
   porn in the 1970s functioned as a kind of substitute or supplemen-
   tal sex education for a lot of straight people, teaching men especially, who were often still educated to look at the whole act as
   sinful and one-sided, the pleasures of cunnilingus, different sexual

positions, and attending to the woman's pleasure.[51] However, the combination of the ubiquity of contemporary online porn with the dearth of sex education has not been as salutary for contemporary forms of sexual knowledge and practice. Do not misunderstand me. I am not anti-porn. As with other forms of sex work, the most pressing issues attaching to it are around labor and the conditions of its production. As a form, I think it has utopian as well as potentially dystopian uses and resonances. But porn without a discourse around how it is supposed to function—fundamentally as a form of fantasy that is designed to get you off—can miseducate viewers about best or even workable practices in the bedroom and other places of sexual encounter. We need a discourse that recognizes the status of fantasy and its workings and that frames porn as fantasy. You may want to realize a number of fantasies in your actual sex life, but such realization takes discussion, consent, and a recognition of the difference of the other person's or persons' fantasies. And, for many, porn may stage fantasies that they may not want to realize in everyday life. For the sexual commons, discourse about sex and discourse as sex will be crucial. Language and desire are two of the building blocks of our social worlds. Sex at its most expansive is also such a constructive entity.

10. The responsibility and pleasure involved in recognizing and realizing the world-building dimensions of sex. As I just argued, sex is a fundamental building material of our social worlds. Desire is what binds us to others and, as Lacan and Laplanche both demonstrate, desire is fundamentally social. It is the intimate presence of the other in the subject. It is also what drives our desire to build social worlds. A central tenet of the sexual commons is that the more that we recognize the sexual dimension of the social the more effective we will be at building just, pleasurable, and sustainable collectivities. On the face of it, this claim may seem wildly optimistic. Sex, of course, is not all about peace, love, and understanding (although, of course, there is nothing funny about the latter, as Elvis Costello, via Nick Lowe, reminds us). Instead, sex also contains aggression, envy, and other seemingly antisocial or destructive facets. As Freud argues in *Civilization and its Discontents*, human culture seems to be shaped by both productive and destructive forces, which he metaphorizes as Eros (a more culturally capacious, and less precise, version of his earlier concept of the sex drive) and Thanatos (a similarly capacious and nebulous reworking of the death drive).[52]

Lacan, recognizing that these drives do not manifest as separate but are expressed in complex manifestations of jouissance, makes them a singular drive and complicates the workings of this drive well beyond Freud's more philosophical reflections in *Civilization and its Discontents*, which was written for a lay audience. Lacan's reworking seems right, at least in terms of our discussion of sex here. Sex can be as destructive and disruptive (although these aspects may also have their uses and pleasures) as it can be connective and productive. Here is where discourse and fantasy become important again. Both discourse and fantasy are imaginary and symbolic ways of mediating the drive. Certainly, actions, including sexual actions, are mediations of the drive. Desire, of course, is never fully realizable in the Lacanian schema. Thus, not all of our sexuality is realized in sex, even for the sluttiest of us. There is always surplus jouissance. Moreover, much sex also informs our other productions, discourses, and actions. It informs what we build together as a commons and it informs the pleasure we take in such building. Freud, of course, called the redirecting of the sexual toward other cultural activities sublimation. Sublimation seems an acceptable term for it, except that it often suggests a kind of repression or a making less explicit of sexuality. Instead, I want to see it as an active and positive force. Sex manifests in everything we do and the world that we build together. Because it fuses with other materials, physical, symbolic, and phantasmatic, we often have more control over how we relate to this version of sexuality. Yet it is also crucial to recognize (and, when we can, take pleasure in) the presence of the drive in all of our actions, thoughts, productions, and communications. Finally, such a broad conception of sex, suggests a key role for the symbolic. The symbolic is where we can "work through," to use Freud's phrase, our relationship to the sexual and the ways in which it infuses imaginary antagonisms and social fantasies (both of which are present everywhere online while masquerading as purely rational discourse).[53] The symbolic, with help from the imaginary, is also where we can produce a fundamentally different relationship to the real, which can in turn be the locus of both psychic and social transformation. Such a reflexive relationship to the symbolic, imaginary, and real are crucial for realizing a version of the commons that will not, pace Joy Division, tear itself apart or be organized around fundamental antagonisms with other collectivities.

The Embodied Commons

Of course, sex cannot function without a relationship to embodiment. However sublimated it becomes and however much we want to emphasize the discursive dimensions of sex, it is still fundamentally embodied. We cannot create just sexual relations without just relationships of embodiment. We also cannot create a just material arrangement of the commons if we do not create just relationships of embodiment. Many of our most pressing issues currently are material, including profound global inequality, the climate emergency, the radical unevenness of health care both within nation states and around the globe, the radical unevenness of life chances, the poisoning of so much of the world ecology, and the sixth great extinction, to name only a few of the most pressing. It is also crucial to realize such issues are also fundamentally shaped by inequalities of class, race, gender, sexuality, and geography. For example, one cannot effectively address ecological destruction without addressing ecological racism and the functioning of what Rob Nixon calls slow violence.[54] We need to strive for symbolic equality within the commons as well. The two should, of course, go hand in hand, but neoliberalism has made an industry out of affirming symbolic inclusion while maintaining ever greater material inequality. The embodied commons will work to produce both.

Any vision of an embodied commons that strives for justice, equality, and flourishing will involve the following affirmations and institutions:

1. Socialist or communist economic institutions. The embodied commons must produce economic institutions that are founded on valorization of labor of all sorts. Such inclusion involves not only what was paid work under capitalism but all the forms of labor, including infrastructural, affective, intellectual, reproductive, cultural, and sexual, that take place within a society. It is important to note that these forms of labor are not mutually exclusive but overlapping. It is only the process of capitalist reification and wage distribution that makes them appear fully distinct. A socialized or communized mode of production is crucial both to produce economic equality and to halt the ecological violence that is being driven primarily by capitalist accumulation on a world scale. In doing so, we need to draw on work in the burgeoning field of eco-Marxism, including the crucial work of Kohei Saito, Imre Szeman, and Jason W. Moore. Once the economy becomes driven by collectively decided upon and articulated needs, especially including embodied needs, we will be able to balance the economic and the ecological, which, as

Brent Ryan Bellamy and Jeff Diamanti have argued, exist in fundamental opposition under capitalism.[55] Democracy, in its most radical versions, needs to be central to such a vision. How such a vision
will be coordinated globally is also an open if crucial question.
Kojin Karatani's proposal for a global socialism that would be made
up of different federated states is certainly one attractive solution.[56]
Even if we would want to imagine a single common, as proposed
by both Hardt and Negri and Pierre Dardot and Christian Laval,
how such a common will be produced and mediated still would
necessarily involve some sort of interface between the local, regional, and global.[57] Still, fundamentally, if we want human (as
well as many other forms of) life to continue on this planet, we
need to end capitalism and develop a workable and ecologically
oriented form of the commons (made up of multiple commons)
and the organizations and institutions, perhaps including states,
that will allow it to flourish.

2. We need institutions that fundamentally will sustain the embodied
flourishing and collective good. These institutions should be free
for the users (as befits a commons) and a central focus of the society that produces them. A central set of institutions would be organized around health care. The focus would not only be on ongoing
and chronic care, but also include pediatric health, reproductive
health, preventative health (which, in a commons, would be fully
detached from the neoliberal discourse of wellness, in which the
responsibility is shifted onto the individual), psychological health,
and sexual and gendered health. There would not be a distinction
between necessary and elective surgery; both would be available
when it makes sense for the person wishing to access it as long as
the society can materially support it. Such options would also be
fully decommodified (as would all other aspects of medical care).
For people to flourish their bodies must be sustained and supported. For such flourishing to be fully realized, we also need to ex-
pand user choice and knowledge in relationship to medical
practice. Transitioning would be free and available on demand as
would abortion. Counseling around these decisions would be offered but not required. We also need to find a way to empower ostensible minors to be able to make consensual choices around what
is done to their bodies and what medical procedures they want to
obtain. The choice to transition as well as the choice to reject unnecessary surgeries around intersex embodiments must be made by

those who are undergoing the procedures, whether they are minors or adults. Recognizing the limitations of agency in relationship to age should not be a reason to efface it completely. Rather than these choices being just a question of ages of consent, they should involve extended discussions between the users and the healthcare professionals, with a recognition of all the complex factors (health, physical development, psychological health) that impinge on the decision. Educational institutions would, of course, also be central to the embodied commons. Ideas, knowledge, and affects are all part of the body and the educational engagement with or production of these will be crucial. An educational system that is not organized around competition but collective learning and problem solving would be one of the most important transformations within democratic socialism. Collective institutions around death and its acceptance will also be crucial. The privatization of death, both in terms of private profit and in terms of the effacement of death and grief from public spaces is one of the most pernicious aspects of capitalist culture. Death is a fundamental dimension of embodiment and yet so much of capitalist culture is organized around its disavowal. Finally, various artistic institutions and practices would be crucial to the commons. Aesthetics are also crucial to human flourishing. They are not merely superstructural or an afterthought but provide the fundamental framework by which we understand and begin to change our embodied relationship to the world.

3. We need practices that reconceptualize the body as trans-corporeal, to use Stacy Alaimo's term, and as part of different corporeal collectivities. Rather than privilege the autonomous, ostensibly self-sufficient, and self-regulating body affirmed by neoliberalism and having its roots in Lockean liberalism, we instead should think of bodies as functioning as part of relational collectivities. Of course, it is crucial to attend to individual forms of bodily needs, experiences of pain, and pathology. Yet the ostensibly autonomous, able-bodied, white, middle-class cis male should no longer be the theoretical norm or standard by which we measure and understand embodiment. Instead, all bodies should be understood as existing in and depending on both an ecosystem and a political-economic system that enables collective flourishing. Within such a framework, all bodies contribute to and are part of the collective. All bodies need support and sustenance to flourish or even to persist. There is no such thing as the independent individual. All

bodies depend on larger ecological, social, and economic systems for their functioning. Moreover, sex, sensuality, and eroticism are also part of the social; they are socially produced and important to human flourishing. The health and needs of anyone within the larger embodied collectivity are the responsibility of the larger collectivity itself, as is the maintenance of a flourishing ecosystem or systems and a just political-economic system. Within such a framework, by thinking of bodies as trans-corporeal and collectively intertwined, we would be able to reconceptualize all bodies as crucial to the work of the collective good and collective flourishing. Such a conception of collectivity would be organized around all kinds of embodiment, including crip embodiment, surgically altered or transitioned embodiment, prosthetic embodiment, and so forth.

4. An embodied commons would also attend to and support the flourishing and conceptual transformation of the flesh, as it has been theorized by Hortense Spillers, C. Riley Snorton, R. A. Judy, Marquis Bey and Alexander Weheliye.[58] As we have explored in earlier chapters, central to this notion of the flesh is that cultural meanings are not just a function of representational distinctions and forms of power. Such distinctions get cut into the flesh in certain, particularly violent or necropolitical contexts, such as slavery and medical experimentation. The flesh is also presented as nonsubjective and fungible (to use Snorton's term) within slavery and, in a more positive register, can be imagined as a form of species being that is destroyed by the reification of the body in capitalist wage work. Those who are enfleshed in slavery are often denied, as Spillers argues, even the privileges of being marked by gender or individuality. A similar dynamic takes place within various forms of experimentation and exploitation of those who are disallowed the status of agential adult or able-bodied citizen. Where anyone is defined as infrahuman, the flesh is at the center of politics. In order to address inequalities around race and the long histories of racial violence within settler colonialism, we need not only a materialist politics that addresses economics and the environment, but also one of the flesh. Thus, we would need to challenge and eradicate the structural systems that make cleavages in humanity between the human and the infrahuman. This would involve a very different conception of the human, as Sylvia Wynter argues, one not based on a Cartesian privileging of the mind over the body (or a splitting of the two) or on Lockean conceptions of the free self as possessing

oneself as property.[59] It also suggests that a genuinely transformational politics cannot just stay on the level of representation but needs to find ways of transforming how we exist in, use, care for, and affectively structure our embodiment. While the fungibility of bodies that were rendered infrahuman was part of the violence of slavery and other systems organized around embodied violence, the connection between bodies that is established within such contexts that exist in opposition to the Enlightenment conception of the individual might point us to an affirmative conception of the flesh as species being that uses it as basis for structuring transindividuality and trans-corporeality. As we saw in chapter 2, such a conception of the flesh is present in Maurice Merleau-Ponty's very different conception of the flesh, in which human embodiment becomes continuous (both touching and touched) with the environment in which it moves.[60] This fundamental connectivity is what he terms the flesh, and we can imagine it as both ecosystemic as well as collective; it can be a structuring dimension of the embodied commons. Of course, we also have to attend to the way in which embodied trauma may create different relationships to such forms of transitivity and this will be crucial as well. Still, a politics oriented around embodiment will enable us to address forms of both bodily violence and potentiality.

5. Finally, the embodied commons should be organized around a rearticulated concept of species being, what I suggest could be called transspecies being. In his 2016 book *Materialism*, Terry Eagleton returns to Marx's conception of species being.[61] For Eagleton, the concept represents a corrective to much recent work on the materiality of the body, which emphasizes its radical particularity. As I have argued throughout this chapter, drawing on Jason Read's conception of transindividuality, we do not need to make a choice between the particular and the universal, or the individual and the collective. They are mutually constitutive categories. Yet Eagleton is surely right that theory has placed too much emphasis on the particular, micrological, and individual in the present moment. I want to affirm his invocation of species being and connect it, in part, to racialized versions of the flesh as I described above. Such a position opens out past what Sylvia Wynter describes as colonial construction of (Western) man and encompasses a broader and more ecumenical conception of humanity. It also points past the human. If we rethink species being in a more eco-Marxist and new

materialist manner, it can enable us to develop a notion of trans-species being. Marx articulates the concept of species being in "Economic and Philosophic Manuscripts of 1844," arguing that humans realize themselves as a species—as a universalizable col-lectivity—through the conscious transformation of nature and "the objective world."[62] Such transformation thus produces nature as a reflection of and support of humans even as humans then see themselves realized through the nature they transform. I want to affirm this vision of self-conscious and embodied transformation of the material world as a central dimension of the embodied com-mons. Yet, in light of critiques of anthropocentrism within posthu-manist and new materialist theories, I think it is crucial to recognize that humans, while typically one of the most powerful actors here, are not the only ones. The ecosystem we work to trans-form also contains many actors from animals and insect species to plants and trees, to various geological entities. The ecosystem trans-forms us as we transform it, and we are dependent on it both eco-nomically and ecologically. We must pay attention to what we do to it even as we have to recognize what it does to us. Our transforma-tions of it can enable human and nonhuman flourishing, but it can also destroy it. Within this framework, nature and the ecosystem are no longer merely raw materials for the creation of value. They are instead co-actors in building a sustainable lifeworld. This dia-lectical relationship between human and nonhuman actors, the commons and its relationship to the ecosystem or systems in which it functions can perhaps be termed transspecies being. It is built on the mutual interactions of different species and different entities. As with trans in transgender, the trans in transspecies is about the ability to transform the conceptual and material dimensions of lived reality. It is toward such a conception of transspecies being that the bodily commons is oriented.

Building with Theory

I began this chapter by excoriating the effects of privatization on everyday life in the present. I then provided an account of the ways in which theory has transformed from modernism to postmodernism, to our present moment of late neoliberalism. In response to this historicization, I have argued for a con-cept of theory that can work at a scale where collective action and struggle is most viable. The sexual and embodied commons that I have just articulated has been my attempt at working at such a scale. For many it may already seem too broad, permissive, synthetic, and unsystematic. To this I can only plead guilty. The vision articulated by this chapter has been willfully proleptic, synthetic, and utopian.[63] It has tried to imagine the largest resonances and collective possibilities for the concepts of sex articulated in the earlier chapters of the book. Given the global nature of the threats facing humans and other denizens of this planet, it is crucial that we employ theory not only to critique what exists but also to imagine what can also exist and at the largest workable scale. Theory is not only a hammer with which to smash the windows of the status quo, it is also the hammer that helps us build a better future. For this reason alone, we need the work of theory at its most bold, wild, and visionary. It is toward building and imagining this better world, and using theory boldly to do so, that the chapter is dedicated.

Epilogue: Following in the Steps of the Hermaphrodite

Metaphors are complicated tropes. When done well they can simultaneously condense, crystallize, and enlarge the meanings of a given passage. They also can produce the spark of new knowledge, in which a worn-out set of associations around a given word become made anew with an unexpected substitution and its implied juxtaposition. Of course, when done badly, metaphors can do violence to the concrete meanings of a concept, word, or figure. They can have a dematerializing effect, rendering general and abstract what was once powerful in its specificity and material context. Such a danger is particularly present in discussing embodied categories and concepts such as intersex and trans. Bo Laurent (best known as Cheryl Chase), who did so much for the visibility of intersex and worked tirelessly to stop unnecessary surgeries, has criticized fields like queer theory and women's studies for appropriating intersex in the name of challenging normativity and "creating a future that is radically different."[1]

Yet this intersex person, at least, wants a future that is radically different. Studying intersex and trans embodiments and desires can have a crucial denaturalizing effect on how we conceptualize sex, gender, and sexuality. Abstractions can be powerful. They function to open out and scale up concepts that otherwise do not speak to a situation larger than their individual context. Moreover, from a deconstructive standpoint, all language is catachresis, a fundamental misnaming and metaphorization. In naming anything, it is less the correctness of the name but rather its force, resonance, and capaciousness that finally matter.

I want to conclude this book by willfully metaphorizing the two embodied figures that sit at its conceptual center: the transgender person and the intersex person. Since I have worked to specify the material embodiment of both throughout most of this book, I will take the risk of metaphorizing both figures in my concluding argument. The two figures, when considered abstractly, suggest different possibilities, promises, and limitations of human interactions with the lifeworld, with technology, and with the constructing of a more just world economy and ecology. Here I metaphorize them as figures of world building. They figure both possibilities and limits.

Considered metaphorically, *transgender* suggests the possibility and necessity of remaking and transforming both our concepts and our material bodies. It suggests the force of human poesis and its ability to produce a different lived and material world. It emphasizes all those actions that attach to the prefix "trans-": transition, transpose, translate, transfix, transform. It suggests the power of humans, as transspecies beings, working in concert with the world and with a recognition of specific ecosystems to transform life possibilities, the systems by which we realize them, and our existences themselves. It is the promise (one derived from the positive dimensions of the Enlightenment), that we can engineer a different relationship to our economic, ecological, political, technological, and embodied lifeworlds. Trans can be a figure for human possibility. One thinks of the complex mix of the technological and the human in the Colombian trans musical artist Arca's videos for her Kick project.

The surgically altered body caries both utopian and dystopian resonances in the videos. Arca's images are as disturbing as they are affirmative, suggesting the violence that attaches to transforming the world and the body even in finally sustainable and just ways. The surgically altered body caries both utopian and dystopian resonances in the videos. One also thinks of terraforming in Kim Stanley Robinson's *Mars Trilogy*.[2] Facing the threats of the climate emergency, global inequality, and growing fascism, we will need the human ability to fundamentally imagine and alter the conditions of our existence and the flourishing of all of those entities with whom we share a lifeworld. Transness points one way forward.

While we often conceptualize the intersex and trans together (and that is finally the goal of this book as well), in the schema I am presenting here, the *intersex* figures all of that which resists or deviates from conscious human transformation. It suggests the accidents, contingencies, and materialities that refuse to respond to human shaping and human ideation. It is the inter: the intertext, the intertwined, the interference, the interregnum, the interjected, the interlarded. It is what emerges in between and against human and linguistic binaries. To borrow from Adorno, it is the preponderance of the object, the body, the flesh, and the ecological. The long history of the failed medical correction of intersex suggests the underside of the Enlightenment. It is the violence done by technology, enclosure, appropriation, extraction, and colonization.

It marks the ways in which humans often do irreparable violence to bodies, ecosystems, cultures, workers, and animals in the name of progress, ideation, and improvement. The intersex is all that eludes the best laid plans. It is the aleatory, the obdurate, the intimately alien. Intersex points out the importance of attending to the resistance of that which we propose to transform. It suggests an ethics and a politics around the forms of violence attaching to human progress. We look to it, too, to discern a way forward.

Of course, in positing these two concepts I risk merely repeating binary thinking. Yet what I am most interested in is thinking these two insights in their necessary yet contradictory relationship to each other. They are a version of the negative dialectic that Adorno posits.[3] They refuse positive synthesis and instead exist in necessary tension and opposition even as they are partially and repeatedly transformed by each other. We need both, and we need what both produce in tension with each other.

Thinking trans and intersex together as I have just redefined them recalls a concept from another Frankfurt school thinker: Walter Benjamin's account of the dialectical image. For Benjamin, the image was Janus-faced, a figuration of both modernity's violence and promise. It also figured the doubleness of the commodity, both the violence that produces it and the utopian dreams contained within its promise.[4] Thinking intersex and trans together produces a more em-bodied version of Benjamin's image: multiply gendered, multiply sexed, the dialectical hermaphrodite (if I may willfully reclaim this term) sits at the gates of the future, both augur and promise. Part monster, part god, and part spherical human from Aristophanes's tale, it indicates that the road ahead will be both necessary and difficult. Asking it to guide us, we follow in its footsteps.

Acknowledgments

This book was one I had no intention of writing. Then it became one I had to write. The initial idea for the book grew out of an invitation from Julietta Singh and Nathan Snaza, at the University of Richmond, to present new work on intersex, modeled on the preface I wrote for my book *Insistence of the Material*. I had originally told myself that I would never write on intersex again. The preface and an earlier article for *English Journal* were enough. The topic was painful for me to write about. I also did not want my intersex embodiment to be fixed as my intellectual calling card. It is an important part of me, but only one part. Among other things, I am also an intellectual, a scholar of literature, culture, and theory. While my intellectualism may have something to do with abstracting from what was being done to my body in my many surgeries, it is not reducible to it. I also have become concerned (a concern I share with Anna Kornbluh, one of my closest intellectual confidants) about the rise of the memoir and autotheory and the effacement of larger forms of social theory and representation. So I was ambivalent about returning to the subject. But then I found a new way of approaching it. I would write a theory talk that addressed the status of embodied sex in the present. It might refer to my experience, but it would not be focused on it. That talk, also titled "In Defense of Sex," met with more affirmation and interest than I expected. Thank you, Nathan and Julietta, for your brilliance, friendship, and generosity. Thank you as well for planting this seed. Thank you, Anna, for constantly being there as someone with whom to think. If anything in this book matches your theoretical precision and capaciousness, I will be happy.

In the early days of planning this book, I thought I would turn the talk into a short book, the different sections of the talk itself functioning as something like an outline for different chapters. I began to present the talk in more venues, including our philosophy colloquium at Illinois State University; my old graduate program at the University of California, Santa Cruz; and Edgewood College. My thanks to Chris Horvath, a deeply knowledgeable scholar of sex, gender, and sexuality himself (I regularly draw upon his knowledge, often over a glass of wine at my favorite haunt, Stave), Carla Freccero, Susan Gillman, Deanna Schemek, and Tyrus Miller, at UCSC, and my old friend, Ashley Byock, at Edgewood. The book began to grow in scope and ambition. At the initial presentation of the talk, I stated, "I am not talking about fucking." But then I started to wonder why not? Being a part of the pro-sex feminist and queer culture of the West Coast in the 1990s and seeing that vision slowly (and then rapidly) erode in the twenty-first century, I felt like I had something to say about sex as desire and act. Similarly, my surgical experiences did not leave my relationship to sex untouched. Far from it, so I had something to say on that account as well.

The book grew, and as I began composing and presenting new writing for it, it started to round into its present form. More recent talks in which I tried out different parts of the book and a grant that I received from the Katholische Universität in Eichstätt, Germany, really helped me refine my argument and provided me with the time to produce the best version of this manuscript. My thanks to Rebekah Sheldon (whose intellectual friendship and seemingly effortless brilliance have deeply shaped this book) for hosting me at Indiana University, Ed Kazarian (another key interlocutor) for bringing me to Rowan University as part of his Theorizing at Rowan series, ISU's own College of Arts and Sciences for hosting my Distinguished Lecture in the fall of 2023, and the Katholische Universität Center for Advanced Study for hosting me for a month in the summer of 2022. I was able to compose all of chapter 4 during that time. I also benefited from conversations with Bonnie Honig, Kerstin Schmidt, and my good friend René Dietrich while at KU, where I also presented as part of the Dialogic Cultures conference.

All origin stories are, of course, backward projections. They are constructions, from the present, of a usable past. I have already given one origin story for this book. Now I want to briefly present another. At the end of my first year of graduate school, I took a Greyhound from Santa Cruz to Los Angeles to visit a friend and fellow grad student. During that ten-hour bus ride (it was Greyhound, after all, and it took its damn time), I read all of Judith Butler's *Gender Trouble*. The book stayed with me. It haunted me. I became a Butler fanatic while having the trouble that many did with how dematerialized her account of embodiment felt. Butler did so much for my thinking and sense of self. Suddenly gender was not necessarily binary or natural. This was a crucial insight for the long-haired intersex kid who was just starting to come to terms with what he had gone through. I wrote one of my first papers (much to my professors' understandable chagrin) in graduate school arguing for a Marxist conception of materialism to supplement Butler's poststructuralist critique. Thirty years later, the letter finally arrived at its destination. *In Defense of Sex* is my fully developed response to *Gender Trouble,* as well as my immodest attempt to write something that resembles it. Interestingly, my first book was my third book idea. My second book was my second, and this book is, in some ways, my original book idea. Time works in funny ways.

I want to thank Richard Morrison and all the people at Fordham University Press. I also want to thank the two remarkably supportive and generous peer reviewers: David A. Rubin and Hil Malatino. If my book comes close to the standard of insight, care, and rigor set with their own scholarship, I will be happy. Finally, Gregory McNamee did a remarkable job editing what was a very messy manuscript. I have felt absolutely supported in the writing of this book from its inception through its completion. I have worked with Richard from my first book, *Hard-Boiled Masculinities,* through this one (two with Minnesota and now two with Fordham). Richard is the ideal editor, supportive, shrewd, critical, and happy to support work that takes risks and thinks big. He has also become a good friend and a fellow music obsessive. My career would be a shadow of its current form without Richard's support and guidance. Given his years of queer activism and his investments in supporting risky work on sex and sexuality, he was the ideal editor for *In Defense of Sex.*

In addition to the folks I thanked above, there have been so many people who have helped me do this work and supported me through the writing process. At my home institution, ISU, I want to recognize the support of Gabe Gudding, Andrew Hartman, Susan Kim, Tara Lyons, Ela Przybylo, Brian Rejack, Amy Robillard, Rebecca Saunders, Aaron Smith, and Julie Webber. I also want to thank the graduate students I have worked with during the writing of this book, including Amish Trivedi, Edmund Ankomah, Hye Hyon Kim, Steven Lazaroff, Ridita Mizan, Blake Reno, Manuel Reza, Heather O'Leary, Karla Rodriguez, Asmita Saha, Amish Trivedi, Jennifer Tullos. Thanks as well to two exceptional undergraduate students who are perhaps the best ones I have taught in my thirty-year career of teaching to date: Kate and Luna Fortner. The Fortner twins are so smart about everything from gender and sex to contemporary culture more broadly that I often found myself learning from them in the classroom. They are remarkable thinkers. I only hope they inherit a society worthy of their thought.

I also want to recognize the wonderful group of professional colleagues and friends who have been central to my thinking around this book and have provided that most important form of support, intellectual comradeship. In addition to the people I already mentioned above, these include: Stacy Alaimo (who provided a wonderful blurb for the book), Robin Baldridge, Dodie Bellamy, Renée Bergland, Emanuela Bianchi, Hunter Bivens, Kaitland Blanchard, Levi Paul Bryant, Gina Buccola, Louis Chude-Sokei, Ulrika Dalh, Scott Davis, Jeffrey R. di Leo, Patty Dunn, Erin E. Edwards, Jennifer Fleissner, Carla Freccero, Gerald Graff, Sean Grattan (who is another close intellectual inter-locutor as well as the book's indexer), Christian Haines, K. Allison Hammer, Jason Hannan, Alex Hartmann, Doug Henwood, Peter Hitchcock, Caren Irr, Jo Isaacson, Earl Jackson Jr., Aaron Jaffe, Adam Kotsko, Leigh Clare La Berge, Ken Lindblom, Eric Longfellow, Annie McClanahan, Sophia McClennen, Jan Mieszkowski, Allen Miller, Ray Nayler (yes, the novelist and a dear friend), Daniel O'Hara, Ann Pelligrini, Ignacio Sanchez Prado, José David Saldívar, Cate Sandilands, Russell Sbriglia, Steven Shaviro, Nicole Simek, Mirinda Simmons, Ali Sperling, Blake Strickland, Robert Tally, Zach Tavlin, Charles Tung, Kirin Wachter-Grene (who is one of my favorite interlocutors, knower of all things kink, and a fellow dark soul), Phillip Wegner, Ara Wilson, Cindy Wu, and Zahi Zalloua.

I thank the members of the Facebook group Comparative Theory, which I run with Anna Kornbluh, Gina Stinnett, and Carlos M. Amador. This group is remarkably vital and has grown beyond any of our expectations. I am sure they are tired of hearing about this book (as are my more general Facebook friends), but they have been instrumental in its conception and final form. Thank you for helping me bring it to fruition.

I deeply value the support of my family, including my parents, Joseph and Giovanna Breu; my sister, Eugenia Baron; my brother-bother-in-law, Randall Baron; and my nieces, Zoe and Alexis Baron. Thanks go as well to nonacademic close friends, including Tom Banks, Andrew Griffin, Robin Hendershot, Megan Lewis, Tim Marks, Suzi Markham, Max Rovner, Alexandra Sullivan, and Doug Zartman.

I want to acknowledge the intellectual debt I continue to owe to the late Elizabeth A. Hatmaker for being such a core intellectual and emotional pres-ence in my life. Finally, I thank Gina Arlene Stinnett for teaching me I could love again and for being present as an interlocutor throughout every part of this book's conception and composition. Your feminism, humor, whip-sharp political mind, and of course your love have sustained me and taught me that tragedy can again turn to happiness. We proved everybody wrong. Good for us!

Notes

Preface

1. Yves Tumor, "Gospel for a New Century," *Heaven to a Tortured Mind*, Warp CDD3054, 2020.

2. Funkadelic, "Free Your Mind and Your Ass Will Follow," *Free Your Mind . . . and Your Ass Will Follow*, Westbound Records, WB 2001, 1970.

3. Paisley Currah, *Sex Is as Sex Does: Governing Transgender Identity* (New York: New York University Press, 2022); Dean Spade, *Normal Life: Administrative Violence, Critical Trans Politics, and the Limits of the Law* (Durham, NC: Duke University Press, 2015).

4. Jacques Lacan, *The Ethics of Psychoanalysis: The Seminar of Jacques Lacan, Book VII*, trans. Dennis Porter (New York: W. W. Norton, 1992).

5. Stacy Alaimo, *Bodily Natures: Science, Environment, and the Material Self* (Bloomington: Indiana University Press, 2010), 2.

6. R. A. Judy, *Sentient Flesh: Thinking in Disorder, Poesis in Black* (Durham, NC: Duke University Press, 2020), 215–51; Duke Ellington, "Harlem Air-Shaft," Sepia Panorama/Harlem Air-Shaft, Victor 26731, 1940.

7. Lauren Berlant, *On the Inconvenience of Other People* (Durham, NC: Duke University Press, 2023), 3.

8. Samuel R. Delany, *Times Square Red, Times Square Blue* (New York: New York University Press, [1999] 2019).

9. Jane Jacobs, *The Death and Life of Great American Cities* (New York: Vintage Books, 1992).

10. Mike Davis, *Planet of Slums* (London: Verso, 2007).

11. Christopher Breu, *Insistence of the Material: Literature in the Age of Biopolitics* (Minneapolis: University of Minnesota Press, 2014), vii–x; Christopher

Breu, "Middlesex Meditations: Understanding and Teaching Intersex," *English Journal* 98, no. 4 (2009): 102–8.

12. Anna Kornbluh, *Immediacy or, The Style of Too Late Capitalism* (London: Verso, 2023), 1–23.

13. I also write this section of the preface in the spirit of Fredric Jameson's list of postmodern tastes in *Postmodernism*. His point is that his personal tastes are not relevant to the larger political-economic argument he is producing. While I think my positionality is relevant to my argument, hopefully the latter cannot be reduced to the former. See Fredric Jameson, *Postmodernism or, The Cultural Logic of Late Capitalism* (Durham, NC: Duke University Press, 1991), 298–300.

14. David A. Rubin's *Intersex Matters* provides a persuasive defense of "intersex" as a category rather than DSD. Key for Rubin is the way in which the category names a real mode of embodied difference that challenges binary conceptions of sex, while the language of DSD wants to skirt the larger implications of such forms of embodied difference. The case for DSD has been articulated most forcefully by the editors of a special issue of *GLQ*. See David A. Rubin, *Intersex Matters: Biomedical Embodiment, Gender Regulation, and Transnational Activism* (Albany: SUNY Press, 2017), 87–95; Alice D. Dreger and April Herndon, "Progress and Politics in the Intersex Rights Movement: Feminist Theory in Action," *GLQ: A Journal of Lesbian and Gay Studies* 15, no. 2 (2009): 199–224.

15. Christopher Breu, *Hard-Boiled Masculinities* (Minneapolis: University of Minnesota Press), 2005.

16. While I only reference some of them going forward, my understanding of intersex, transgender, and nonbinary subjectivities is informed by a range of different texts. For intersex, see Rubin, *Intersex Matters*; Hil Malantino, *Queer Embodiment: Monstrosity, Medical Violence, and Intersex Experience* (Lincoln: University of Nebraska Press, 2019); Katrina Karkazis, *Fixing Sex: Intersex, Medical Authority, and Lived Experience* (Durham, NC: Duke University Press, 2008); Georgiann Davis, *Contesting Intersex: The Dubious Diagnosis* (New York: New York University Press, 2015); Sharon E. Preves, *Intersex and Identity: The Contested Self* (New Brunswick, NJ: Rutgers University Press, 2008); Elizabeth Reis, *Bodies in Doubt: An American History of Intersex* (Baltimore: Johns Hopkins University Press, 2009); Suzanne J. Kessler, *Lessons from the Intersexed* (New Brunswick, NJ: Rutgers University Press, 1998). See also, in addition to the special issue of *GLQ* mentioned in note 14, Morgan Holmes, ed., *Critical Intersex* (New York: Routledge, 2009), and Alice Domurat Dreger, ed., *Intersex in the Age of Ethics* (Hagerstown, MD: University Publishing Group 1999). The literature on transgender subjectivity is too voluminous to cite here, but for a powerful sense of the field in all its diversity see the work published in *Transgender Studies Quarterly (TSQ)*; Susan Stryker and Stephen Whittle, eds., *The Transgender Studies Reader* (New York: Routledge, 2006), and Susan Stryker and Aren Z. Aizura, eds., *The Transgender Studies Reader 2* (New York: Routledge, 2013). For theorizations of nonbinary subjectivities, see Charlie McNabb, *Nonbinary Gender Identities: History, Culture, Resources* (Lanham,

MD: Rowman & Littlefield, 2018); Sebastian Cordoba, *Nonbinary Gender Identities: The Language of Becoming* (New York: Routledge, 2023); Alex Iantaffi and Meg-John Barker, *Life Isn't Binary: On Being Both, Beyond, and In-Between* (London: Jessica Kingsley Publishers, 2020); Leah DeVun, *The Shape of Sex: Nonbinary Gender from Genesis to the Renaissance* (New York: Columbia University Press, 2021); Ben Vincent, *Non-Binary Genders: Navigating Communities, Identities, and Healthcare* (Bristol, UK: Policy Press, 2000); and the essays in Motmans Joz, Timo Ole Nieder, and Walter Pierre Bouman, *Non-Binary and Genderqueer Genders* (New York: Routledge, 2020) and the special issue of *WSQ* edited by Red Washburn and JV Fuqua, "Nonbinary," *WSQ* 51, nos. 3–4 (Fall/Winter 2023). On "genderqueer" as a critical understanding of nonbinary gender embodiments (one I find compelling as a descriptor in relationship to gender, although "nonbinary" has been the more popular usage), see Robin Dembroff, "Beyond Binary: Genderqueer as Critical Gender Kind," *Philosophers' Imprint* 20, no. 9 (2020): 1–23. Kadji Amin provides an important complication of nonbinary conceptualized as an identity in "We Are All Nonbinary: A Brief History of Accidents," *Representations* 158 (2022): 106–19.

Introduction: Sex for the Twenty-First Century

1. The epigraph is from Jacques Lacan, *The Four Fundamental Concepts of Psychoanalysis: The Seminar of Jacques Lacan Book XI*, trans. Alan Sheridan (New York: W. W. Norton, 1998), 1.

2. Gila Ashtor, *Homo Psyche: On Queer Theory and Erotophobia* (New York: Fordham University Press, 2021), 19.

3. Kate Julian, "Why Are Young People Having So Little Sex," *The Atlantic*, December 2018, https://www.theatlantic.com/magazine/archive/2018/12/the-sex-recession/573949/.

4. David M. Halperin, "Introduction: The War on Sex," in *The War on Sex*, ed. David Halperin and Trevor Hoppe (Durham, NC: Duke University Press, 2017), 1–64.

5. Oliver Davis and Tim Dean, *Hatred of Sex* (Lincoln: University of Nebraska Press, 2022).

6. On extimacy, see Jacques Lacan, *The Ethics of Psychoanalysis, 1959–1960: The Seminar of Jacques Lacan Book VII*, trans, Dennis Porter (New York: W. W. Norton, 1992), 139, and Jacques-Alain Miller, "Extimity," *The Symptom* 9, https://www.lacan.com/symptom/extimity.html.

7. Ben Smith, "Junot Díaz in Limbo," *Semafor*, July 28, 2023, https://www.semafor.com/article/11/27/2022/junot-diaz-in-limbo

8. Cynthia Barounis, *Vulnerable Constitutions: Queerness, Disability, and the Remaking of American Manhood* (Philadelphia: Temple University Press, 2019), 197–209.

9. Samuel R. Delany, *Times Square Red, Times Square Blue* (New York: New York University Press, [1999] 2019); David Wojnarowicz, *The Waterfront Journals*

(New York: Grove Press, 1997); Thea Hillman, *Intersex (For Lack of a Better Word)* (San Francisco: Manic D Press, 2008).

10. Jordy Rosenberg, "Afterword: One Utopia, One Dystopia," in *Transgender Marxism*, ed. Jules Joanne Gleason and Elle O'Rourke (London: Pluto Press, 2021), 259–95.

11. Michel Foucault famously advances his critique of the repressive hypothesis in the opening pages of the first volume of *The History of Sexuality.* See Foucault, *The History of Sexuality: An Introduction* (New York: Vintage Books, 1978), 3–35.

12. The paradigmatic text for arguments about sexual repression that combines Marxist and psychoanalytic theory is, of course, Herbert Marcuse's *Eros and Civilization*, which often feels like the text that Foucault is indirectly inditing in *History of Sexuality Volume 1.* See Herbert Marcuse, *Eros and Civilization: A Philosophical Inquiry into Freud* (Boston: Beacon Press, 1955).

13. Ela Przybylo, *Asexual Erotics: Intimate Readings of Compulsory Sexuality* (Columbus: Ohio State University Press, 2019).

14. See Foucault, *History of Sexuality Volume 1*, 92–102, and Jacques Lacan, *The Four Fundamental Concepts of Psychoanalysis*, trans. Alan Sheridan (New York: W. W. Norton, 1998).

15. Gayle Rubin, "Thinking Sex: Notes for a Radical Theory of the Politics of Sexuality," in *Deviations: A Gayle Rubin Reader* (Durham, NC: Duke University Press, 2011), 137–81; Amber Hollibaugh, *My Dangerous Desires: A Queer Girl Dreaming Her Way Home* (Durham, NC: Duke University Press, 2000); Susie Bright, *Sexwise* (Charleston, SC: BookSurge Publishing, 2009).

16. Andrea Dworkin, *Intercourse* (New York: Free Press, 1987); Catherine A. MacKinnon, *Only Words* (Cambridge, MA: Harvard University Press, 1996).

17. Lorna Bracewell, *Why We Lost the Sex Wars: Sexual Freedom in the #MeToo Era* (Minneapolis: University of Minnesota Press, 2021).

18. David Harvey, *A Brief History of Neoliberalism* (Oxford: Oxford University Press, 2007); Michel Foucault, *The Birth of Biopolitics: Lectures at the Collège de France, 1978–1979*, trans. Graham Burchell (New York: Picador, 2010); Wendy Brown, *Undoing the Demos: Neoliberalism's Stealth Revolution* (New York: Zone Books, 2017).

19. Alberto Toscano, *Late Fascism: Race, Capitalism, and the Politics of Crisis* (London: Verso, 2023). It is important to note that Toscano's book is speculative about the ways in which the concept of fascism can be applied and redefined in relationship to present dynamics. He is explicitly not trying to create a new periodizing concept.

20. Wendy Brown, *In The Ruins of Neoliberalism: The Rise of Antidemocratic Politics in the West* (New York: Columbia University Press, 2019), 9–10.

21. Jodi Dean, "Neofeudalism: The End of Capitalism?," *Los Angeles Review of Books*, May 12, 2020, https://lareviewofbooks.org/article/neofeudalism-the-end-of-capitalism/; McKenzie Wark, *Capital Is Dead: Is This Something Worse?* (London: Verso, 2019).

22. Jean Laplanche, "Implantation, Intromission," trans. Luke Thurston, in Jean Laplanche, *Essays on Otherness* (New York: Routledge, 1999), 133–37.

23. Jacques Lacan, . . . *Or Worse: The Seminar of Jacques Lacan Book XIX*, trans. A. R. Price (New York: Polity, 2018), 4.

24. Paisley Currah, *Sex Is as Sex Does: Governing Transgender Identity* (New York: New York University Press, 2022).

25. Paul B. Preciado, *Testo Junky: Sex, Drugs, and Biopolitics in the Pharmaco-pornographic Era*, trans. Bruce Benderson (New York: Feminist Press, 2013), 33.

26. Rebekah Sheldon, *The Child to Come: Life After the Human Catastrophe* (Minneapolis: University of Minnesota Press, 2016), 19.

27. Susan Stryker and Aren Z. Aizura, "Introduction: Transgender Studies 2.0," in *The Transgender Studies Reader 2*, ed. Susan Stryker and Aren Z. Aizura (New York: Routledge, 2013), 7.

28. Kadji Amin, "Taxonomically Queer?: Sexology and New Queer, Trans, and Asexual Identities" *GLQ* 29, no. 1 (2023): 91–107.

29. Jennifer F. Boylan, "Loving Freely," *New York Times*, October 14, 2015, www.newyorktimes.com/2015/10/14/opinion/loving-freely/html.

30. Jay Prosser, *Second Skins: The Body Narratives of Transsexuality* (New York: Columbia, 1998); Preciado, *Testo Junky.*

31. Amanda Montañez, "Visualizing Sex as a Spectrum," *Scientific American* blog, August 29, 2017, https://blogs.scientificamerican.com/sa-visual/visualizing-sex-as-a-spectrum/.

32. Sara Ahmed, "Gender Critical = Gender Conservative," *FeministKilljoys* blog, https://feministkilljoys.com/2021/10/31/gender-critical-gender-conservative/.

33. Judith Butler, *Who's Afraid of Gender?* (New York: Farrar, Straus, and Giroux) 2024.

34. Didier Anzieu, *The Skin Ego*, trans. Naomi Segal (New York: Routledge, 2016); Jacques Lacan, "The Mirror Stage as Formative of the I Function as Revealed in Psychoanalytic Experience," in *Écrits: The First Complete Edition in English*, trans. Bruce Fink (New York: W. W. Norton, 2006), 75–81; Sigmund Freud, "The Ego and the Id," in *The Standard Edition of the Complete Psychological Works of Sigmund Freud*, trans. James Strachey (London: Hogarth Press, 1961), 19:3–66.

35. Ben Spatz, *What a Body Can Do: Technique as Knowledge, Practice as Research* (New York: Routledge, 2015), 171–214.

36. Hortense Spillers, "Mama's Baby, Papa's Maybe: An American Grammar Book," *Diacritics* 17, no. 2 (Summer 1987): 64–81; R. A. Judy, *Sentient Flesh: Thinking in Disorder, Poiēsis in Black* (Durham, NC: Duke University Press, 2020); C. Riley Snorton, *Black on Both Sides: A Racial History of Trans Identity* (Minneapolis: University of Minnesota Press, 2017); Alexander G. Weheliye, *Habeas Viscus: Racializing Assemblages, Biopolitics, and Black Feminist Theories of the Human* (Durham, NC: Duke University Press, 2014); Marquis Bey, *Black Trans Feminism* (Durham, NC: Duke University Press, 2022).

37. See Hil Malatino, *Queer Embodiment: Monstrosity, Medical Violence, and Intersex Experience* (Lincoln: University of Nebraska Press, 2019); David A. Rubin, *Intersex Matters: Biomedical Embodiment, Gender Regulation, and Transnational Activism* (Albany: SUNY Press, 2017).

38. Anne Fausto-Sterling, *Sex/Gender: Biology in a Social World* (New York: Routledge, 2012), 10.

39. Thomas Laqueur, *Making Sex: Body and Gender from the Greeks through Freud* (Cambridge, MA: Harvard University Press, 1990), 43, 243.

40. Lacan, *The Four Fundamental Concepts of Psychoanalysis*, 235.

41. Alenka Zupančič, *What Is Sex?* (Cambridge, MA: MIT Press, 2017), 4.

42. Laqueur, *Making Sex*, 43, 243.

43. See Stacy Alaimo, *Bodily Natures: Science, Environment, and the Material Self* (Bloomington: Indiana University Press, 2010); Karen Barad, *Meeting the Universe Halfway: Quantum Physics and the Entanglement of Matter and Meaning* (Durham, NC: Duke University Press, 2007); Samantha Frost, *Biocultural Creatures: Toward a New Theory of the Human* (Durham, NC: Duke University Press, 2017).

44. Tim Dean, *Beyond Sexuality* (Chicago: University of Chicago Press, 2000), 22–60.

45. Sigmund Freud, "Three Essays on the Theory of Sexuality," in *The Standard Edition of the Complete Psychological Works of Sigmund Freud*, 7:123–243.

46. The tradition of psychoanalytic Marxism is too long and complex to cite, but the Tomšič I directly reference is: Samo Tomšič, *The Capitalist Unconscious: Marx and Lacan* (London: Verso, 2015).

47. Sophie Lewis, *Full Surrogacy Now: Feminism against Family* (London: Verso, 2019).

48. Kevin Floyd, Jen Hedler Phillis, and Sarika Chandra, eds., *Totality Inside Out: Rethinking Crisis and Conflict Under Capital* (New York: Fordham University Press, 2022); Colleen Lye and Christopher Nealon, eds., *After Marx: Literature, Theory, and Value in the Twenty-First Century* (Cambridge: Cambridge University Press, 2022).

49. Kevin Floyd, *The Reification of Desire: Toward a Queer Marxism* (Minneapolis: University of Minnesota Press, 2009); Petrus Liu, *The Specter of Materialism: Queer Theory and Marxism in the Age of the Beijing Consensus* (Durham, NC: Duke University Press, 2023); Christopher Chitty, *Sexual Hegemony: Statecraft, Sodomy, and Capital in the Rise of the World System*, ed. Max Fox (Durham, NC: Duke University Press, 2020).

50. Colleen Lye and Christopher Nealon, "Marxist Literary Study and the General Law of Capitalist Accumulation," in *After Marx: Literature, Theory, and Value in the Twenty-First Century*, ed. Colleen Lye and Christopher Nealon (Cambridge: Cambridge University Press, 2022), 1–22.

51. Georg Lukács, *History and Class Consciousness: Studies in Marxist Dialectics*, trans. Rodney Livingstone (Cambridge, MA: MIT Press, 1971), 197–209.

52. Manuel Reza is one of the graduate students I work with and made this observation in a presentation on queer Marxism in my "Marxism Then and Now" seminar in the Spring of 2023.

53. Eve Kosofsky Sedgwick, *Epistemology of the Closet* (Berkeley: University of California Press, 1990), 82–86.

54. Ann Pellegrini and Avgi Saketopoulou, *Gender without Identity* (New York: The Unconscious in Translation, 2023).

55. Madhavi Menon, *Indifference to Difference: On Queer Universalism* (Minneapolis: University of Minnesota Press, 2015), 18.

56. See Chitty, *Sexual Hegemony*, and Rosemary Hennessy, *Profit and Pleasure: Sexual Identities in Late Capitalism*, 2nd ed. (New York: Routledge, 2017).

57. Nancy Fraser, *Justice Interruptus; Critical Reflections on the "Postsocialist" Condition* (New York: Routledge, 1997), 41–68.

58. Giovanni Arrighi, *The Long Twentieth Century: Money, Power, and the Origins of Our Times*, rev. ed. (London: Verso, 2010).

59. Fredric Jameson, "Reification and Utopia in Mass Culture," *Social Text* 1 (Winter 1979): 130–48, at 131–32.

60. Jordy Rosenberg, "The Molecularization of Sexuality: On Some Primitivisms of the Present," *Theory and Event* 17, no. 2 (2014), muse.jhu.edu/article/546470.

61. Theodor W. Adorno, "Subject and Object," in *The Essential Frankfurt School Reader*, ed. Andrew Arato and Eike Gebhardt (New York: Continuum, 1993), 497–511.

62. For Adorno's understanding of dialectics, see Theodor W. Adorno, *Negative Dialectics*, trans. E. B. Ashton (London: Continuum, 1966). Lacan's understanding runs throughout his entire corpus and thus is harder to point to specific accounts of it, but see Jacques Lacan, "The Subversion of the Subject and the Dialectic of Desire in the Freudian Unconscious," in *Écrits*, 671–702.

63. Slavoj Žižek, *Tarrying with the Negative: Kant, Hegel, and the Critique of Identity* (Durham, NC: Duke University Press, 1993), 125–61. Žižek has become controversial in recent years owing to a couple of badly thought-through journalistic posts around trans issues, among other things. I still find his basic theoretical insights, what is worked out in his books rather than his unfortunate forays into hot-take journalism, still quite valuable and on the side of liberation.

64. Theodor W. Adorno, *Lectures on Negative Dialectics: Fragments of a Lecture Course 1965/1966* (Cambridge: Polity Press, 2010), 6.

65. Bruce Fink: *The Lacanian Subject: Between Language and Jouissance* (Princeton, NJ: Princeton University Press, 1995), 25.

66. Anne Fausto-Sterling, *Sexing the Body: Gender Politics and the Construction of Sexuality* (New York: Basic Books, 2000), 78–114; Fausto-Sterling, *Sex/Gender*, 3–26.

67. Jean Laplanche, *Essays on Otherness* (New York: Routledge, 1999), 9.

68. Michael Hardt and Antonio Negri, *Commonwealth* (Cambridge, MA: Harvard University Press, 2011); Stefano Harney and Fred Moten, *The Undercommons: Fugitive Planning and Black Study* (New York: Autonomedia, 2013); Christian Haines and Peter

Hitchcock, "Introduction: No Place for the Commons," *The Minnesota Review* 93 (2019): 55–61.

69. Jason W. Moore, *Capitalism in the Web of Life: Ecology and the Accumulation of Capital* (London: Verso, 2015).

1. The Ascent of Gender and Decline of Sex

1. The epigraph is from Hil Malatino, *Queer Embodiment: Monstrosity. Medical Violence, and the Intersex Experience* (Lincoln: University of Nebraska Press, 2019), 2.

2. Donna J. Haraway, "A Cyborg Manifesto," in *The Cultural Studies Reader*, 3rd ed., ed. Simon During (New York: Routledge, 2007), 314–34; *Blade Runner: Final Cut*, dir. Ridley Scott (Los Angeles: Warner Bros, 2007), DVD.

3. *Blade Runner 2049*, dir. Denis Villeneuve (Los Angeles: Warner Bros, 2018), DVD.

4. Christopher Breu, *Insistence of the Material: Literature in the Age of Biopolitics* (Minneapolis: University of Minnesota Press, 2014), 22.

5. Fredric Jameson, *Postmodernism or, The Cultural Logic of Late Capitalism* (Durham, NC: Duke University Press, 1991), 281.

6. Stacy Alaimo, *Bodily Natures: Science, Environment, and the Material Self* (Bloomington: Indiana University Press, 2010), 2.

7. Dean Spade, *Normal Life: Administrative Violence, Critical Trans Politics, and the Limits of the Law* (Durham, NC: Duke University Press, 2011); Toby Beauchamp, *Going Stealth: Transgender Politics and U.S. Surveillance Practices* (Durham, NC: Duke University Press, 2019).

8. See Judith Butler, *Gender Trouble: Feminism and the Subversion of Identity* (New York: Routledge, 1990), and Susan Stryker, "My Words to Victor Frankenstein above the Village of Chamounix: Performing Transgender Rage," in *The Transgender Studies Reader*, ed. Susan Stryker and Stephen Whittle (New York: Routledge, 2006), 244–57.

9. Judith Butler, *Bodies That Matter: On the Discursive Limits of "Sex"* (New York: Routledge, 1994).

10. Stacy Alaimo and Susan Hekman, "Introduction: Emerging Models of Materiality in Feminist Theory," in *Material Feminisms*, ed. Stacy Alaimo and Susan Hekman (Bloomington: University of Indiana Press, 2008), 1–19, at 11.

11. Claire Colebrook, "On Not Becoming Man: The Materialist Politics of Unactualized Potential," in Alaimo and Hekman, *Material Feminisms*, 52–84, at 67.

12. Susan Stryker, "(De)Subjugated Knowledges: An Introduction to Transgender Studies," in Stryker and Whittle, *The Transgender Studies Reader*, 1–17, at 8–10.

13. Gayle Salamon, *Assuming a Body: Transgender and Rhetorics of Materiality* (New York: Columbia University Press, 2010).

14. Jay Prosser, *Second Skins: The Body Narratives of Transexuality* (New York: Columbia University Press, 1998); C. Jacob Hale, "Tracing a Ghostly Memory in My

Throat: Reflections on FTM Feminist Voice and Agency," in *Men Doing Feminism*, ed. Tom Digby (New York: Routledge, 1998).

15. Hil Malatino, *Queer Embodiment*, 24.

16. K. Allison Hammer, *Masculinity in Transition* (Minneapolis: University of Minnesota Press, 2023); Cynthia Barounis, *Vulnerable Constitutions: Queerness, Disability, and the Remaking of American Manhood* (Philadelphia: Temple University Press, 2019).

17. See the 2019 short documentary film, *A Normal Girl*, which features Pagonis.

18. Paul B. Preciado, *Testo Junkie: Sex, Drugs, and Biopolitics in the Pharmacopornographic Era*, trans. Bruce Benderson (New York: Feminist Press, 2013), 23.

19. David A. Rubin, *Intersex Matters: Biomedical Embodiment, Gender Regulation, and Transnational Activism* (New York: SUNY Press, 2017), 64.

20. Rebekah Sheldon, *The Child to Come: Life after the Human Catastrophe* (Minneapolis: University of Minnesota Press, 2016), 19.

21. Dan Irving, "Normalized Transgressions: Legitimizing the Transsexual Body as Productive," in *The Transgender Studies Reader* 2, ed. Susan Stryker and Aren Z. Aizura (New York: Routledge, 2013), 15–29.

22. Michel Foucault, *The Birth of Biopolitics: Lectures at the Collège de France, 1978–1979*, trans. Graham Burchell (New York: Palgrave, 2004), esp. 215–65.

23. David Harvey, *A Brief History of Neoliberalism* (Oxford: Oxford University Press, 2005), 75–76.

24. Marquis Bey, *Black Trans Feminism* (Durham, NC: Duke University Press, 2022).

25. Louis Althusser, *On the Reproduction of Capitalism: Ideology and Ideological State Apparatuses*, trans. G. M. Goshgarian (London: Verso, 2014), 189.

26. Iain Morland, "Gender, Genitals, and the Meaning of Being Human," in Lisa Downing, Iain Morland, and Nikki Sullivan, *Fuckology: Critical Essays on John Money's Diagnostic Concepts* (Chicago: University of Chicago Press, 2015), 69–98; Jules Gill-Peterson, *Histories of the Transgender Child* (Minneapolis: University of Minnesota Press, 2018).

27. Dana Kaplan and Eva Illouz, *What Is Sexual Capital?* (London: Polity, 2022), esp. 33–42.

28. Erin L. Durban, "Postcolonial Disablement and/as Transition: Trans* Haitian Narratives of Breaking Open and Stitching Together," *Transgender Studies Quarterly* 4, no. 2 (2017): 195–207.

29. Thomas Laqueur, *Making Sex: Body and Gender from the Greeks to Freud* (Cambridge, MA: Harvard University Press, 1992).

30. Joan Wallach Scott, *Only Paradoxes to Offer: French Feminists and the Rights of Man* (Cambridge, MA: Harvard University Press, 1996).

31. Helen King, *The One Sex Body on Trial: The Classical and Early Modern Evidence* (Burlington, VT: Ashgate, 2013).

32. Sylvia Wynter and Katherine McKittrick, "Unparalleled Catastrophe for Our Species? Or, to Give Humanness a Different Future: Conversations," in *Sylvia Wynter: On Being Human as Praxis*, ed. Katherine McKittrick (Durham, NC: Duke University Press, 2015), 9–89.

33. Sander Gilman, *Sexuality, An Illustrated History: Representing the Sexual in Medicine and Culture from the Middle Ages to the Age of AIDS* (New York: Wiley, 1989).

34. C. Riley Snorton, *Black on Both Sides: A Racial History of Trans Identity* (Minneapolis: University of Minnesota Press, 2017), 17–53.

35. Achille Mbembe, *Necropolitics* (Durham, NC: Duke University Press, 2019).

36. Hortense Spillers, "Mama's Baby, Papa's Maybe: An American Grammar Book," *Diacritics* 17, no. 2 (1987): 64–81.

37. R. A. Judy, *Sentient Flesh: Thinking in Disorder, Poiēsis in Black* (Durham, NC: Duke University Press, 2020), 215–51; Bey, *Black Trans Feminism*, 39–65.

38. Sigmund Freud, "Three Essays on Sexuality," in *The Standard Edition of the Complete Psychological Works of Sigmund Freud*, trans. James Strachey (London: Hogarth Press, 1955–61), 7:125–248.

39. In addition to the authors I have already cited, see Anne Fausto-Sterling, *Sexing the Body: Gender Politics and the Construction of Sexuality*, rev. ed. (New York: Basic Books, 2020). Bo Laurent is famous for her activism and starting the ISNA (Intersex Society of North America).

40. On genealogy as historical methodology see Friedrich Nietzsche, *On the Genealogy of Morals and Ecce Homo*, trans. Walter Kaufmann and R. J. Hollingdale (New York: Vintage Books, 2012), and Michel Foucault, "Nietzsche, Genealogy, History," in *Language, Counter Memory, Practice: Selected Essays and Interviews by Michel Foucault*, ed. Donald F. Bouchard (Ithaca, NY: Cornell University Press, 1980), 139–64.

41. My understanding of the concept of gender in the ancient world comes from conversations with Emanuela Bianchi and Allen Miller.

42. Nikki Sullivan, "The Matter of Gender," in Downing, Morland, and Sullivan, *Fuckology*, 19–40.

43. Jennifer Germon, *Gender: A Genealogy of an Idea* (New York: Palgrave Macmillan, 2009).

44. Pierre Bourdieu, *Distinction: A Social Critique of the Judgment of Taste*, trans. Richard Nice (Cambridge, MA: Harvard University Press, 1984), 169–225.

45. Eve Kosofsky Sedgwick, *Epistemology of the Closet* (Berkeley: University of California Press, 1990), 82–86.

46. Jacques Lacan, "The Mirror Stage as Formative of the *I* Function as Revealed in Psychoanalytic Experience," in *Écrits: The First Complete Edition in English*, trans. Bruce Fink (New York: W. W. Norton, 2006), 75–81.

47. Anna Kornbluh, *Immediacy or, The Style of Too Late Capitalism* (London: Verso, 2023), 45.

48. Jack Halberstam, *Female Masculinity* (Durham, NC: Duke University Press, 1998), 144.

49. See Lacan's discussion of the Copernican revolution as a model for the Freudian revolution in Jacques Lacan, *Transference: The Seminar of Jacques Lacan Book VIII*, trans. Bruce Fink (Cambridge: Polity Press, 2015), 90–92; Jean Laplanche, "The Unfinished Copernican Revolution," in *Essays on Otherness*, trans. Luke Thurston (New York: Routledge, 1999), 52–83.

50. Iain Morland, "Cybernetic Sexology," in Downing, Morland, and Sullivan, *Fuckology*, 101–32, at 105.

51. Rubin, *Intersex Matters*, 49–69; Jennifer Germon, *Gender: A Genealogy of an Idea* (New York: Palgrave, 2009), 85–120. See also Germon's powerful introduction, which links the concept of gender with the effacement intersex as a recognized form of embodiment.

52. Ara Wilson, "Gender Before the Gender Turn," *Diacritics* 49, no. 1 (2021): 13–39.

53. Gayle Rubin, "The Traffic in Women: Notes on the 'Political Economy' of Sex" in *Deviations: A Gayle Rubin Reader* (Durham, NC: Duke University Press), 66–87.

54. Halberstam, *Female Masculinity*.

55. Jason W. Moore, *Capitalism in the Web of Life: Ecology and the Accumulation of Capital* (London: Verso, 2015), 17.

56. Judith Butler, *Who's Afraid of Gender?* (New York: Farrar, Straus, and Giroux, 2024), 23.

57. Alaimo and Hekman, "Introduction," 7.

58. Donna J. Haraway, *The Companion Species Manifesto: Dogs, People, and Significant Otherness* (Chicago: Prickly Paradigm Press, 2003), 1; Samantha Frost, *Biocultural Creatures: Toward a New Theory of the Human* (Durham, NC: Duke University Press, 2016), 4.

59. Mel Y. Chen, *Animacies: Biopolitics, Racial Mattering, and Queer Affect* (Durham, NC: Duke University Press, 2012), 1–20.

60. Sophie Lewis, *Full Surrogacy Now: Feminism against Family* (London: Verso, 2021).

61. Silvia Federici, *Beyond the Periphery of the Skin: Rethinking, Remaking, and Reclaiming the Body in Contemporary Capitalism* (San Francisco: PM Press, 2020).

2. Sex as Extimacy

1. For an account of the real as uncoded or undifferentiated materiality, see Jacques Lacan, "The Mirror Stage as Formative of the *I* Function as Revealed in Psychoanalytic Experience," in *Écrits: The First Complete Edition in English*, trans. Bruce Fink (New York: W. W. Norton, 2006), 75–81. For the real as the excluded see the following quotation from Seminar I: "I put forward the quasi-algebraic formula, which has the air of being too transparent, too concrete—the real, or what is perceived

as such, is what resists symbolization absolutely." In Jacques Lacan, *The Seminar of Jacques Lacan Book I: Freud's Papers on Technique, 1953–1954*, trans. John Forrester (New York: W. W. Norton, 1991), 66. For the real as "the impossible," see Jacques Lacan, *Seminar XI: The Four Fundamental Concepts of Psychoanalysis*, trans. Alan Sheridan (New York: W. W. Norton, 1978), 167. For a quick account of the real as material vs. the real as excluded/impossible (what he terms R_1 vs. R_2), see Bruce Fink, *The Lacanian Subject: Between Language and Jouissance* (Princeton, NJ: Princeton University Press, 1995), 24–31.

2. Gilles Deleuze and Félix Guattari, *Anti-Oedipus: Capitalism and Schizophrenia*, trans. Robert Hurley, Mark Seem, and Helen R. Lane (Minneapolis: University of Minnesota Press, 1983), 9.

3. Slavoj Žižek, *Disparities* (London: Bloomsbury, 2019), 69.

4. Samantha Frost, *Biocultural Creatures: Toward a New Theory of the Human* (Durham, NC: Duke University Press, 2016), 33, 17.

5. Gila Ashtor, *Exigent Psychoanalysis: The Interventions of Jean Laplanche* (New York: Routledge, 2021), 9.

6. Marquis Bey, *Black Trans Feminism* (Durham, NC: Duke University Press, 2022), 231.

7. Theodor W. Adorno, *Negative Dialectics*, trans. E. B. Ashton (New York: Continuum), 354–58, at 354.

8. Tim Dean, *Beyond Sexuality* (Chicago: University of Chicago Press, 2000); Patricia Gherovici, *Transgender Psychoanalysis: A Lacanian Perspective on Sexual Difference* (New York: Routledge, 2017).

9. Alenka Zupančič, *What Is Sex?* (Cambridge, MA: MIT Press, 2017), 44–61.

10. See Anne Fausto-Sterling, *Sexing the Body: Gender Politics and the Construction of Sexuality* (New York: Basic Books, 2000), 45–114.

11. Hortense Spillers, "Mama's Baby, Papa's Maybe: An American Grammar Book," *Diacritics* 17, no. 2 (Summer 1987): 64–81; R. A. Judy, *Sentient Flesh: Thinking in Disorder, Poiēsis in Black* (Durham, NC: Duke University Press, 2020); C. Riley Snorton, *Black on Both Sides: A Racial History of Trans Identity* (Minneapolis: University of Minnesota Press, 2017); Alexander G. Weheliye, *Habeas Viscus: Racializing Assemblages, Biopolitics, and Black Feminist Theories of the Human* (Durham, NC: Duke University Press, 2014); Karl Marx, "Economic and Philosophic Manuscripts of 1844," in *The Marx-Engels Reader*, 2nd ed., ed. Robert Tucker (New York: W. W. Norton, 1978); Maurice Merleau-Ponty, *The Visible and the Invisible*, trans. Alphonso Lingis (Evanston, IL: Northwestern University Press, 1968); Herbert Marcuse, *Eros and Civilization: A Philosophical Inquiry into Freud* (Boston: Beacon Press, 1974); Bey, *Black Trans Feminism*.

12. Luke Thurston, "Ineluctable Nodalities: On the Borromean Knot," in *Key Concepts of Lacanian Psychoanalysis*, ed. Dany Nobus (New York: Other Press, 1998), 148.

13. Jacques Lacan, *The Sinthome: The Seminar of Jacques Lacan Book XXIII*, trans. A. R. Price (Cambridge: Polity Press, 2016), 24 (italics in original).

14. Alain Badiou, *Lacan: Anti-Philosophy* 3 (New York: Columbia University Press, 2018), 1–2.

15. Jacques Lacan, *The Ethics of Psychoanalysis, 1959–1960: The Seminar of Jacques Lacan Book VII*, trans. Dennis Porter (New York: W. W. Norton, 1992), 55.

16. Lacan, *The Ethics of Psychoanalysis*, 139.

17. Jacques-Alain Miller, "Extimity," *The Symptom* 9 (2008), https://www.lacan.com/symptom/extimity.html. I have cleaned up the syntax of this translation, which was riddled with errors. I take responsibility for any changed understanding that comes with editing the quotations from this text.

18. Adele E. Clarke, Janet K. Shim, Laura Mamo, Jennifer Ruth Fosket, and Jennifer R. Fishman, "Biomedicalization: A Theoretical and Substantive Introduction," in *Biomedicalizaton: Technoscience, Health, and Illness in the U.S.*, ed. Adele E. Clarke, Janet K. Shim, Laura Mamo, Jennifer Ruth Fosket, and Jennifer R. Fishman (Durham, NC: Duke University Press, 2010), 1–46.

19. Christopher Breu, "*Resident Evil's* Lisa Trevor: The Monster Is Me," *Gamers with Glasses*, https://www.gamerswithglasses.com/features/resident-evils-lisa-trevor-the-monster-is-me.

20. Jasbir K. Puar, *The Right to Maim: Debility, Capacity, Disability* (Durham, NC: Duke University Press, 2017), 13.

21. Anne Fausto-Sterling, *Sex/Gender: Biology in a Social World* (New York: Routledge, 2012), 5. The chart on the same page articulates ten different possible understandings of sex (although I find the idea of brain sex questionable, as does Fausto-Sterling for the most part), including the differences between fetal forms of sex and the biological production of various forms of sex during puberty and so forth.

22. Karen Barad, *Meeting the Universe Halfway: Quantum Physics and the Entanglement of Matter and Meaning* (Durham, NC: Duke University Press, 2007), 175–89.

23. Frost, *Biocultural Creatures*, 1–29.

24. Julietta Singh, *Unthinking Mastery: Dehumanism and Decolonial Entanglements* (Durham, NC: Duke University Press, 2018), 1–3.

25. Stacy Alaimo and Susan Hekman, "Introduction: Emerging Models of Materiality in Feminist Theory," in *Material Feminisms*, ed. Stacy Alaimo and Susan Hekman (Bloomington: Indiana University Press, 2008), 1–19, at 1.

26. Judith Butler, *Gender Trouble: Feminism and the Subversion of Identity* (New York: Routledge, 1990), 128–49.

27. Sigmund Freud, "The 'Uncanny,'" in *The Standard Edition of the Complete Psychological Works of Sigmund Freud*, trans. James Strachey (London: Hogarth Press, 1955–1961), 17:217–52.

28. Stacy Alaimo, *Bodily Natures: Science, Environment, and the Material Self* (Bloomington: Indiana University Press, 2010). 3.

29. For an account of social reproduction in relationship to trans embodiment and subjectivity see Noah Zazanis, "Social Reproduction and Social Cognition: Theorizing (Trans)gender Identity Development in Community Context," in

Transgender Marxism, ed. Jules Joanne Gleeson and Elle O'Rourke (London: Pluto Press, 2021), 33–46.

30. Anja Heisler Weiser Flower, "Cosmos against Nature in the Class Struggle of the Proletarian Trans Women," in Gleeson and O'Rourke, *Transgender Marxism*, 230–58.

31. Frost, *Biocultural Creatures*, 4.

32. Jean Laplanche, *Freud and the Sexual; Essays 2000–2006*, trans. John Fletcher, Jonathan House, and Nicholas Ray (New York: International Psychoanalytic Books, 2011), 11.

33. Laplanche, *Freud and the Sexual*, 19.

34. Judith L. Herman, *Trauma and Recovery: The Aftermath of Violence—from Domestic Abuse to Political Terror* (New York: Basic Books, 1997), 7–32.

35. Jean Laplanche, "Implantation, Intromission," trans. Luke Thurston, in *Essays on Otherness* (New York: Routledge, 1999), 133–37.

36. Sigmund Freud, "From the History of an Infantile Neurosis," in *The Standard Edition of the Complete Psychological Works of Sigmund Freud*, 17:1–133.

37. Avgi Saketopoulou, *Sexuality beyond Consent: Risk, Race, Traumatophilia* (New York: New York University Press, 2023), 7.

38. Karl Marx, "The Eighteenth Brumaire of Louis Bonaparte," in Tucker, *The Marx-Engels Reader*, 594–617.

39. See Samo Tomšič, *The Capitalist Unconscious: Marx and Lacan* (London: Verso, 2015). Žižek's sociopolitical reworking of Lacan runs throughout his voluminous oeuvre, but for one particularly influential version of it, see Slavoj Žižek, *Tarrying with the Negative: Kant, Hegel, and the Critique of Ideology* (Durham, NC: Duke University Press, 1993), 200–238.

40. Jacques Lacan, *The Logic of Phantasy: The Seminar of Jacques Lacan Book XIV*. The English translation is available only at http://www.lacaninireland.com/web/wp-content/uploads/2010/06/14-Logic-of-Phantasy-Complete.pdf. The quotation is on page 1.

41. Anna Kornbluh, *Marxist Film Theory and Fight Club* (London: Bloomsbury, 2019), 57–64.

42. For an overview of some of the best work published in *Screen*, see Mandy Merck, ed., *The Sexual Subject: Screen Reader in Sexuality* (New York: Routledge, 1992).

43. Didier Anzieu, *The Skin Ego*, trans. Naomi Segal (New York: Routledge, 2016), 39–48.

44. Julietta Singh, *Unthinking Mastery: Dehumanism and Decolonial Entanglements* (Durham, NC: Duke University Press, 2018).

45. Judith Butler, *Bodies That Matter: On the Discursive Limits of "Sex"* (New York: Routledge, 1993), 93–120.

46. Kadji Amin, "We Are All Nonbinary: A Brief History of Accidents," *Representations* 158, no. 1 (2022): 106–19.

47. Jacques Lacan, "The Mirror Stage as Formative of the I Function as Revealed in Psychoanalytic Experience," in *Écrits*, 75–81; Sigmund Freud, "The Ego and the

Id," in *The Standard Edition of the Complete Psychological Works of Sigmund Freud*, 19:3–66.

48. Sigmund Freud, "Remembering, Repeating, and Working Through (Further Recommendations on the Technique of Psycho-Analysis II)," in *The Standard Edition of the Complete Psychological Works of Sigmund Freud*, 12:147–56.

49. Anna Kornbluh, *Immediacy or, The Style of Late Capitalism* (London: Verso, 2023), 44-64.

50. Lauren Berlant, *The Queen of America Goes to Washington City: Essays on Sex and Citizenship* (Durham, NC: Duke University Press, 1997), 177–78.

51. Jodi Dean, *Comrade* (London: Verso, 2019).

52. Jodi Dean, *Crowds and Party* (London: Verso, 2016), 22–29.

53. Alain Badiou, *Being and Event*, trans. Oliver Feltham (London: Continuum, 2005), 391–440.

54. Marx, "Economic and Philosophic Manuscripts of 1844."

55. Michel Foucault, *Confessions of the Flesh: The History of Sexuality, Volume 4*, trans. Robert Hurley (New York: Pantheon Books, 2021), 36.

56. Michel Foucault, *Discipline and Punish: The Birth of the Prison*, trans. Alan Sheridan (New York: Vintage Books, 1977).

57. Aníbal Quijano and Immanuel Wallerstein, "Americanity as a Concept, or the Americas in the Modern World System," *International Social Science Journal* 44, no. 4 (1992): 549–57.

58. Jason W. Moore, *Capitalism in the Web of Life: Ecology and the Accumulation of Capital* (London: Verso, 2015), 242.

59. Spillers, "Mama's Baby, Papa's Maybe," 64–81.

60. Russ Castronovo, *Necro Citizenship: Death, Eroticism, and the Public Sphere in the Nineteenth-Century United States* (Durham, NC: Duke University Press, 2001).

61. Hazel V. Carby, *Reconstructing Womanhood: The Emergence of the Afro-American Woman Novelist* (Oxford: Oxford University Press, 1989).

62. Ariane Cruz, *The Color of Kink: Black Women, BDSM, and Pornography* (New York: New York University Press, 2016); Elizabeth Freeman, *Time Binds: Queer Temporalities, Queer Histories* (Durham, NC: Duke University Press, 2010), 137–70; Kirin Wachter-Grene, "Cold Kink: Race and Sex in the African American Underworld," in *Noir Affect*, ed. Christopher Breu and Elizabeth A. Hatmaker (New York: Fordham University Press, 2020), 78–98.

63. Sigmund Freud, "'A Child Is Being Beaten': A Contribution to the Study of the Origin of Sexual Perversions," in *The Standard Edition of the Complete Psychological Works of Sigmund Freud*, 17:179–204, esp. 180.

64. Jean Laplanche, *Life and Death in Psychoanalysis*, trans. Jeffrey Mehlman (Baltimore: Johns Hopkins University Press, 1970), 85–102.

65. Achille Mbembe, *Necropolitics* (Durham: Duke University Press, 2019), 25.

66. Marx, "Economic and Philosophic Manuscripts of 1844," 73.

67. Georg Lukács, *History and Class Consciousness* (Cambridge, MA: MIT Press, 1971), 83–110.

68. Mel Chen, *Animacies: Biopolitics, Racial Mattering, and Queer Affect* (Durham, NC: Duke University Press, 2012).

69. Melinda Cooper, *Counterrevolution: Extravagance and Austerity in Public Finance* (New York: Zone Books, 2024), 7–26.

70. Marcuse, *Eros and Civilization*, 179.

3. Bioaccumulation and the Dialectics of Embodiment

1. David Harvey, *A Brief History of Neoliberalism* (Oxford: Oxford University Press, 2005) 178–79.

2. Karl Marx, *Capital*, vol. 1, trans. Ben Fowkes (New York: Vintage Books, 1977), 873–76.

3. Jason W. Moore, *Capitalism in the Web of Life: Ecology and the Accumulation of Capital* (London: Verso, 2015); Tithi Bhattacharya, "Introduction: Mapping Social Reproduction Theory," in *Social Reproduction Theory: Remapping Class, Recentering Oppression*, ed. Tithi Bhattacharya (London: Pluto Press, 2017), 1–20; Maya Gonzalez and Jeanne Neton, "The Logic of Gender: On the Separation of Spheres and the Process of Abjection," in *Contemporary Marxist Theory: A Reader*, ed. Andrew Pendakis, Jeff Diamanti, Nicholas Brown, Josh Robinson, and Imre Szeman (London: Bloomsbury, 2014), 149–74; Aníbal Quijano, "Coloniality of Power, Eurocentrism, and Latin America," in *Coloniality at Large: Latin America and the Postcolonial Debate*, ed. Mabel Moraña, Enrique Dussel, and Carlos A. Jáuregui (Durham, NC: Duke University Press, 2008), 181–224.

4. Macarena Gómez-Barris, *The Extractive Zone: Social Ecologies and Decolonial Perspectives* (Durham, NC: Duke University Press, 2017), 4.

5. Pratik Chakrabarti, *Medicine and Empire: 1600–1960* (London: Bloomsbury, 2014).

6. Jasbir K. Puar, *The Right to Maim: Debility, Capacity, Disability* (Durham, NC: Duke University Press, 2017), x.

7. Erin L. Durban, "Postcolonial Disablement and/as Transition: Trans* Haitian Narratives of Breaking Open and Stitching Together," *Transgender Quarterly* 4, no. 2 (2017): 195–207.

8. Walter Benjamin, "Theses on the Philosophy of History," in *Illuminations*, trans. Harry Zohn (New York: Schocken Books, 1968), 253–64.

9. Edward W. Said, *Orientalism* (New York: Vintage Books, 1978), 1–30.

10. Achille Mbembe, *Necropolitics*, trans. Steven Corcoran (Durham, NC: Duke University Press, 2019); Roberto Esposito, *Bios: Biopolitics and Philosophy*, trans. Timothy Campbell (Minneapolis: University of Minnesota Press, 2008), 45–77, 110–45.

11. For Foucault's classic theorizations of biopolitics, see Michel Foucault, *The History of Sexuality Volume One: An Introduction*, trans. Robert Hurley (New York: Vintage Books, 1978), 135–59; Michel Foucault, *"Society Must be Defended": Lectures at the Collège de France, 1975–1976*, trans. David Macey (New York: Picador,

2003); Michel Foucault, *Security, Territory, Population: Lectures at the Collège de France, 1977–78*, trans. Graham Burchell (New York: Picador, 2007); Michel Foucault, *The Birth of Biopolitics: Lectures at the Collège de France, 1978–1979*, trans Graham Burchell (New York: Picador, 2010).

12. Karl Marx, *Capital*, vol. 3, trans. David Fernbach (New York: Penguin Books, 1981), 958–59.

13. John Bellamy Foster, *Marx's Ecology: Materialism and Nature* (New York: Monthly Review Press, 2000), 141–77; Kohei Saito, *Karl Marx's Ecosocialism: Capital, Nature, and the Unfinished Critique of Political Economy* (New York: Monthly Review Press, 2017), 63–140.

14. Jason W. Moore, *Capitalism in the Web of Life: Ecology and the Accumulation of Capital* (London: Verso, 2015), 75–87.

15. Jordan Peele, dir., *Us* (Los Angeles: Universal Pictures, 2019).

16. Johanna Isaacson, "Beach Blanket Barbarism," *Commune Magazine*, June 7, 2019, https://communemag.com/beach-blanket-barbarism/.

17. Colleen Lye and Christopher Nealon, "Introduction: Marxist Literary Study and the General Law of Capitalist Accumulation," in *After Marx: Literature, Theory and Value in the Twenty-First Century*, ed. Colleen Lye and Christopher Nealon (Cambridge: Cambridge University Press, 2022), 1–22, at 8.

18. Christopher Breu, "Biopolitics and/as Infrastructure," in *Biotheory: Life and Death under Capitalism*, ed. Jeffrey R. Di Leo and Peter Hitchcock (New York: Routledge, 2020), 119–35.

19. Michael Denning, "Wageless Life," *New Left Review* 66 (November–December 2022), 83–97.

20. Kevin Floyd, with Brent Ryan Bellamy, Sarah Brouillette, Sarika Chandra, Chris Chen, and Jen Hedler Phillis, "Introduction: Totality Inside Out," in *Totality Inside Out: Rethinking Crisis and Conflict under Capital*, ed. Kevin Floyd, Jen Hedler Phillis, and Sarika Chandra (New York: Fordham University Press, 2022), 1–28, at 3.

21. Moore, *Capitalism in the Web of Life*, 53.

22. Karl Marx, *Capital*, 1: 874.

23. Petrus Liu, *The Specter of Materialism: Queer Theory and Marxism in the Age of the Beijing Consensus* (Durham, NC: Duke University Press, 2023), 21–51.

24. Nikolas Rose, *The Politics of Life Itself: Biomedicine, Power, and Subjectivity in the Twenty-First Century* (Princeton, NJ: Princeton University Press, 2007), 253.

25. Eli Clare, *Brilliant Imperfection: Grappling with Cure* (Durham, NC: Duke University Press, 2017), 14, italics in original.

26. Rebekah Sheldon, *The Child to Come: Life after the Human Catastrophe* (Minneapolis: University of Minnesota Press, 2016), 19.

27. See chapter 2 for my theorization of these dynamics and the accompanying bibliography.

28. Donna J. Haraway, *When Species Meet* (Minneapolis: University of Minnesota Press, 2008), 149–264.

29. Rose, *The Politics of Life Itself*, 6; Kaushik Sunder Rajan, *Biocapital: The Constitution of Postgenomic Life* (Durham, NC: Duke University Press, 2006), 23.

30. Deidre Cooper Owens, *Medical Bondage: Race, Gender, and the Origins of American Gynecology* (Athens: University of Georgia Press, 2017).

31. Harriet A. Washington, *Medical Apartheid: The Dark History of Medical Experimentation on Black Americans from Colonial Times to the Present* (New York: Anchor Books, 2006).

32. Washington, *Medical Apartheid*, 29–30, 3.

33. Iain Morland, "Gender, Genitals, and the Meaning of Being Human," in Lisa Downing, Iain Morland, and Nikki Sullivan, *Fuckology: Critical Essays on John Money's Diagnostic Concepts* (Chicago: University of Chicago Press, 2015), 67–98.

34. C. Riley Snorton, *Black on Both Sides: A Racial History of Trans Identity* (Minneapolis: University of Minneapolis Press, 2017), 17–54.

35. Michel Foucault, *The Birth of the Clinic: An Archaeology of Medical Perception*, trans. A. M. Sheridan Smith (New York: Vintage, 1994), xii.

36. Fredric Jameson, *A Singular Modernity* (London: Verso, 2013).

37. Silvia Federici, *Caliban and the Witch: Women, the Body, and Primitive Accumulation* (New York: Autonomedia, 2004).

38. Silvia Federici, *Beyond the Periphery of the Skin: Rethinking, Remaking, and Reclaiming the Body in Contemporary Capitalism* (Oakland: PM Press, 2020).

39. Jeffrey Jerome Cohen, "Monster Culture (Seven Theses)," in *The Monster Theory Reader*, ed. Jeffrey Andrew Weinstock (Minneapolis: University of Minnesota Press, 2020), 37–56, at 41.

40. Michel Foucault, *Abnormal: Lectures at the Collège de France, 1974–1975*, trans. Graham Burchell (New York: Picador, 1999).

41. David A. Rubin, *Intersex Matters: Biomedical Embodiment, Gender Regulation, and Transnational Activism* (Albany: SUNY University Press, 2017); Alice Dreger, *Hermaphrodites and the Medical Invention of Sex* (Cambridge, MA: Harvard University Press, 1997); Foucault, *Abnormal*.

42. Rubin, *Intersex Matters*, 32.

43. Foucault, *Birth of the Clinic*, xiii, xiv.

44. Georges Canguilhem, *A Vital Rationalist: Selected Writings from Georges Canguilhem*, trans. Arthur Goldhammer (New York: Zone Books, 1994), 93.

45. Joanne Meyerowitz, *How Sex Changed: A History of Transsexuality in the United States* (Cambridge, MA: Harvard University Press, 2002), 14–98; Jules Gil-Peterson, *Histories of the Transgender Child* (Minneapolis: University of Minnesota Press, 2018), 59–96.

46. Kadji Amin, "Taxonomically Queer? Sexology and the New Queer, Trans, and Asexual Identities" *GLQ* 29, No. 1 (2023): 91-107.

47. Christopher Chitty, *Sexual Hegemony: Statecraft, Sodomy, and Capital in the Rise of the World System*, ed. Max Fox (Durham, NC: Duke University Press, 2020).

48. Kevin Floyd, *The Reification of Desire: Toward a Queer Marxism* (Minneapolis: University of Minnesota Press, 2009).

49. Adele E. Clarke, Laura Mamo, Jennifer Ruth Fosket, Jennifer R. Fishman, and Janet K. Shim, "Biomedicalization: A Theoretical and Substantive Introduction" in *Biomedicalization: Technoscience, Health, and Illness in the U.S.*, ed. Adele E. Clarke, Laura Mamo, Jennifer Ruth Fosket, Jennifer R. Fishman, and Janet K. Shim (Durham, NC: Duke University Press, 2010), 47–88.

50. Rubin, *Intersex Matters*, 92.

51. Rose, *The Politics of Life Itself*, 11; Sarah Franklin and Margaret Lock, "Animation and Cessation: The Remaking of Life and Death," in *Remaking Life and Death: Toward an Anthropology of the Biosciences*, ed. Sarah Franklin and Margaret Lock (Houston, TX: School of American Research Press, 2003), 3–22.

52. Wendy Brown, *Undoing the Demos: Neoliberalism's Stealth Revolution* (New York: Zone Books, 2015).

53. Foucault, *Birth of Biopolitics*, 228.

54. Rose, *The Politics of Life Itself*, 13, 27.

55. Franklin and Lock, "Animation and Cessation," 13.

56. Franklin and Lock, "Animation and Cessation," 13.

57. Christopher Breu, *Insistence of the Material: Literature in the Age of Biopolitics* (Minneapolis: University of Minnesota Press, 2014), 22–23.

58. Paisley Currah, *Sex Is as Sex Does: Governing Transgender Identity* (New York: New York University Press, 2022).

59. Jordy Rosenberg, "The Molecularization of Sexuality: On Some Primitivisms of the Present," *Theory and Event* 17, no. 2 (2014), muse.jhu.edu/article/546470.

60. The Care Collective, *The Care Manifesto: The Politics of Interdependence* (London: Verso, 2020).

4. The Sexual and Bodily Commons

1. The epigraph is from Jean-Luc Nancy, *Sexistence*, trans. Steven Miller (New York: Fordham University Press, 2021), 40.

2. Lauren Berlant and Michael Warner, "Sex in Public," *Critical Inquiry* 24, no. 2 (Winter 1998): 547–66.

3. Jacques Lacan, *On Feminine Sexuality and the Limits of Love and Knowledge, 1972–1973: The Seminar of Jacques Lacan Book XX*, trans. Bruce Fink (New York: W. W. Norton, 1999), 9.

4. Michel Foucault, *The Birth of Biopolitics: Lectures at the Collège de France, 1978–1979*, trans. Graham Burchell (New York: Picador, 2010); David Harvey, *A Brief History of Neoliberalism* (Oxford: Oxford University Press, 2005); Wendy Brown, *Undoing the Demos: Neoliberalism's Stealth Revolution* (New York: Zone Books, 2015).

5. Nancy Fraser, *Justus Interruptus: Critical Reflections on the "Postsocialist" Condition* (New York: Routledge, 1997), 41–67.

6. Cinzia Arruzza, Tithi Bhattacharya, and Nancy Fraser, *Feminism for the 99%: A Manifesto* (London: Verso, 2019).

7. The dialectic between the individual and the collective appears throughout Adorno's writings. For a swift account of it, see "Sociology and Empirical Research," in *The Adorno Reader*, ed. Brian O'Conner (London: Blackwell, 2000) 175–91.

8. Elisabeth R. Anker, *Ugly Freedoms* (Durham, NC: Duke University Press, 2022).

9. Jason Read, *The Politics of Transindividuality* (Chicago: Haymarket Books, 2017), 5; Stacy Alaimo, *Bodily Natures: Science, Nature, and the Material Self* (Bloomington: Indiana University Press, 2010), 2.

10. Karl Marx and Friedrich Engels, "The German Ideology," in *The Marx-Engels Reader*, 2nd ed., ed. Robert C. Tucker (New York: W. W. Norton, 1978), 146–200.

11. Jason W. Moore, *Capitalism in the Web of Life: Ecology and the Accumulation of Capital* (London: Verso, 2015), 3.

12. The scholarship on animal studies and posthumanism is too voluminous to list here, but two foundational texts are Cary Wolfe, *Zoontologies: The Question of the Animal* (University of Minnesota Press, 2003), and Rosi Braidotti, *The Posthuman* (Cambridge, MA: Polity Press, 2013).

13. R. A. Judy, *Sentient Flesh: Thinking in Disorder, Poiēsis in Black* (Durham, NC: Duke University Press, 2020).

14. David Harvey, *The Condition of Postmodernity: An Enquiry into the Origins of Cultural Change* (London: Blackwell, 1989), 10–38.

15. Kadji Amin, "Taxonomically Queer?: Sexology and New Queer, Trans, and Asexual Identities," *GLQ* 29, no. 1 (2023): 91–107.

16. Fredric Jameson, *Postmodernism or, The Cultural Logic of Late Capitalism* (Durham, NC: Duke University Press, 1991), 21–34.

17. Linda Hutcheon, *The Politics of Postmodernism*, 2nd ed. (New York: Routledge, 2002).

18. Brian McHale, *Postmodernist Fiction* (New York: Routledge, 1987), 1–25.

19. Fredric Jameson, *Valences of the Dialectic* (London: Verso, 2010), 9–10; Christopher Breu, "After Anti-Theory: Ten Theses on the Limits of Anti-Theory," in *What's Wrong with Anti-Theory?*, ed. Jeffrey R. Di Leo (London: Bloomsbury, 2020), 250–71.

20. Jean-François Lyotard, *The Postmodern Condition: A Report on Knowledge*, trans. Geoff Bennington (Minneapolis: University of Minnesota Press, 1984).

21. Colleen Lye and Christopher Nealon, "Introduction: Marxist Literary Study and the General Law of Capitalist Accumulation," in *After Marx: Literature, Theory, and Value in the Twenty-First Century*, ed. Colleen Lye and Christopher Nealon (Cambridge: Cambridge University Press, 2022), 2.

22. See the essays collected in Levi R. Bryant, Nick Srnicek, and Graham Harman, eds., *The Speculative Turn: Continental Materialism and Realism* (Melbourne: re.press, 2011).

23. Quentin Meillassoux, *After Finitude: An Essay on the Necessity of Contingency*, trans. Ray Brassier (London: Continuum, 2010); Ray Brassier, *Nihil Unbound: Enlightenment and Extinction* (New York: Palgrave, 2007); Eugene

Thacker, *In the Dust of This Planet: Horror of Philosophy Volume One* (Winchester, UK: Zero Books, 2011).

24. Levi R. Bryant, *The Democracy of Objects* (Ann Arbor, MI: Open Humanities Press, 2011).

25. Karen Barad, *Meeting the Universe Halfway: Quantum Physics and the Entanglement of Matter and Meaning* (Durham, NC: Duke University Press, 2007); Mel Y. Chen, *Animacies: Biopolitics, Racial Mattering, and Queer Affect* (Durham, NC: Duke University Press, 2012).

26. On value form, see Michael Heinrich, *An Introduction to the Three Volumes of Marx's Capital*, trans. Alexander Locascio (New York: Monthly Review Press, 2012). There are many debates within value theory that are too numerous to list here. For two different takes on eco-Marxism, see Kohei Saito, *Marx's Ecosocialism: Capital, Nature, and the Unfinished Critique of Political Economy* (New York: Monthly Review Press, 2017), and Moore, *Capitalism in the Web of Life*.

27. The Care Collective, *The Care Manifesto: The Politics of Interdependence* (London: Verso, 2020).

28. Richard Slotkin, *Regeneration through Violence: The Mythology of the American Frontier, 1600–1860*, rev. ed. (Norman: University of Oklahoma Press, 2000).

29. Read, *The Politics of Transindividuality*, 2.

30. Michael Hardt and Antonio Negri, *Commonwealth* (Cambridge, MA: Harvard University Press, 2009), viii. For my own critique of Hardt and Negri's investment in ideas of "immaterial production," see Christopher Breu, *Insistence of the Material: Literature in the Age of Biopolitics* (Minneapolis: University of Minnesota Press, 2014).

31. Christian P. Haines and Peter Hitchcock, "Introduction: No Place for the Commons," *The Minnesota Review* 93 (2019): 55–61.

32. Dean Spade, *Mutual Aid: Building Solidarity during This Crisis (and the Next)* (London: Verso, 2020), 27.

33. Elizabeth Maddock Dillon, "The Plantationocene and the Performative Commons: A Brief History of Uncommoning," *The Minnesota Review* 93 (2019): 83–93; Maurizio Lazzarato, *The Making of the Indebted Man*, trans. Joshua David Jordan (Los Angeles: Semiotext(e), 2012); Karl Marx, *Capital, Volume I*, trans. Ben Fowkes (New York: Vintage Books, 1977), 877–904.

34. Dillon, "The Plantationocene and the Performative Commons," 83; Samuel R. Delany, *Times Square Red, Times Square Blue* (New York: New York University Press, [1999] 2019); José Esteban Muñoz, *Cruising Utopia: The Then and There of Queer Futurity* (New York: New York University Press, 2009), 33–48.

35. Anna Kornbluh, *The Order of Forms: Realism, Formalism, and Social Space* (Chicago: University of Chicago Press, 2019), 2.

36. Imre Szeman, "Energy Commons," *The Minnesota Review* 93 (2019): 94–101.

37. Cesare Casarino, "Farewell to the University (without Nostalgia), or Thoughts on the Relationship between the University and the Common," *The Minnesota Review* 93 (2019): 141–49.

38. Fred Moten and Stefano Harney, *The Undercommons: Fugitive Planning and Black Study* (New York: Autonomedia, 2013).

39. Susan Hegeman, "The Indigenous Commons," *The Minnesota Review* 93 (2019): 133–40, at 133.

40. Loretta J. Ross and Rickie Solinger, *Reproductive Justice: An Introduction* (Berkeley: University of California Press, 2017).

41. Muñoz, *Cruising Utopia*, 11, 12.

42. Delany, *Times Square Red, Times Square Blue*, xvii.

43. Michel Foucault, *The History of Sexuality, Volume One: An Introduction*, trans. Robert Hurley (New York: Vintage Books, 1978); Michel Foucault, *The Use of Pleasure: Volume Two of The History of Sexuality*, trans. Robert Hurley (New York: Vintage Books, 1985).

44. See my discussion of all of these dynamics in chapter 2. For trauma's relationship to sexuality, see Jean Laplanche, *Essays on Otherness* (New York: Routledge, 1999), 64–66, and Judith Herman, *Trauma and Recovery* (New York: Basic Books, 1997). On the drive, see Jean Laplanche, "The Drive and Its Source-Object: It's Fate in Transference," in *Essays on Otherness*, 117–32. For a brief but resonant formulation of the drive by Lacan, see Jacques Lacan, "On Freud's 'Trieb' and the Psychoanalyst's Desire," in *Écrits: The First Complete Edition in English*, trans. Bruce Fink (New York: W. W. Norton, 2006), 722–25.

45. Muñoz, *Cruising Utopia*, 33–48; David Wojnarowicz, *The Waterfront Journals* (New York: Grove Press, 1997).

46. Sophie Lewis, *Full Surrogacy Now: Feminism Against Family* (London: Verso, 2021), 1–29.

47. Herbert Marcuse, *Eros and Civilization: A Philosophical Inquiry into Freud* (Boston: Beacon Press, 1955), 172–96.

48. Theodor W. Adorno, "Subject and Object," in *The Essential Frankfurt School Reader*, ed. Andrew Arato and Eike Gebhardt (New York: Continuum, 1993), 497–511.

49. Oliver Davis and Tim Dean, *Hatred of Sex* (Lincoln: University of Nebraska Press, 2022), xiii–xv.

50. Jacques Lacan, *The Four Fundamental Concepts of Psychoanalysis: The Seminar of Jacques Lacan Book XI*, trans. Alan Sheridan (New York: W. W. Norton, 1998), 1.

51. Delany, *Times Square Red, Times Square Blue*, 78.

52. Sigmund Freud, "Civilization and Its Discontents," in *The Standard Edition of the Complete Psychological Works of Sigmund Freud*, trans. James Strachey (London: Hogarth Press, 1955–61), 21:59–145.

53. Sigmund Freud, "Remembering, Repeating, and Working-Through (Further Recommendations on the Technique of Psychoanalysis II)," in *The Standard Edition of the Complete Psychological Works of Sigmund Freud*, 12:147–56.

54. Rob Nixon, *Slow Violence and the Environmentalism of the Poor* (Cambridge, MA: Harvard University Press, 2011).

55. Brent Ryan Bellamy and Jeff Diamanti, "Materialism and the Critique of Energy," in *Materialism and the Critique of Energy*, ed. Brent Ryan Bellamy and Jeff Diamanti (Chicago: MCM' Press, 2018), ix–xxxvii.

56. Kojin Karatani, *The Structure of World History: From Modes of Production to Modes of Exchange*, trans. Michael K. Bourdaghs (Durham, NC: Duke University Press, 2014), 285–307.

57. Pierre Dardot and Christian Laval, *Common: On Revolution in the Twenty-First Century* (New York: Bloomsbury, 2019); Hardt and Negri, *Commonwealth*.

58. Hortense Spillers, "Mama's Baby, Papa's Maybe: An American Grammar Book," *Diacritics* 17, no. 2 (Summer 1987): 64–81; Alexander G. Weheliye, *Habeas Viscus: Racializing Assemblages, Biopolitics, and Black Feminist Theories of the Human* (Durham, NC: Duke University Press, 2014); C. Riley Snorton, *Black on Both Sides: A Racial History of Trans Identity* (Minneapolis: University of Minnesota Press, 2017); R. A Judy, *Sentient Flesh: Thinking in Disorder, Poiēsis in Black* (Durham, NC: Duke University Press, 2020); Marquis Bey, *Black Trans Feminism* (Durham, NC: Duke University Press, 2022).

59. Katherine McKittrick, ed., *Sylvia Wynter: On Being Human as Praxis* (Durham, NC: Duke University Press, 2015), 1–89. The section I cited is an interview by McKittrick with Wynter.

60. Maurice Merleau-Ponty, *The Visible and the Invisible*, trans. Alphonso Lingus (Evanston, IL: Northwestern University Press, 1968), 130–55.

61. Terry Eagleton, *Materialism* (New Haven, CT: Yale University Press, 2016).

62. Karl Marx, "Economic and Philosophic Manuscripts of 1844," in Tucker, *The Marx-Engels Reader*, 32.

63. My thinking about the utopian is shaped by Phillip E. Wegner, *Invoking Hope: Theory and Utopia in Dark Times* (Minneapolis: University of Minnesota Press, 2020) and Sean Austin Grattan, *Hope Isn't Stupid: Utopian Affects in Contemporary American Literature* (Iowa City: University of Iowa Press, 2017).

Epilogue: Following in the Steps of the Hermaphrodite

1. Vernon Rosario, "An Interview with Cheryl Chase," *Journal of Gay and Lesbian Psychotherapy* 10, no. 2 (2006): 93–104.

2. Kim Stanley Robinson, *Red Mars* (New York: Random House, 2021); *Green Mars* (New York: Random House, 2021); and *Blue Mars* (New York: Random House, 2021).

3. Theodor Adorno, *Negative Dialectics*, trans. E. B. Ashton (New York: Continuum, 2004), 187–89.

4. Walter Benjamin, *The Arcades Project*, trans. Howard Eiland and Kevin McLaughlin (Cambridge, MA: Harvard University Press, 1999), 462.

Index

accumulation by dispossession, 10, 22, 28, 36, 96, 101–3, 109–10, 114, 116–119, 121, 123, 125, 128–30, 138, 149

Adorno, Theodor, 31–33, 70, 137, 159, 174–75, 187nn61–62, 187n64, 192n7, 200n7, 202n48, 203n3

Agamben, Giorgio, 96

Ahmed, Sara, 16, 185n32

Aizura, Aren Z., 14, 182n16, 185n27, 189n21

Alaimo, Stacy, xiii, 21, 42–43, 45, 68, 78–80, 82, 98, 100, 137, 167, 181n5, 186n43, 188n6, 188nn10–11, 191n57, 193n25, 193n28, 200n9

Althusser, Louis, 49, 111, 142, 189n25

Amin, Kadji, 14, 89, 124, 140, 183n16, 185n28, 194n46, 198n46, 200n15

Anker, Elisabeth R., 137, 200n8

Antifoundational, 25, 43, 141

Anzieu, Didier, 17, 88, 94, 185n34, 194n43

Arca, 174

Arrighi, Giovanni, 28, 187n58

Arruzza, Cinzia, 136, 199n6

asexuality, 1–2, 8, 158

Ashtor, Gila, 1, 69, 183n2, 192n5

avatar, 11–12, 31, 40–41, 44; culture, 39, 50; fantasies, 66; fetishism, 12, 40, 129

Ayler, Albert, 97

Badiou, Alain, 72, 92–93, 99, 193n14, 195n53

Barad, Karen, 21, 35, 68, 76, 78–80, 144, 186n43, 193n22, 210n25

Barker, Meg-John, 183n16

Barounis, Cynthia, 5, 47, 183n8, 189n16

BDSM, 26, 84, 150

Beauchamp, Toby, 42, 44, 188n7

Bellamy, Brent Ryan, 112, 166, 203n55

Benjamin, Walter, 36, 103–5, 107–8, 119, 126, 175, 196n8, 203n4

Berlant, Lauren, xiv, 7, 91, 134, 181n7, 195n50, 199n2

Bey, Marquis, 17–18, 48, 53, 69–71, 93, 96, 168, 185n36, 189n24, 190n37, 192n6, 192n11, 203n58

Bhattacharya, Tithi, 102, 114, 196n3, 199n6

Bianchi, Emanuela, 180n41

bioaccumulation, 96, 100, 106, 108, 115–18, 123, 127

Bladerunner, 39, 188n2

Blade Runner 2049, 39–41, 57, 188n3

Bohr, Niels, 79

Borromean knot, 68, 71–72, 74, 76, 79, 88, 115

Bouman, Walter Pierre, 183n16

Bourdieu, Pierre, 57, 190n44

Boylan, Jennifer Finney, 14, 185n29

Bracewell, Lorna, 9, 184n17

Braidotti, Rosi, 200n12

Brassier, Ray, 144, 200n23

Breu, Christopher, 181n11, 182n11, 188n4, 193n19, 195n62, 197n18, 199n57, 200n19, 201n30

Bright, Susie, 9, 184n15

Brouillette, Sarah, 112, 197n20

Brown, James, 97

Brown, Nicholas, 196n3

Brown, Wendy, 9–10, 127, 135, 184n18, 184n20, 199n52

Bryant, Levi, 144, 200n22, 201n24

Burke, Tarana, 160

Christopher Breu (he/they) is Professor of English at Illinois State University. He is the author of *Insistence of the Material: Literature in the Age of Biopolitics* and *Hard-Boiled Masculinities*. He is also co-editor (with Elizabeth A. Hatmaker) of *Noir Affect* (Fordham).